THE
POET
AT THE
PIANO

Kurt — This is
not what it appears to
be! It's on creativity —
(ie how to write
sensous + be original.)

This time next year —
Jn will we send out
Jon packets!!!

Love, Jon

MICHIKO KAKUTANI

THE POET AT THE PIANO

*Portraits of Writers, Filmmakers,
Playwrights, and Other
Artists at Work*

PETER BEDRICK BOOKS
NEW YORK

LIBRARY OF CONGRESS CATALOGING-IN-PUBLICATION DATA

KAKUTANI, MICHIKO.
THE POET AT THE PIANO.

1. AUTHORS—20TH CENTURY—INTERVIEWS.   2. MOTION
PICTURE PRODUCERS AND DIRECTORS—INTERVIEWS.   3. ENTER-
TAINERS—INTERVIEWS.   I. TITLE.
[PN453.K34   1989   700'.92'2   88-8009
ISBN 0-87226-210-3

BOOK DESIGN BY TASHA HALL

∞

For my parents

POET, BE SEATED AT THE PIANO.
PLAY THE PRESENT, ITS HOO-HOO-HOO,
ITS SHOO-SHOO-SHOO, ITS RIC-A-NIC,
ITS ENVIOUS CACHINNATION.

—*Wallace Stevens,*
from "Mozart, 1935"

My thanks and appreciation
to Arthur Gelb,
a gifted editor,
for his support, encouragement,
and enthusiasm.

CONTENTS

. . .

PLAYWRIGHTS AND PRODUCERS

PERFORMERS

INTRODUCTION

. . .

ALL THE PROFILES IN THIS VOLUME WERE WRITTEN during the last eight years; and all except one (John Updike) first appeared in *The New York Times*. The stories were the result of assignments for the paper; and in that sense the collection may seem eclectic, even somewhat random—certainly it does not aspire to be comprehensive.

What the pieces do have in common is a glimpse of an artist—a writer, a playwright, a musician, a director, or an actor—at work. The shorter ones are really little more than impressionistic sketches of someone, caught at a certain moment, in a certain mood, in a certain light. Others attempt, at somewhat greater length, to illuminate an artist's career and peculiar angle of vision, to explore some of the imaginative transactions that have occurred between his life and art.

Nearly every piece in this volume was based on tape-recorded conversations. Although I have little trust in the reliability of mechanical devices and always take my notebook along, I've found that having someone's voice on tape has its advantages. It helps ensure factual accuracy, and it helps capture elusive verbal rhythms and inflections—and often, the reporter learns, the *way* people express things can be as revealing as what they actually say. The shorter pieces were written on deadline for the daily paper, and certain material cut for space reasons has been restored;

other minor changes have been made for the sake of clarity. Otherwise, the pieces stand as they were written.

When I first started working for the culture department of the *Times*, back in 1979, I remember I was amazed at how easy it was to get people to agree to do an interview. As I quickly discovered, however, such agreements do not guarantee that anything resembling a spontaneous conversation will ensue. Take, for instance, my experience with Philip Roth, a writer who'd once cited Henry James and the nightclub comedian Henny Youngman as his two primary influences. For years, mutual acquaintances had been telling me about the Youngman side of his character—his clowning, his gift for mimicry (he supposedly did a very good Jack Benny), and his tireless Rabelaisian wit. Yet when we finally met in 1981 for a talk about *Zuckerman Unbound*, only the Jamesian side of Roth was on display. We sat in the lobby of the Algonquin hotel for several hours, and like his heroes, who carefully cloak their more outrageous impulses beneath a "responsible manner," Roth spoke throughout in decorous, precise phrases about the "unreckoned consequences of literature" and the hazards of his vocation. He told no jokes—rarely even smiled.

If Roth's demeanor failed to jibe with my expectations (always a hazard for reporters), he was nonetheless unfailingly gracious and generous with his time—as were the rest of the subjects in this book. The one exception was Gore Vidal, who greeted me with the line, "Oh, I guess you're here to do your hatchet job," and later added, "I suppose you'll call me a narcissist—well, a narcissist is someone better looking than you are." I later heard he was angry with the *Times* for having run several negative reviews of his novels over the years.

Why, then, did Vidal agree to do an interview in the first place? Why, in fact, do people talk at all to reporters—complete strangers who come into their lives for a few minutes, ask them nosy questions, and then retreat to the newsroom to write up their stories? Obviously, some people have a responsibility to be heard on important issues—politicians, say, and public officials. Others may want to make certain philosophical or political points; they may enjoy speaking to an attentive audience—or they may simply want, on some level, like Miss Coldfield in *Absalom, Absalom!*, to have their stories or their points of view clarified, remembered, and set down in print.

Then, there are some artists who believe that interviews can help make their work more accessible to the public. They want to clarify their motives and talk about their techniques—in the hope that such discussions may shed light on their craft, prevent misinterpretations, perhaps inspire or provoke others. Norman Mailer—who featured more than a dozen interviews in his last collection of nonfiction *(Pieces and Pontifications)*—apparently sees them as a forum from which he can sound off about various issues, test his intellectual reflexes, and generally think out loud. As for John Updike, who's also included interviews in his anthologies, he seems to regard them as contributions to the public record, contrived but useful situations in which "one is forced to say things" "not always said elsewhere."

Of course in this day of author tours and press junkets, the more pragmatic question of exposure becomes an important issue as well. Though an artist with a new project (a book, a movie, a show, etc.) may well feel that his work should speak for itself, the demands of the market-place—and pressure from agents, studios, publishers, etc.—argue for pub-licity, and this often means talking to the press. Stories in newspapers and magazines, after all, can help bring a work of art to the attention of an audience that might otherwise not exist.

Certainly there are some artists—most notably, J. D. Salinger and Thomas Pynchon—who actively avoid speaking to the press. And there are others, like Samuel Beckett and Sam Shepard, who have earned a reputation for being reclusive.

It was my experience with Shepard that he was neither evasive nor unduly reticent—just difficult to get hold of. When I tried to reach him in the winter of 1984, he was completing an acting stint on the movie *Country,* and he told me he'd be glad to talk—in between takes on the set.

Since he was reluctant to phone me, and since I never knew when he'd be on a break, I ended up phoning his trailer—somewhere on location in L.A.—every twenty minutes or so. The story was eventually pieced to-gether out of six or seven ten-to-fifteen-minute chats.

The late Tennessee Williams was also cooperative—and elusive. Hav-ing agreed to let me follow his last Broadway play, *Clothes for a Summer Hotel,* through rehearsals and out-of-town tryouts, he cheerfully added that he would spend whatever free time he had with me—we would have plenty of time to talk about the development of *Clothes,* and its relation-ship to his earlier work.

As it turned out, the show's first engagement at the Annenberg Center in Philadelphia fell through; and the producer abruptly accepted a book-ing at Washington's Kennedy Center—more than two weeks ahead of the original schedule. The next few days were frantic for Williams and the cast—hours before the Washington opening, the show was still missing an appropriate ending—and the reviews they received from the local critics were so devastating that the following weeks in Chicago were also devoted to furious rewriting and restaging. Certainly the last thing on Williams's mind at that point was talking to a reporter: He was spending the better part of every day holed up in a hotel room with the show's director, José Quintero, cutting characters and scenes, writing new transitions, and later, presenting the changes to the cast.

A distinct pattern emerged over the following days: Every evening over bottles of Ruffino Chianti, Williams would talk of moving to Tahiti "where they at least gracefully pretend I'm not an old fossil." He would then declare that it had been a stressful day, that it was time for him to go to bed, and he would apologize for not being able to do an interview. I, in turn, would apologize for having to bother him with questions at such a time; and we would both agree to speak further the following day. Every morning I would get up early, in hopes of chatting with the playwright over breakfast, and every morning he would fail to emerge from his room. Lunchtime usually found him working incommunicado; and by evening, he'd again be too tired to talk.

Eventually, I discovered that he took the occasional hour off to scour the winter streets of Chicago for a swimming pool (for the last ten years, he said, he'd made it a habit to go swimming every morning, and forgoing this pleasure disrupted his work routine), and it was during these walks that he seemed most at ease talking about his work.

In the next three years before his death, I would talk with Williams several more times; there would be a follow-up story on the aftermath of *Clothes'* disastrous Broadway run, and another story on *Something Cloudy Something Clear*, a new play that opened Off Off Broadway in 1981. The piece included in this volume was written the evening he died.

Usually the process of interviewing makes for a very artificial—and fleeting—sort of intimacy. A talk with Jorge Luis Borges, the blind Latin American writer, ended with my reading *Robinson Crusoe* aloud to him as he prepared to take a nap. The one with Brian De Palma, the director of *Dressed to Kill* and *Carrie*, was punctuated by the fuses in his office blowing out—and concluded at a nearby restaurant after a futile search for candles. Most of the time, the nature of newspaper deadlines does not allow ongoing dialogues with a subject to develop. Unlike magazine writers, newspaper reporters rarely have days or weeks in which to follow someone around, waiting for a "telling" scene, a "revealing" offhand gesture or remark. And the subjects themselves tend to have schedules that preclude spending extended periods of time with a reporter—the big exception, in this collection, being Joseph Papp, who saw me repeatedly over a period of months, and generously gave me complete access to all his meetings and rehearsals. In the course of a week's interviews, Joan Didion allowed me to accompany her home on a visit to her parents; and Mary McCarthy spent four complete afternoons talking with me in Paris.

The other interviews, as a rule, were conducted in a single session—over lunch, tea, or dinner, followed, in some cases, by a conversation on the phone. The magazine piece on Ingmar Bergman, for instance, grew out of a single afternoon spent with the director at his home on the Swedish island of Fårö. All in all, I spent roughly five times as much time traveling to see him (a plane flight to London, another to Stockholm, a third to Visby, followed by a car and ferry ride), as I did in his actual presence.

If this creates certain pressures for the reporter, it doubtless creates commensurate ones for the subject of the interview. If he's an artist who's spent the last year (two, five, ten years) working on a project in the solitude of his own imagination, how can he possibly articulate to a stranger—in the space of a couple of hours—the sources and means of his art? And if he's a well-known public figure, used to dispensing regular interviews, how can he respond spontaneously to questions he's heard dozens of times over the years?

To make matters worse, many artists worry that talking too much about a subconscious process may alter, perhaps even damage, the magical element in their art (Rilke resisted psychoanalysis for this very reason). Others simply feel that their work should stand on its own, that explications or annotations of any sort are superfluous—that such addenda actually deflect attention from the work, focusing it, instead, on the trivialities of personality. Too much confusion already exists, they may argue, between an artist's life and work; and any sort of public pronouncement that hints at autobiographical sources only serves to diminish the importance of imagination and craft.

"It is very bad for a writer to talk about how he writes," Hemingway once declared. "He writes to be read by the eye and no explanations or dissertations should be necessary. You can be sure that there is much more there than will be read at any first reading and having made this it is not the writer's province to explain it or to run guided tours through the more difficult country of his work."

No doubt Hemingway, who made this statement in a *Paris Review* interview, frequently saw more attention being paid to the details of his life than to his work. And to some degree, he both encouraged it and fell victim to it. By the time he killed himself in 1961, he was probably as famous for his macho posturing as he was for his celebrated writing style.

Of course, artists had begun collecting this sort of fame as far back as the Renaissance, and the Romantic poets helped galvanize the public's fascination with the artistic sensibility by willfully courting notoriety. Byron, for instance, liked to dress in black because it made him look like a young, metropolitan Hamlet; and to underscore his sensitive nature, he even made a public show of eating only biscuits and soda water (though he was once caught out at a restaurant, wolfing down mutton and potatoes).

Still, the lives of artists have never been of more popular interest than in this media-conscious century—talent, in our society, is scrutinized, glamorized, and often amply rewarded. Indeed, there has been a tendency, in America especially, to turn works of art into commodities of entertainment, and the artist, himself, into a personality worthy of gossip-column mentions. More people, sadly enough, are familiar with Norman Mailer's public and private high jinks—running for mayor, stabbing his wife, exchanging blows with Gore Vidal—than they are with the text of *The Naked and the Dead.* And while many people have heard about the sexual hijinks in Roth's *Portnoy's Complaint,* fewer have read the author's fine earlier works, like *Letting Go* or *When She Was Good.*

Noting that a controversial writer in America gets invited to appear on talk shows, while a controversial writer in Eastern Europe gets threatened with exile or imprisonment, Philip Roth observes that the differences are "almost comically vivid: In my situation, everything goes and nothing matters; in their situation, nothing goes and everything matters. Every word they write has endless implications, whereas in the States, one often doesn't have the sense of making an impact at all."

Why has the artist acquired this sort of celebrity in the West? For one thing, the relationship between artists and their audiences has changed. Unlike their predecessors in earlier societies, today's writers can no longer take for granted a following of like-minded fellows—contemporaries who share a body of values and aesthetic assumptions. Instead, they're forced to come to terms with a vast public already distracted by television and other diversions. And while a novelist or poet can choose to ignore this audience, individuals working in film and musical theater (forms overlapping with popular entertainment, and requiring substantial financing) do not always have this luxury.

Secondly, contemporary artists, themselves, have chosen to focus increasingly on their own psyches, and the details of their domestic lives—resulting in a blurring of the lines between fact and fiction, autobiography and art. As Alfred Kazin once noted, "A writer can never be sure that his emotions, his habits, his childhood, his loves and enmities, are not crucial to his work. The modern writer is likely to feel that his life and his work speak for each other; when an interviewer gently presses him to tell more, he will gladly try, for in the writer's own mind clarity about a seemingly personal matter seems to advance that moral clarity which is tantamount to literary power." "It is the modern writer's sense," he goes on, "that he inhabits some mysterious power over his own life, that his gift and his life are really versions of each other, that his habits and beliefs occupy some mysterious center of creativity that is still not the same thing as 'himself' but is his private god, his daemon, the mystery of his creativity."

This interest in the self is not new certainly (think of Byron's self-dramatization in poems like "Childe Harold"), but it has been heightened by this century's familiarity with psychology, and the growing sense, in the wake of World War II and the disruptions of the sixties, that the world of public events is overwhelming, even absurd—and hence intractable to imaginative assaults; that the only thing the artist might presume to know, to borrow a phrase from Henry James, is that "obstinate finality"—himself.

Consider, for instance, just how many recent novels have focused on the literary vocation itself. The late Bernard Malamud examined the creative problems and familial dilemmas of a biographer in *Dubin's Lives;* and in *The World According to Garp*, John Irving recounted the adventures of a novelist who writes a book called *The World According to Bensenhaver.* In *Sophie's Choice*, William Styron portrayed an aspiring novelist remarkably similar to his own younger self, and in his *Zuckerman Bound* trilogy, Philip Roth reinvented his own life as an American writer. John Fowles's *Mantissa* described the difficulties an author faces in dealing with his recalcitrant muse; and John Updike's two Bech novels (*Bech: A Book* and *Bech Is Back*) used material about writers and writing that the author says he might not have otherwise been able to use.

Nor are novelists the only ones engaged in such acts of self-contemplation. In the tradition of Strindberg and Eugene O'Neill, playwrights—from Arthur Miller to Lanford Wilson, Tennessee Williams to Neil

Simon and Sam Shepard—have been turning out more and more works in which the autobiographical impulse plays a major, if not pivotal, role. And like Fellini and Truffaut, such American filmmakers as Woody Allen and Martin Scorsese have established their medium as a forum for self-examination as well. Some works—including Scorsese's *The King of Comedy*, and Sondheim and Lapine's musical *Sunday in the Park with George*, and Philip Roth's novel *Zuckerman Unbound*—have narrowed the autobiographical focus further, zeroing in on the consequences of being an artist and the palpable effects of fame.

Success, in fact, is an issue addressed by many artists in this volume, for in many cases, it has had specific and lasting effects on their work. Norman Mailer, for one, points out that early acclaim—and notoriety—irrevocably altered the nature of his work. When *The Naked and the Dead* made him one of America's brightest new literary voices at the age of twenty-five, he says he realized that "the kind of writing I was going to do would be altogether different from the kind of writing I thought I would do." Having aspired to write "huge collective novels about American life," he had planned to go out and collect experience—something his new celebrity now precluded. Instead of being the observer—the role for which he'd prepared himself as a young man—he suddenly found he'd become one of the observed. He began writing about himself—and the blustering protagonist of *Armies of the Night* was born.

Since most of the artists in this volume are still active, it's difficult to talk about the overall shape of their careers. A few, such as Ingmar Bergman and Saul Bellow, seem to be tracing the classic arc of vocation enjoyed by Henry James (in which youthful apprenticeship slowly and inexorably gives way to mastery and magisterial finesse), while others—like Tennessee Williams and Arthur Miller—have had the frustrating task of competing with earlier selves. In the case of Williams, the work grew increasingly abstract over the years; in contrast, the work of two of his heirs—Lanford Wilson and Sam Shepard—has moved from a kind of wild expressionism to embrace more conventional narrative forms. Norman Mailer—who has experimented with a variety of voices, personas, and forms—notes that he tries to "start off in a new direction with every book"; and Philip Roth similarly talks of the "self-conscious and deliberate zigzag" of his career. Asked about his next book, Milan Kundera says, "The only thing I know is it will be composed of seven parts—as are all my books. I realized more and more how one is determined by obsessions, even the obsessions of proportions. I realized all my books had the same architecture, and even if I wanted to write a book composed of six parts, I would find myself writing a seventh."

As most of these artists point out, certain compensations come with maturity and success: confidence and command of technique accumulate with the passage of time; and for filmmakers and playwrights, access to funding and talented collaborators tends to become easier as well. Styron notes that he no longer struggles over "le mot juste" as he did in his youth; and Mailer says that his own reduced expectations—he no longer talks, as he did in the sixties, of waging a war "for the mind of man"—have had certain liberating effects. Yet at the same time, these individuals all speak nostalgically of the days when they were starting out, when the urgent need to articulate new ideas gave them a sense of mission, and the desire to make some sort of mark on the world pushed them to achievement. Updike recalled feeling, as a young man, that he "was the only conduit whereby a large body of American reality was going to get into print"; and Shepard remembered the thrill that came with the early belief that "with words you could do anything."

As an artist becomes established, he must deal not only with the public expectations created by earlier successes, but must also learn ways to reinvent his own ambition and talent. "You live off your own guts day to day," says Philip Roth. "You don't always know what you're doing. You're not like a brain surgeon—a man my age who is a surgeon is not going to be caught off guard in the operating room. He's good at it by now. He doesn't have to invent each operation from scratch. There's a procedure he can follow. The same thing's true of a lawyer. He isn't six months into a case and says, 'This is awful, I can't handle it.' I have confidence in my skull, but the project may exceed it. Most men my age doing what they've been doing for twenty-five years aren't thrown by what they do. But with almost every book I've done, there were points where I didn't think I'd make it."

To make matters worse, many of the things that came easily in the beginning grow increasingly elusive: new ideas are harder to come by (Norman Mailer goes so far as to argue that he formed most of his theories during the fifties and has since been engaged in an "occupation of territories I reconnoitered years ago") and the artist is forced either to deal with less accessible material or to find new ways of working variations on old themes. A heightened critical sense may result in creative inhibitions—"you discard things you'd have leapt at twenty years ago as not enough to work on now," says Lanford Wilson—and the development of a distinctive voice (a mark, in itself, of artistic maturity) may eventually lead to an awareness of creative limitations.

"I notice as I write it comes out as sort of Updike prose," says John Updike. "I sit down in such different moods, wearing such different clothes, and out this comes—like a kind of handwriting. It's always mine, and there's no way I can seem to get around it. Isn't it funny you have only one voice? And obsessions—how the same kinds of moments keep recurring in fiction. It really seems to me that a writer sitting in New England should be able to write a perfectly persuasive novel about slum life in Mexico City. In theory. But in practice, we do seem tied to our own lives to a degree. I've not accepted this docilely. I think I've tried to stretch my imagination as far as it will go, but there's a point beyond which you're just transcribing other people's research and not writing out of a felt sense of things.

"In novel after novel, the amorous get together, there's the romantic failure, the economic struggle. God, we've done it so many times. It's like you're a portraitist and you sat down and were horrified to find the nose is between the eyes, and the mouth is still under the nose. And so it is with human nature. For all the variation, the people in novels seem to behave on such a limited number of principles."

How to cope with this sense of suffocation? Some artists have learned to move from one form to another, in the process stretching their imaginative muscles. Besides writing novels and short stories, Updike has played with poetry and essays, and in recent years, has emerged as one of our finest literary critics. Joan Didion and V. S. Naipaul regularly shuttle back and forth between fiction and reportage, and Norman Mailer recently added the role of movie director (he directed a film version of his novel *Tough Guys Don't Dance*) to his repertoire.

In the end, it's impossible to generalize about artists or their work—it's best to let the individuals speak for themselves. By and large, the people in this book are pretty eloquent when it comes to discussing their craft—though one might keep in mind Gertrude Stein's observation that "remarks are not literature." Which brings me to a final point about this volume: Its real purpose, its usefulness if any, is to provide a kind of prologue or introduction—to send the reader back to the artist's work itself.

AUTHORS

.   .   .

SAUL BELLOW

. . .

"'I SOMETIMES ENJOY SAYING THAT ANYBODY'S LIFE can be encompassed in about ten wonderful jokes. One of my favorites is about an American singer who makes his debut at La Scala. He sings his first aria to great applause. And the crowd calls '*Ancora, viva, viva.*' He sings it a second time, and again they call for an encore. Then a third time and a fourth . . . Finally, panting and exhausted, he asks, 'How many times must I sing this aria?' Then someone tells him, 'Until you get it right.' That's how it is with me—I always feel I haven't gotten it quite right, and so I go on singing."

Saul Bellow tells this story with great relish. Sitting down in a black leather easy chair, he gazes out through the window of his high-rise apartment to the dark waters of Lake Michigan beyond and throws his head back and laughs. His conversation, like his books, is at once colloquial and lofty, intellectual and passionate, filled with jokes heard on the Chicago streets and the high seriousness of Academe. The author himself bears a certain resemblance to his own heroes: earnest, elegantly dressed, and deeply thoughtful, he, too, is "a hungry observer" of everything around him.

At sixty-six, Bellow has written nine novels and created in his work an immediately recognizable fictional world, a world animated by an acutely moral imagination and populated by assorted cranks, con men, and fast-talking salesmen of reality who goad and challenge his anxious heroes. Poor, put-upon Moses Herzog, Eugene Henderson, that absurd seeker of higher qualities, wise old Artur Sammler, and Albert Corde in *The Dean's December*—all are men caught in the middle of a spiritual crisis, overwhelmed by the sheer "muchness" of the world and frightened by the stubborn fact of death. Rejecting both easy optimism and easy despair, they struggle to maintain a private life amidst the noisy distractions of contemporary culture and they wonder if their problems are simply their share of "the big-scale insanities of the twentieth century."

Like these characters who are continually searching for a way to apprehend reality, Bellow likes to use fiction as a kind of tool for investigating the society around him; he sees the novelist as "an imaginative historian, who is able to get closer to contemporary facts than social scientists possibly can." But while the confusions of the modern world, manifested in everything from sexual profligacy to random violence, have always reverberated in his characters' lives—a phenomenon that became more pronounced in *Mr. Sammler's Planet*—specific public issues have remained largely in the background. With his latest novel *The Dean's December*, such matters as oppression in Eastern Europe, the plight of the American "underclass," student militancy, and the deterioration of life in American cities are more directly addressed.

What brought about this heightened focus on political and social issues? For one thing, Bellow says he realized after writing *To Jerusalem and Back*, an account of his 1975 trip to Israel, that "it was as easy to write about great public matters as about private ones—all it required was more confidence and daring." The winning of the Nobel Prize in 1976 no doubt provided some of that necessary confidence, and he made plans to write a nonfiction book about Chicago. After making hundreds of pages of notes, however, he decided to abandon that approach and write a novel.

"I found a more congenial way to do it, my own way, developed over many decades," he says. "But I think I've begun to write differently—I had never really attempted anything of this sort before, though I've been all my life an amateur student of history and politics. It became clear to me that no imagination whatsoever had been applied to the problems of demoralized cities. All the approaches have been technical, financial, and bureaucratic, and no one has been able to take into account the sense of these lives.

"I thought I had to cut loose with this book," he goes on. "It seems many of my contemporaries don't take many personal risks—they shoot fish in a barrel. They write about wounded adolescents—there's no problem there. Sexual adventures—there's no problem there. Wounded ethnicity. They appear occasionally to be bold, to challenge the powers that be, but they're generally pretty safe. I think I'm speaking out quite frankly about the deterioration of life in American cities [in this book], and I wouldn't be surprised if I drew some flack. But if you've told yourself all your life that you're a friend of the truth, there comes a time when you must put up or shut up. They're not going to be able to shrug this one off, though there are some very powerful shruggers around."

By now, Bellow points out, he is somewhat accustomed to drawing flack—at least from certain quarters of the literary establishment. For all the honors he has received—a Pulitzer and three National Book Awards as well as the Nobel—he sees himself as going against the mainstream of contemporary literature. He has long rejected the fashionable nihilism of what he calls the "wastelanders," those who believe—as he put it in a 1966 speech—that it is "enlightened to expose, to disenchant, to hate, and to experience disgust." And he is equally skeptical of the willful aestheticism of the "new fiction" practitioners.

As far as Bellow is concerned, those writers who substitute analysis for imagination have estranged literature from the common world and removed one of its original and most important purposes: the raising of moral questions. Contemporary writers, he adds, are also easily tempted by the sensational, for they are faced with "the Ancient Mariner problem"—like Coleridge's seaman, "they need something to buttonhole the wedding guests with, as they go from wedding to wedding or orgy to orgy; they need something that has the power to penetrate distraction.

"People make careers of invoking the horrible—genocide, the Holocaust, dropped atom bombs, labor camps, and so on. It seems to me unforgivable for artists to manipulate these disasters, if they don't genuinely feel them. You have no business putting them in a book in order to make an effect—unearned bitterness, I think I've called it. Of course there's the peculiar American temperament which leads us in that direction—the tradition of Sunday moralism, the power of the pulpit, chastisement, correction, scolding, Old New England. Now they have syndicated columns and television playing upon the guilt of the public, which is more voluminous than these Great Lakes. It's a way to get the attention of the public. This is what television has to do. And this is what musicians, painters, and writers have to do. So they find themselves in competition with the power of politics, the power of the media, and the powers invoked by these powers—like money and sexuality. The Moral Majority gives you a fast moral fix; most novels give you a fast sexual fix. So the question becomes, What is really interesting, genuinely and permanently interesting?"

Such strong opinions have been voiced by Bellow in both his essays and his novels, and they have occasionally made for controversy. Touring universities in the sixties, Bellow was denounced by students during his lectures, and the critic Richard Poirier contended, in an essay written for *Partisan Review,* that *Herzog* and *Mr. Sammler's Planet* were "efforts to test out, to substantiate, to vitalize, and ultimately to propagate a kind of cultural conservatism."

It is an observation Bellow rejects. "People who stick labels on you are in the gumming business," he says by way of reply. "What good are these categories? They mean very little, especially when the people who apply them haven't had a new thought since they were undergraduates and now preside over a literary establishment that lectures to dentists and accountants who want to be filled in on the thrills. I think these are the reptiles of the literary establishment who are grazing on the last Mesozoic grasses of Romanticism. Americans in this respect are quite old-fashioned: they're quite willing to embrace stale European ideas—they should be on Tenth Avenue where the rest of the old importers used to be.

"They think they know what writers should be and what writers should write, but who are these representatives who practice what Poirier preaches? They're, for the most part, spiritless, etiolated, and the liveliest of them are third-rate vaudevillians. Is this literary life? I'd rather inspect gas mains in Chicago."

With their old-fashioned characters, their passion for big ideas and problems of the spirit, Bellow's own books clearly belong to a different tradition. The Old Testament, Shakespeare, and the great nineteenth-century Russian novels—these were the books Bellow read as a boy, and these were the books which, in large measure, gave him a sense of what great literature ought to do. Indeed, his choice of vocation, he says, was animated by the traditional challenge "to account for the mysterious circumstance of being."

"I don't think I was a very sophisticated person," he says, recalling his youth in Chicago as the son of an onion importer who had immigrated from Russia. "Chicago is not a city that produces sophisticated people, but it was in Chicago where this child of Jewish immigrants got the *idée fixe* of becoming an American author, and he had to find a way to prove he wasn't hallucinated, that he could write English sentences, and that he could hold the attention of a reader or two. In those days, the WASP establishment wouldn't listen till you established your credentials—there are people even now who don't."

To establish those credentials, Bellow wrote two books that filled what he calls "formal requirements": *Dangling Man,* the story of a young Chicagoan awaiting induction into the war, was his B.A.; *The Victim,* a portrait of a journalist and his importunate, anti-Semitic alter ego, his Ph.D. Both these somber books won modest critical acclaim, but their author, who was living in Paris on a Guggenheim at the time, says he was already sinking "into a depression by trying to do the wrong things." In a kind of manic reaction, he began another book, a book that he would write "in a purple fever" over the next three years. The book was the exuberantly picaresque *Augie March.*

Augie March marked Bellow's discovery of his own voice. It was a supple voice, infused with the rhythms and idioms of Yiddish, a voice that was capable of articulating a moral vision and lofty philosophical speculation in the most colloquial of terms. "I loosened up," Bellow recalls, "and found I could flail my arms and express my impulses. I was unruly at first and didn't have things under control, but it was at least a kind of spontaneous event. It was my liberation."

Augie March, Bellow said at the time, came easily—all he had to do "was to be there with buckets to catch it"—and it won the National Book Award in 1953. But, in retrospect, the experience proved somewhat disconcerting, for it revealed to Bellow certain prejudices within the literary community.

"I began to discover," he says, "that while I thought I was simply laying an offering on the altar like a faithful petitioner, other people thought I was trying to take over the church. It came at a strange point when I think the WASP establishment was losing confidence in itself, and it felt it was being challenged by Jews, blacks, and ethnics, and some people were saying there was a Jewish Mafia, and other people, who should have had more sense, spoke of—well, they didn't use the word conspiracy, but they saw it as an unwelcome eruption. I began to talk of Malamud, Roth, and me as Hart, Shaffner & Marx, and there was a pathetic absurdity under it all—all we wanted was to add ourselves to the thriving enterprise we loved; no one wanted to take over. That's a motive worthy of the Mafia, and I don't think Hart, Shaffner & Marx were Mafiosi.

"I think of myself as an American of Jewish heritage," he goes on.

"When most people call someone a 'Jewish writer,' it's a way of setting you aside. They don't talk about the powers of the 'Jewish writers' who wrote the Old Testament; they say to write novels you need to know something about manners, which is something you have to be raised in the South to know. I felt many writers [during the fifties and early sixties] treated their Jewish colleagues with unpardonable shabbiness, and anti-Semitism after the Holocaust is absolutely unforgivable."

With the breakthrough in style achieved in *Augie March*, there also came a shift in tone. Whereas the first two books shared a certain depressive quality—underlined by the fact that their heroes did little to resolve the condition of their alienation—*Augie March* was a wildly extroverted work, ending with its hero looking forward to his next adventure. Later books such as *Henderson the Rain King* and *Herzog* would go somewhat further: each ended with its protagonist taking the first step toward an affirmation of his life, and their development would also help reveal what Bellow refers to as "the two sides of my psyche"—the brooding side and the exuberant. "Sometimes I feel I've written two sorts of books," he says. "The high-minded ones and the delightful ones. I prefer the delightful ones myself—*Henderson the Rain King* and *Humboldt's Gift*, I think, fall into that category. The high-minded ones are preparation of sorts for the delightful ones.

"For many years," he goes on, "Mozart was a kind of idol to me—this rapturous singing for me that's always on the edge of sadness and melancholy and disappointment and heartbreak, but always ready for an outburst of the most delicious music. I found Mozart temperamentally so congenial. I'm not claiming the same range of talent, but I often feel an affinity with him."

Certainly many of Bellow's characters have shared temperamental affinities with their author—a fact that Bellow acknowledges by quoting Alberto Moravia, who once told him, "Every novel is some kind of higher autobiography." In *The Dean's December*, for instance, Albert Corde takes a trip to Bucharest to help his wife attend her dying mother—as Bellow himself did several years ago—and Corde shares, more or less, his creator's age, occupation, and place of residence. Like many of Bellow's heroes, Corde is also something of a lapsed intellectual, who takes pride and pleasure in exercising his mind, but also worries about the inadequacy of all his theories. As Mr. Sammler puts it, "Intellectual man had become an explaining creature. Fathers to children, wives to husbands, lecturers to listeners, colleagues to colleagues, doctors to patients, man to his own soul explained. . . . For the most part, in one ear and out the other. The soul wanted what it wanted."

Bellow himself holds curiously ambivalent attitudes toward academia. He believes, on one hand, that "it's in the university and only in the university that Americans can have a higher life," and yet he also contends that professors "are so eager to live the life of society like everybody else that they're not always intellectually or spiritually as rigorous as they should be." By institutionalizing the avant-garde magazines and giving writers the security of tenure, he argues, universities effectively destroyed the independent literary culture that once existed in this country.

Still, Bellow finds that an academic community provides him with people "to talk to about the things that concern me most," and he has served, since 1964, on the prestigious Committee on Social Thought at the University of Chicago. His decision to leave New York and return to Chicago in the early sixties, he says, was motivated, in part, by what he saw as the increased politicization of writers in New York.

When he first arrived in New York during the forties, a "young hick" bent on "going to the big town and taking it," a sense of community existed among writers associated with *Partisan Review*. Bellow became friends with such writers and critics as Meyer Schapiro, Dwight Macdonald, Delmore Schwartz, and Clement Greenberg—"they were not always friendly friends, but they were always stimulating friends"—and he enjoyed the "open spirit of easy fraternization" that animated their discussions. Politics, generally in the form of Marxism, tended to be mostly theoretical.

"Then," Bellow recalls, "a new generation turned up—a lot of people out of Columbia University, a lot of students of Lionel Trilling, who got into enterprises like *Commentary*—and suddenly the whole atmosphere in New York became far more political than it had been before. With the Vietnam War and other issues, people became organized in camps, and while I was opposed to the war, I just refused to line up with the new groups. I didn't like it, and it seemed to me a good time to leave New York, because I'd been drawn there in the first place by my literary interests, and there seemed to be no room for an independent writer in New York anymore. It became harder to find people to talk to, and it was harder to stay out of the draft—you were always being solicited for this cause or that, always being drafted for one thing or another.

"People have said in their memoirs that I was guarded, cautious, career-oriented, but I don't think that's so—after all, there was nothing easier in New York during those days than the life of the extremist, and that's continued to be so. I was not comfortable with the extremist life, and so I thought I might as well go back to the undiluted U.S.A., go back to Chicago. It's vulgar but it's vital and it's more American, more representative."

In Chicago, Bellow finds that he can keep up with his old high-school friends, as well as a cross-section of society including contractors, lawyers, doctors, physicists, historians, policemen, and retired social workers—some of whom surface in his fiction. "You meet people," he says. "They reveal or conceal themselves, and you read them or try. They struggle with their souls or don't. They either generate interest or not. It forms a picture for you. The people who interest me the most do concern themselves with the formation of a soul. The others are what Hollywood used to call the cast of thousands."

When he is working on a book, Bellow spends his mornings at an electric typewriter, set up by a window overlooking Lake Michigan. After nine novels, the craft has been mastered, but the magical aspect of the art remains. Bellow, in fact, has spoken in the past of "a primitive prompter or commentator within, who from earliest years has been advising us, telling us what the real world is"—a commentator not unlike Henderson's little voice that constantly cries, "I want, I want"—and he attributes his best writing to this unconscious source.

"I think a writer is on track when the door of his native and deeper intuitions is open," he says. "You write a sentence that doesn't come from that source and you can't build around it—it makes the page seem somehow false. You have a gyroscope within that tells you whether what you're doing is right or wrong. I've always felt a writer is something of a medium, and when something is really working, he has a certain clairvoyant power; he has a sense of what's going on. Whenever I've published a book that's received wide attention, I've heard from thousands of people around the world who have been thinking the same thing—as though I'd anticipated things. I didn't mean to, but I've learned one does."

Since he won the Nobel Prize for Literature in 1976, of course, those letters from readers have increased, as have the demands on Bellow's time. He is asked to deliver speeches, serve on committees, and sign all manner of petitions. As far as he is concerned, these responsibilities act as distractions from his true vocation.

"I could spend the rest of my life now functioning on committees," he says, "standing up for all the right things and denouncing all the bad ones. What good this does your art, I leave to the expert guessers to guess at. I have yet to feel I've intimidated Brezhnev by signing protests."

"The Nobel changes things in different ways," he continues. "For one thing, you feel that you have more authority, and if the Academy was mistaken in giving you the prize, you try to make the best of it, and recover your balance and your normal poise and not feel oppressed by the weight of this honor. I don't intend to let this laurel wreath of heavy metal sink me. I'm treading water very successfully, thank you. I know people like John Steinbeck thought it was the kiss of death, but I've decided to choose my own death kiss. No one's going to lay it on me."

December 1981

JORGE LUIS BORGES

.   .   .

THE KEY HAD BEEN MISPLACED, AND JORGE LUIS Borges was locked out of his room. Having just spent twelve hours on a plane from Buenos Aires, the Argentinian author was now feeling tired and a bit lost. Still, as his own gnomic fables, filled with mazes and mirrors, will attest, that feeling of dislocation is a familiar one for him, and he seemed resigned to sit in the lobby of his host's building, waiting for someone to open the door, as he passed the afternoon talking to a stranger.

At eighty-three, Borges is a shy, fragile-seeming man, gentlemanly in manner and locution. Long acknowledged as a literary master within the Spanish-speaking world, he achieved international recognition in 1961, when he and Samuel Beckett both won the International Publishers' Prize, and since then has been a perennial Nobel Prize nominee. He recently joined the ranks of prominent foreign writers—V. S. Naipaul, Joseph Brodsky, and Czeslaw Milosz—who have delivered the William James Lecture at the New York Institute for the Humanities.

Such public acclaim comes as something of a surprise to Borges, who has led a hermetic, unworldly life—a life defined almost entirely by books. "To me, reading has been a way of living," he says. "I think the only possible fate for me was a literary life. I can't think of myself in a bookless world. I need books. They mean everything to me."

The "chief event" in his life, he once wrote, was his "father's library"—and his own work has reflected his obsessively literary upbringing. His stories, like his conversation, are filled with allusions to other books, often turning them into fanciful philosophical pranks. "Pierre Menard, Author of the *Quixote*," for instance, examines T. S. Eliot's famous dictum that every new work of art alters our perception of previously existing works of art. And "The Garden of Forking Paths" similarly illuminates the nature of cause and effect by postulating a world composed of intersecting planes in which events may occur independently of one another.

Over the years, the baroque, metaphor-filled prose of his youth—inspired largely by Shakespeare and Sir Thomas Browne—has given way to a new concision of style: "When I began, my writing was very strange. Now I try to write in very simple words. When I was young, I used to think the invention of metaphor was possible. Now I don't—except for very essential ones: stars and eyes, life and dreams, death and sleeping, time and the river."

Despite this evolution, Borges's fictions share an insistent air of unreality. Indeed, the fantastical events and fabulous beasts that populate his fiction—transparent tigers, wizards who conjure up visions in a bowl of ink, encyclopedias that do not chronicle events but cause them—demonstrate that his real literary affinities lie less with the avant-garde than with those other masters of the marvelous such as Kafka, H. G. Wells, and G. K. Chesterton. "I think I share their amazement at things," he says. "Things are a kind of fairy tale to me. I suppose I'm still a boy, though I'm an old man."

In some of the stories, that sense of wonder is expressed in recurrent images of the mirror, the maze, and the labyrinth—images that express Borges's view of the world as mysterious, strange, and ultimately unknowable. In "The Total Library," he writes about a library that would contain everything, including a "detailed history of the future, Aeschylus' 'Egyptians,' the exact number of times the water of the Ganges have reflected the flight of a falcon, the secret and true name of Rome, the encyclopedia Novalis would have composed." And in "Funes the Memorious," a man afflicted with total recall—he is unable to forget anything he has ever seen or experienced—finds he is incapable of thinking, incapable of making connections.

This dizzying sense of infinity—a sickening awareness of the " 'muchness' of the world"—Borges explains, was nurtured by his own childhood nightmares and the dense, stifling atmosphere of Buenos Aires. "You have the plains and the pampas, but it is a tropical city," he says. "You feel the endless number of events, of people, of leaves, of mosquitoes, of all kinds of insects, of serpents. Begetting and mirrors are hateful because they multiply the number of things."

Even though some of his more realistic stories portray the gauchos and landscapes of Argentina with vivid specificity, Borges—unlike so many of his American contemporaries—tends to avoid both autobiographical detail and psychological analyses of character in his fiction. "I try to do my best not to work in my own opinions, because opinions come and go," he says. "I am also very shy—I don't go in for confessions, those sorts of things."

Born into an English-Spanish family that had played an important role in Argentina's nineteenth-century struggle for independence—"we were not wealthy; my father had only six slaves"—Borges was a delicate, near-sighted child, who spent most of his time in his father's extensive English library. At the age of six he wrote a ten-page pamphlet on Greek mythology; and at nine he translated Oscar Wilde's story "The Happy Prince" into Spanish. After attending school in Europe, he returned to Argentina, where he edited various avant-garde journals and became a leading exponent of Ultraism, a form of Spanish expressionism.

For several years, Borges worked as an assistant at a small municipal library in Buenos Aires, but lost the job in 1946, when his anti-Perónist activities resulted in his being assigned to work as a government inspector of chickens and rabbits instead. In 1955, following Perón's fall, he was appointed director of the National Library of Argentina; ironically enough, that was the same year in which he found he could no longer see well enough to read or write.

His father and great-grandfather had gone blind before him, and Borges said he knew for years that blindness was "my fate, my doom." "I know two twilights," he said, "the twilight of the dove—morning; and the twilight of the raven—evening. One is blindness, one is old age."

Still, he continues, "gradual blindness is hardly a tragedy. First the colors and shapes begin to go. The first colors I lost were black and red. Then three colors—blue, green, and yellow—were left. Yellow was the last to go, but now even that has left me. The whole thing turned sort of brownish—everything is very dim."

In an odd way, Borges's blindness seems to have reinforced the qualities of his own fiction. No doubt the awareness of his hereditary fate imparted a special urgency to his meditations on destiny and free will, and by forcing him to rely increasingly on memory and imagination, the loss of sight further blurred the lines, in his work, between reality and dreams.

Except for the occasional lecture trip abroad, Borges says he spends most of his time these days "dreaming away my life." Since his marriage ended—he was married for the first time at sixty-eight and was divorced three years later—he has lived quietly by himself in Buenos Aires. A secretary takes down the stories and poems he dictates; and friends stop by to chat and to read aloud to him. Having made a promise to his mother years ago, he continues to say the Lord's Prayer every night. "I don't know whether there's anybody at the other end of the line, but being an agnostic means all things are possible, even God. This world is so strange, anything may happen or may not happen. Being an agnostic makes me live in a larger, more futuristic kind of world. It makes me more tolerant."

"I don't understand my own country," he goes on. "But the world is not meant to be understood by men. Every night, I dream. I have nightmares—of being lost, of being in an unknown city. I don't remember the name of the hotel, or I can't find my way home in Buenos Aires.

"Maybe I feel lost because the world is meaningless. Those who think of it as a cosmos—not a chaos—maybe feel very safe. I do not. Sometimes there are strange hints that there is a secret order in the universe. Perhaps it is realized after death, but I hope death will blot me out. I would welcome oblivion. After eighty-three years of putting up with Borges—I am sick of him. But until then, what else can I do but dream and write?"

Borges pauses and his face brightens suddenly. A key to the apartment he is staying in has been found, allowing him to go upstairs now and take his afternoon nap. "Ah, the key," he murmurs. "It's like one of my stories—it seems some kind of symbol, no?"

October 1982

JOHN CHEEVER

. . .

JOHN CHEEVER, WHOSE POISED, ELEGANT PROSE established him as one of America's finest storytellers, died yesterday at his home in Ossining, New York. He was seventy years old.

Long regarded by critics as a kind of American Chekhov, Cheever possessed the ability to find spiritual resonance in the seemingly inconsequential events of daily life. In four novels (*The Wapshot Chronicle, The Wapshot Scandal, Bullet Park,* and *Falconer*) and more than a hundred short stories, he chronicled both the delights and dissonances of contemporary life with beauty and compassion.

"There is always the possibility that as one grows old, one won't be able to write," he said in a recent interview. "Some very distinguished men turn out some very undistinguished work. But writers have very little to say about continuing to write. I did wake one morning and think 'Ahh, but I don't *have* to write another novel.' And then I realized I had no choice. The need to write comes from the need to make sense of one's life and discover one's usefulness. For me, it's the most intimate form of communicating about love and memory and nostalgia. As close as I am to my son, there are still things I can't say to him that I can say in fiction. I feel on this particular afternoon or in this particular light that to write is a sort of giftedness."

Cheever's voice was the voice of a New England gentleman—gener-

ous, graceful, at times amused, and always preoccupied with the fundamental decencies of life. "The constants that I look for," he once wrote,
"are a love of light and a determination to trace some moral chain of
being."

Flooded in light—river light, morning light, and late autumn light—
his stories were also illuminated with a spiritual radiance. In fact, for all
his meditations on the sad, sometimes humorous inadequacies of modern
America, Cheever was, at heart, a moralist, concerned with what he called
"the enduring past" and the nostalgia created by memory and desire.

Over the years, Cheever's style became increasingly refined, his narratives more compressed, but it always retained its essential lyricism. His
prose was lapidary in precision, sensuous and visual in effect. He could
describe the ironic—"It was one of those rainy late afternoons when the
toy department of Woolworth's on Fifth Avenue is full of women who
appear to have been taken in adultery and who are now shopping for a
present to carry home to their youngest child"; shape the poetic—"The
light was like a blow, and the air smelled as if many wonderful girls had
just wandered across the lawn"; and conjure the surreal—"Then it is dark;
it is night where kings in golden suits ride elephants over the mountains."

"He can take a watch chain," Ralph Ellison once said, "and tell you
the whole man."

Many of Cheever's descriptions had to do with a certain stratum of
upper-middle-class people who lived in such places as the Upper East
Side, certain New England hamlets, and the suburbs of Connecticut and
Westchester. These characters talked a lot about lawn parties and boarding schools, commuter schedules and country-club socials. Their children
went to dancing schools and horseback-riding lessons, and on the surface,
everyone, as Cheever wrote in one of his stories, "seemed so very, very
happy and so temperate in all their habits and so pleased with everything."

Focusing on his decorous style and his characters' privileged lives,
critics tended at first to regard Cheever as an urbane, graceful *"New Yorker*
writer"—perhaps the quintessential *New Yorker* writer, but a social realist
somewhat like John O'Hara, nonetheless. His tableau, they said, was
limited by place and social class; his range confined to what he knew from
direct experience. "The imaginative identification with the upper middle
class which allows him to depict their mores and dilemmas with such
vivacity," wrote Robert Towers in *The New York Review of Books,* "entails
a narrowness of social range and a sentimental snobbery which can get
the best of him when his guard is down."

Yet as his novels *Bullet Park* and *Falconer* later made clear, there had always been a darker aspect to Cheever's work. Cheever country was defined as much by what his characters wanted to remember as by how they lived. Raised on "the boarding-school virtues: courage, good sportsmanship, chastity, and honor," they usually tried to be decent but more often than not ended up succumbing to alcoholism, adultery, and assorted suburban sins.

There was some kind of terrible missing link between what they had been brought up to expect and what they found in Shady Hill or Bullet Park, and they were afflicted by nostalgia, failures of will, and a kind of spiritual fatigue. In the short story titled "The Death of Justina," for instance, a man looks out his train window and wonders "why, in this most prosperous, equitable, and accomplished world—where even the cleaning women practice Chopin preludes in their spare time—everyone should seem to be so disappointed."

In addition, strange, supernatural events had a way of intruding into Cheever's naturalistic landscapes, imbuing the most ordinary of lives with a kind of mortal peril. A woman pours lighter fluid instead of oil and vinegar on the salad greens. A mother turns her daughter into a swimming pool. A man is ripped to shreds by his own dogs. Two of his most widely anthologized stories depicted just such happenings. In "The Enormous Radio," a broken radio broadcasts the sad secrets of apartment dwellers around the building; and in "The Swimmer," a man swims home via his neighbors' swimming pools, only to find his own house empty, his family vanished.

In many ways, this use of myth and parable reflected a classical concern with the dignity and failings of man. To Cheever, life was "a perilous moral journey," and those who went astray were deprived of grace—or more practically, serenity—in their daily lives. This was not puritanical moralizing on Cheever's part, for his aim was always "to celebrate a world that lies spread out around us like a bewildering and stupendous dream." It was instead a simple ethic of loyalty: to family and place and the past.

This old-fashioned piety came to Cheever naturally. Born on May 27, 1912, in Quincy, Massachusetts, just outside Boston, he was the second son of a family of shipmasters. "Calvin played no part at all in my religious education," he wrote later, "but his presence seemed to abide in the barns of my childhood and to have left me with some undue bitterness."

Uncompromising in their Yankee rectitude, the elder Cheevers gave their son permission to pursue a career as a writer only after he had given his solemn promise that he would "not seek fame or wealth."

They were not a happy family, the Cheevers. "A self-made man who lost everything," as the author once described his father, Frederick Lincoln Cheever was left virtually bankrupt by the stock market crash of 1929, and soon after moved away, leaving his wife, Mary, to support the family with a gift shop—an arrangement the young Cheever found deeply embarrassing.

He and his brother Fred became increasingly close, "unseemly close" as the author later said, and the theme of brotherly love and discord would appear repeatedly in his work.

Not particularly excited by the prospect of attending Harvard, the seventeen-year-old writer engineered his expulsion from Thayer Academy for smoking. He promptly wrote up the experience, sold the story to Malcolm Cowley at *The New Republic,* and moved to New York to write.

Unlike many of his compatriots who were swept up in the heady ideological atmosphere of the 1930s, Cheever remained apolitical. He lived in a cheap room in Greenwich Village, subsisted on stale bread and buttermilk, and occasionally summarized novels for Metro-Goldwyn-Mayer when he needed money.

At the age of twenty-three, he sold his first story to *The New Yorker,* and he soon became a regular contributor to the magazine, eventually earning "enough money to feed the family and buy a new suit every other year."

Although Cheever consistently maintained that "fiction is not crypto-autobiography," he conceded that his first novel, *The Wapshot Chronicle,* was "a posthumous attempt to make peace with my father's ghosts." He refrained from publishing it until his father died in 1957, and, in fact, the book did tell of the decline in fortunes—both material and spiritual—of a New England family remarkably similar to his own. The novel won a National Book Award in 1958, despite the contention of some critics that it failed to hold up as a full-fledged novel.

While working on a sequel to *The Wapshot Chronicle,* Cheever continued to write short stories. Set in that period "when the city of New York was still filled with a river light, when you heard the Benny Goodman quartets from a radio in the corner stationery store, and when almost everybody wore a hat," the stories of this period seemed infused with a sadness that was new to the author's work. He had discovered, he said, "an excitement in sadness, a nakedness about it."

At the same time, he was turning increasingly toward the church—an inclination reflected in his writing by a growing preoccupation with light. "It seems to me that man's inclination toward light, toward brightness, is very near botanical," he said. "One not only needs it, one struggles for it. It seems to me to be that one's total experience is the drive toward light—spiritual light."

In 1964, Cheever completed *The Wapshot Scandal*, "an extraordinarily complex book built around non sequiturs," as he described it, that followed the second generation of Wapshots as they left New England for such unlikely places as a missile base in the Far West and a New York suburb, where they encountered casual adultery, suicide, alcoholism, and insolvency.

The horrors of modern life—irrationality, alienation, and ennui—came to full fruition in Cheever's next novel, *Bullet Park*, published in 1969. In this highly symbolic tale, a man named Paul Hammer sets out to immolate the son of Eliot Nailles on the altar of the local church. Nailles rescues his son at the last moment, then resumes his life, "as wonderful, wonderful, wonderful, wonderful as it had been." Episodic in construction, eclectic in point of view, the book drew protest from critics like Benjamin DeMott, who called it a "grand gatherum of late twentieth-century American weirdos"; praise as "a magnificent work of fiction" from others, such as John Gardner.

By this time, Cheever, like so many of his characters, had left the city for the suburbs. He and his family—his wife, the former Mary Winternitz, whom he married in 1941, and their three children, Susan, Benjamin Hale, and Federico—had moved to Ossining, a town on the Hudson River where the author could spend his spare time raising Labrador retrievers, cutting his own firewood, and riding horses.

"Except that he does not commute," his friend E. J. Kahn, Jr., once said, "John leads a fairly orthodox commuter's life." During the 1960s and early 1970s, that life, it seems, included a good bit of drinking at cocktail parties, and Cheever gradually realized that he was an alcoholic. He had a near-fatal heart attack in 1972 and grew increasingly pessimistic about his work. "I felt suicidal," he said later, recalling that dark period. "I felt my life and career were over. I wanted to end it."

In 1975, though, Cheever was persuaded by his family to enter Smithers, a rehabilitation center in New York City. Upon his release, he said he knew he wanted to write again, and within a year had completed what he called "a very dark book that possessed radiance." The book was *Falconer*, a story of a fairly ordinary suburbanite who goes to prison for murdering his brother, escapes, and finds a kind of redemption.

It was drawn, in part, from Cheever's own observations made while teaching English at Sing Sing prison, but it was also nourished by his own sense of confinement during the past years and his newfound sense of liberation.

Falconer was both a critical and commercial success, and for the author it was a kind of personal victory as well. "Cheever's is the triumph of a man in his sixties," said his friend Bernard Malamud at the time. "Here he'd been having a dreadful time—he was an alcoholic, most of his books were out of print, he was not much in the public eye, but he stayed with it. And through will and the grace literature affords, he saved himself."

June 1982, on his death

JOAN DIDION

. . .

In her book *The White Album*, Joan Didion
writes: "Kilimanjaro belongs to Ernest Hemingway. Oxford, Mississippi,
belongs to William Faulkner . . . a great deal of Honolulu has always
belonged for me to James Jones. . . . A place belongs forever to whoever
claims it hardest, remembers it most obsessively, wrenches it from itself,
shapes it, renders it, loves it so radically that he remakes it in his image."
California belongs to Joan Didion.

Not the California where everyone wears aviator sunglasses, owns a
Jacuzzi, and buys his clothes on Rodeo Drive. But California in the sense
of the West. The old West where Manifest Destiny was an almost palpable
notion that was somehow tied to the land and the climate and one's own
family—an unspoken belief that was passed down to children in stories.

Didion's California is a place defined not so much by what her unwav-
ering eye observes, but by what her memory cannot let go. Although her
essays and novels are set amid the effluvia of a new golden state peopled
by bored socialites, lost flower children, and unsentimental engineers, all
is measured against the memory of the old California. And in telling what
has happened to California in the past few decades, Didion finds a metaphor for some larger, insidious process at work in American society. The
theatrics of James Pike, Episcopal bishop of California, become a parable

of the American penchant for discarding history and starting tabula rasa; the plight of a San Bernardino woman accused of murdering her husband, a lesson in misplaced dreams.

The California Didion lives in, though, is very much the latter-day California. Brentwood Park is one of those sedate residential sections of Los Angeles; her street, one that is lined with Tudor-style homes, white Colonials, and pillared mansions. The rooms of her house possess all the soothing order and elegance of a *Vogue* photo spread: sofas covered in floral chintz, lavender loveseats the exact color of the potted orchids on the mantelpiece, porcelain elephant end tables, and dozens of framed pictures of family and friends.

Still, this is the kind of day that can give Joan Didion a migraine. In the first place, there is car trouble: Her husband's new pearl-gray Jaguar was dented this morning by a neighbor pulling out of her driveway, and her own 1969 yellow Corvette Sting Ray—a Corvette exactly like the one Maria drove in *Play It As It Lays*—needs a new transmission. Then there are the rats. "The exterminator took one look at the backyard and said we were sure to have rats in the avocado tree," she says. "That's when I started thinking about bubonic plague." Today, though, it isn't so much the rats or the cars that are bothering Didion. It's the dining-room curtains: instead of *gathering* the new curtains, the decorator has *pleated* them. The perfect geometric regularity of those folds triggers migraines, she thinks. She is making a new set of curtains herself.

Wearing a faded blue sweatshirt over brown corduroy Levis, Didion at forty-four strikes anyone who sees her for the first time as the embodiment of the women in her own novels: like Lily McClellan in *Run River*, she is "strikingly frail" (Didion is five feet two, and weighs ninety-five pounds); like Maria in *Play It As It Lays*, she used to chain-smoke and wear chiffon scarves over her red hair; and like Charlotte in *A Book of Common Prayer*, she possesses "an extreme and volatile thinness . . . she was a woman . . . with a body that masqueraded as that of a young girl."

There is a certain sadness in the face that indicates a susceptibility to what she calls "early morning dread"; even indoors, she wears oversized sunglasses to protect her light-sensitive eyes. An almost Southern softness lingers in her voice—she identifies it as an Okie accent picked up in Sacramento high schools—and bright laughter punctuates her unfinished sentences. It is a voice so soft, so tentative at times, that one frequently has to strain to hear her.

The "Didion woman" has by now become a familiar literary figure.

Women who have misunderstood the promises of the past, they are habitués of a clearly personal wasteland, wandering along highways or through countries in an effort to blot out the pain of consciousness. They lose their men to suicide, divorce, and cancer; their children to abortion, bad genes, and history. They are outsiders, but they are also survivors, fatalists who keep on playing the game regardless of the odds.

In her highly praised collection of essays, *Slouching Towards Bethlehem*, Didion meticulously portrayed herself as one also well acquainted with the edge. She wrote of "bad nerves," of drinking "gin and hot water to blunt the pain and . . . Dexedrine to blunt the gin." Her new book, *The White Album*, is something of a sequel to that first anthology.

Novelist and poet James Dickey has called Didion "the finest woman prose stylist writing in English today." And she has created, in her books, one of the most devastating and distinctive portraits of modern America to be found in fiction or nonfiction—a portrait of America where "disorder was its own point." A gifted reporter with an eye for the telling detail—the frayed hem, the shaking hand—she is also a prescient witness, finding in her own experiences parallels of the times. The voice is always precise, the tone unsentimental, the view unabashedly subjective. She takes things personally.

The title of the new book comes, of course, from the Beatles' *White Album*, a record Didion found ominous and disturbing, an album inextricably connected to the Manson murders and the dissonance of the sixties. Didion's own *White Album* contains a number of images from the Manson years: Linda Kasabian awaiting trial in a dress Didion bought for her at I. Magnin; Huey Newton lecturing the press on the "American capitalistic-materialistic system"; students at San Francisco State College breaking the tedium of the academic calendar with a campus revolt.

The White Album, though, is not solely concerned with the sixties. Or, for that matter, with Didion's alienation. Whereas Yeats's poem "The Second Coming" ("Things fall apart; the center cannot hold . . .") served as a perfect epigraph for *Slouching Towards Bethlehem*, no such image exists to sum up *The White Album*. This second volume of essays is not so absolute in its pessimistic vision of the world, not so unquestioningly bleak about history. As Didion herself puts it, "*The White Album* is more tentative. I don't have as many answers as I did when I wrote *Slouching.*"

The White Album includes a shrewd essay on Hollywood as "the last extant stable society"; a tribute to Georgia O'Keeffe; and a charming portrait of one Amado Vazquez, a Mexican gardener who raises orchids in Malibu. The collection, in fact, demonstrates Didion's range as an essayist, her ability not only to portray the extraordinary and apocalyptic, but also to appreciate the ordinary.

"I am alienated," explains Didion, "I would say I *am* a victim. But you don't live every day of your life walking around talking about how alienated you are—you'd start sounding like Woody Allen's *Interiors.*"

Both Didion and her husband, John Gregory Dunne, the author of *Vegas, True Confessions,* and *Quintana & Friends,* have made their lives the subject of their reportage. Their thoughts on divorce, their adoption of their daughter, Quintana, and their nervous breakdowns have all been meticulously chronicled in print. The candor frequently stuns.

"[In person] Joan gives everyone the impression of being very private," observes Ralph Graves, now editorial director of Time Inc. who was editor of *Life* magazine when Didion wrote her column. "Then she'll turn around and write this inside-of-the-stomach stuff that you'd think you'd need to know her five years to find out. This mousy, thin, quiet woman tells you as much about herself as Mailer." For Didion, though, it is merely part of the contract a writer makes with the reader: as she once told her husband, "If you want to write about yourself, you have to give them something."

Why has she chosen this relentless self-scrutiny? One suspects that writing holds for her a kind of talismanic power—the process of putting her life on paper somehow helps to exorcise private demons. Writing, after all, is a means of creating a momentary stay against confusion, of making order out of disorder, understanding out of fear.

In her newest book, Didion does not shirk from exposing herself. "You are getting a woman who somewhere along the line misplaced whatever slight faith she ever had in the social contract, in the meliorative principle . . . I have felt myself a sleepwalker . . . alert only to the stuff of bad dreams, the children burning in the locked car in the supermarket parking lot . . . I have trouble maintaining the basic notion that keeping promises matters in a world where everything I was taught seems beside the point."

She tells us how she went blind for six weeks from a condition diagnosed as multiple sclerosis (the disease has been in remission for the past seven years), and how, in the summer of 1968, she checked into the psychiatric clinic at St. John's Hospital in Santa Monica. She even tells us the doctor's diagnosis: "Patient's thematic productions emphasize her fundamentally pessimistic, fatalistic, and depressive view of the world around her. . . ."

Yet this familiar Didion persona masks a writer whose own life is a wealth of contradictions. She is a westerner who mourns the passing of the frontier ethic, but lives in Los Angeles because the city amuses her. She is a romantic who believes "that salvation [lies] in promises made and somehow kept outside the range of normal social experience," but delights in practical, domestic routines. She is an introvert who says she has always been an outsider, but she enjoys attending glitzy Hollywood parties. She is a writer who has dwelled on the atomization of modern society, but maintains what she describes as a "boring, bourgeois" life.

Didion's friends jokingly refer to her as the "Kafka of Brentwood Park," which amuses her husband no end. "Joan's really a rather cheerful person who drives a bright yellow Corvette," says Dunne. "In person, she doesn't have a dark view of life. She just doesn't expect a lot from it or from people."

Dunne, a large, gregarious man, gives the appearance of managing Didion's life. He tends to do most of the talking, frequently answering questions directed at Didion; he always answers the phones and screens the calls. But, according to their friends, it is Didion who handles all their finances and Didion who smooths over situations created by Dunne's volatile temper. "John does not play Leonard Woolf to her Virginia," notes the writer Josh Greenfeld. "She's more John's Leonard Woolf. John may seem strident and tough, but what you see in John you get in Joan. She is every bit as tough as he is." Another friend describes Didion as "fragile," as in the phrase, "a fragile, little stainless-steel machine."

Didion, too, thinks of herself as an optimist. It's an optimism somewhat akin to F. Scott Fitzgerald's definition of a first-rate intelligence: "the ability to hold two opposed ideas in the mind at the same time, and still retain the ability to function." To believe that nothing matters and yet to believe more strongly that it is worth recording anyway.

Her awareness of "the edge" is, in part, a literary idea that derives from what seized her imagination as a child. The people she read about in the fiction of Conrad, James, and Faulkner convinced a young Didion that "salvation lay in extreme and doomed commitments," and later provided models for the characters in her own novels.

"I have a theatrical temperament," explains Didion. "I'm not interested in the middle road—maybe because everyone's on it. Rationality, reasonableness bewilder me. I think it comes out of being a 'daughter of the Golden West.' A lot of the stories I was brought up on had to do with extreme actions—leaving everything behind, crossing the trackless wastes, and in those stories the people who stayed behind and had their settled ways—those people were not the people who got the prize. The prize was California."

We are on a flight from Los Angeles to Sacramento, where Didion's parents live. As the plane circles over the coast toward the valley, Didion turns to look out the window. "It kills me when people talk about California hedonism," she says deliberately. "Anybody who talks about California hedonism has never spent a Christmas in Sacramento."

Didion's family—five generations on her mother's side—come from Sacramento. Although it is the state capital, it remains a valley town where the summers are hot and plagued by drought, and where the winters are cold and menaced by flood. The land here is flat, the rivers and fields stretching clean to the horizon. It is, in short, a landscape of extremes.

In writing of the Sacramento of her childhood, Didion frequently uses the word *Eden,* and to the early settlers it probably was—or at least a reasonable facsimile of Paradise. The confluence of the muddy, silt-rich Sacramento and the swiftly flowing American made the region a fertile garden. It is only within the past three decades that the cultivated fields have given way to tract housing, subdivisions, and aerospace factories; the dusty roads along the levee to eight-lane freeways.

Even as we drive through town, Didion peruses a map provided by the rent-a-car company. She is unaccustomed to finding her way home via the new highways, for the Sacramento she knows so well is a town of the past. "All that is constant about the California of my childhood is the rate at which it disappears," she wrote in *Slouching Towards Bethlehem.* "California is a place in which a boom mentality and a sense of Chekhovian loss meet in uneasy suspension."

The road leading to the Didions' Tudor house once ran through hop fields; today it is flanked by a thriving industrial park. Inside, their living room is a comfortable assemblage of mementos and assorted knickknacks collected by Eduene Jerrett Didion at local craft fairs. A small, forthright woman, she met John Dunne for the first time at her daughter's wedding and told him: "You know those little old ladies in tennis shoes you've heard about? Well, I'm one of them." Her husband is a quiet, shy man. A former Army Air Corps officer who later served on the Sacramento draft board, Frank Didion now dabbles in real estate.

Joan's bedroom is still the faded carnation pink she painted it when she was a freshman at Berkeley, but bougainvillea and ivy have overgrown the windows, giving the chamber a dark, cavelike effect. Didion returned to this room to finish each of her five books. She wrote the last 150 pages of *A Book of Common Prayer* here in fourteen days. After all, there are no distractions in Sacramento: the phones are answered, the meals are prepared, and her parents leave her alone to work.

On a dressing table here, as in her study back in Brentwood, there is a small framed photograph of the Sierras near Donner Pass. The tale of the Donner party has a peculiar hold on Didion's imagination. Traveling from Illinois to California in 1846, the Donner-Reed party was forced by a sudden blizzard to encamp in the Sierras. Faced with starvation, they ate their own dead. Of the eighty-seven who embarked, forty survived. Joan's great-great-great-grandmother, Nancy Hardin Cornwall, was a member of the original Donner party, but she had left the ill-fated group at Humboldt Sink in Nevada to cut north through Oregon.

Nancy Hardin Cornwall's own forebears lived on the frontier, moving from the Carolinas to Georgia to Arkansas to Missouri with the nation's westward migration, and Didion clings to that heritage. "I used to be strongly convinced that the closing of the frontiers was the central event, the turning point in American history," she says. "I am not flatly convinced of that anymore, but I myself feel better the farther west I am." The frontier legacy, she feels, has made her different, has ingrained in her a kind of hard-boiled individualism, an "ineptness at tolerating the complexities of postindustrial life."

It has also made her something of a libertarian, wary of governmental panaceas and distrustful of utopian promises. Like her parents, Didion voted for Goldwater in 1964. Since then, she has voted only twice. "I never had faith that the answers to human problems lay in anything that could be called political," she explained once. "I thought the answers, if there were answers, lay someplace in man's soul."

Joan was a fearful child—scared of ski lifts, of rattlesnakes in the river, even of comic books filled as they were with violence and monsters. She worried that the funicular at Royal Gorge would crash, that the bridge over the Sacramento River would fall.

During the war years, Frank Didion was transferred from base to base, and the family moved with him. The transience made Joan something of an outsider, and she remained one even when the Didions finally settled again in Sacramento.

If she was ill at ease with people, Joan at least found more congenial company in books. "I tended to perceive the world in terms of things read about it," she says. "I still do." When she was five, Joan wrote her first story: A tale of a woman who dreamed she was freezing to death in the Arctic, only to wake up and find herself in the scorching heat of the Sahara.

By fifteen, she was learning to type and learning how sentences worked by copying over chapters from Ernest Hemingway and Joseph Conrad. Her own stories of that period all had one theme—suicide. In some, the hero walked through the streets of San Francisco to jump off the Golden Gate Bridge; in others, he simply walked into the sea.

One summer when she was in the eighth grade and her parents had a beach cottage, Joan determined to find out for herself how it would feel to walk into the ocean. After telling her parents that she and her brother, Jimmy, were going to a square dance, she dropped Jimmy off at the Greyhound bus terminal, told him to wait for her, and went on to the shore herself. Then, note pad in hand, she gingerly walked into the ocean. The night was dark, and she had no sooner waded in knee-deep than a wave hit her in the face. Sopping wet, her romantic notions of suicide considerably dampened, she made her way back to the terminal, retrieved her brother, and sneaked back into the house.

At Berkeley, Didion majored in English literature, and after graduating in 1956 headed for New York. Her passport there was first prize in the *Vogue* magazine Prix de Paris writing competition, which she received for a piece on the San Francisco architect William Wilson Wurster. Her editor at *Vogue*, Allene Talmey, was a perfectionist who insisted on the right adjective, the "shock" verb, the well-turned caption. "At first she wrote captions," recalls Talmey. "I would have her write three hundred to four hundred words and then cut it back to fifty. We wrote long and published short and by doing that Joan learned to write." One of her first efforts: "Opposite, above: All through the house, colour, verve, improvised treasures in happy but anomalous coexistence. Here, a Frank Stella, an Art Nouveau stained-glass panel, a Roy Lichtenstein. Not shown: A table covered with brilliant oilcloth, a Mexican find at fifteen cents a yard." Joan went on to write stories about furniture, homes, and personalities—exercises that helped fine-tune her prose.

Homesick for California, Didion began to make notes for a book set in the Sacramento Valley. The book was *Run River,* an earnest first novel about a failed marriage. By the end of the book, there are two suicides, a murder, and an abortion; only Lily McClellan survives. Already, many of the obsessional themes of Didion's work are in evidence: a pervasive sense of emotional weariness that surfaces in passionless couplings and the rote acting out of expected roles; a yearning after control and order by those who see their lives falling apart; a fatalistic realization that every act has irremediable consequences.

All of Didion's time in New York, though, was not spent over a typewriter. She liked parties. At twenty-five or so, she says, "I decided it was pathological for a grown woman to be shy, and I began pushing myself to make a contribution. Instead of being shy, I became 'reticent.'" She did not talk a great deal, but maintained a kind of Jamesian distance that insulated her from the rigors of cocktail patter and heightened her reportorial eye.

For several years, Didion attended many of those parties in the company of another writer. After living together for several years, they broke up. "I remember leaving [him] . . . one bad afternoon in New York, packing a suitcase and crying while he watched me," Didion wrote in a *Life* column. "When I asked him finally how he could watch me, he told me that a great many things had happened to him during the ten years before I knew him and nothing much touched him anymore. I remember saying that I never wanted to get the way he was, and he looked at me a long while before he answered. 'Nobody wants to,' he said. 'But you will.'"

A good friend over the years had been an ambitious young writer at *Time* magazine, John Gregory Dunne. The two frequently discussed their work with each other, and Dunne helped her correct the galleys to *Run River.* In 1963 they got an apartment together, and a year later, they were married. "I wonder how the marriage would have worked if we hadn't known each other so many years when we were really close friends," said Dunne once. "People have a hard time believing this, but there is no professional competition between us. I think the reason is the six years of friendship when we were both starting off together." Didion agrees: "Writers are very boring to live with. If I weren't married to a writer, I couldn't be as self-absorbed as I am."

By the time they were married, New York had begun to wear on Didion's nerves—and working at a newsmagazine on Dunne's—and three months later they left for California. In 1966, they adopted a baby girl whom they named Quintana Roo after the Yucatán territory.

Didion says she once believed "that I could live outside history, that the currents of the time in which I lived did not touch or affect me." Then, sometime in 1966, she says, she became "paralyzed by the conviction that the world as I had understood it no longer existed. If I was to work again at all, it would be necessary for me to come to terms with disorder." Los Angeles provided a perfect vantage point from which to watch the disorders of the sixties, and Didion's chronicle of that period, *Slouching Towards Bethlehem,* was published in 1968.

At the time Didion was acclaimed for *Slouching,* Dunne had yet to achieve the fame that *True Confessions* would later bring him. In the summer of 1968, suffering from a protracted case of writer's block, Dunne began driving the highways—sometimes to San Bernardino, sometimes to Reno, sometimes to Mexicali. One morning he told Didion he was going out to buy a loaf of bread. He did: 457 miles away at a Safeway in San Francisco. Finally, he moved to a residential motel just off the Strip in Las Vegas, and for eighteen months lived there among hookers, card sharks, and comedians. Didion bought him three sets of clean sheets and a wastepaper basket; she did not see the apartment until the day he headed home.

After sharing a *Saturday Evening Post* column with her husband and writing another column for *Life,* Didion began her second novel. In 1970, *Play It As It Lays* was published and nominated for a National Book Award. Her editor on the book, Henry Robbins, remembers his first reaction: "It was a brilliant book but cold, almost icy. A devastating book. When I finished it, I wanted to call her up and ask her if she was all right. I *did* see it as the experience of despair."

Arranged in eighty-four staccato-paced takes, the elliptical prose is pared down, perfectly clean. The setting is the desert; the cast, careless Hollywood hedonists; the emotional climate, bleak as the surroundings. Having experienced a bad affair, a worse marriage, the birth of a brain-damaged child and the abortion of another, Maria Wyeth suffers from exhaustion, disillusionment, and emotional bankruptcy. And yet, she survives. It is Maria, at the end of the book, who can say, "I know what 'nothing' means, and keep on playing. Why, BZ would say. Why not, I say."

Play It As It Lays grew out of a scene Didion once observed at the Sands Hotel in Las Vegas: At midnight, a woman in a white gown walked across the casino floor to answer a phone. Didion began asking herself, "Who is this woman? What had occurred in her past that she should at this very moment be paged in the middle of Las Vegas?"

A Book of Common Prayer, published in 1977, similarly grew out of a single image. In the spring of 1973, Didion and Dunne had gone to South

America to attend a film festival. While there, she contracted a case of paratyphoid and her weight dropped to seventy pounds. The entire trip took on a hallucinatory quality, and an image of the Panama airport lodged in Didion's imagination. She became "obsessed with a picture of the airport—its heat, the particular color of the stucco, and especially the light which gets absorbed."

The central character in *A Book of Common Prayer*, Charlotte Douglas, is also *de afuera*, an outsider. Thinking she can escape the past, she comes to the imaginary country of Boca Grande, where she is shot in a revolution—a casualty of her own romanticism. A technically difficult novel, the book received mixed reviews. As a number of critics pointed out, the device of a dispassionate, uninvolved narrator results in an oblique narrative that fails to win our complete sympathy for Charlotte's plight.

Given the current visibility of the women's movement, there are those who place Didion's work in that nebulous genre—"women's novels." The women in her novels, after all, are haunted by the issues of mothers and daughters, blood and babies, and they are usually victims of men who have in some way failed them. The men in the novels—Ryder Channing in *Run River*, Ivan Costello in *Play It As It Lays*, and Warren Bogart in *A Book of Common Prayer*—are remarkably similar. All are brash, irreverent skeptics capable of almost cruel belligerence and possessed of a powerful sexual charm. They are corrupters of innocence, destroyers of idealism.

As for the heroines, they are adept at coping with the immediate, the practical, but have trouble connecting the past with the future. Like Charlotte in *A Book of Common Prayer*, each believes she can remain "a tourist, a traveler with good will and good credentials and no memory."

Didion, however, maintains that her female characters "don't really have specifically women's problems; they have rather more general problems." Indeed, Didion is skeptical of the women's movement. As she writes in *The White Album*: "To those of us who remain committed mainly to the exploration of moral distinctions and ambiguities, the feminist analysis . . . [denies] one's actual apprehension of what it is like to be a woman, the irreconcilable difference of it—that sense of living one's deepest life underwater, that dark involvement with blood and birth and death."

Didion occasionally forces herself to do reporting (which she dislikes) to replenish her image bank, to gather new material for her novels. And in both *Play It As It Lays* and *A Book of Common Prayer*, the reporter's eye is very much in evidence, grounding the melodramatics of the plot in a precision of detail. Didion has carefully observed the manners and mores of Los Angeles's moneyed set and expertly records those observations with a mordant wit. "Le island. Le weekend. Les monkey-gland injections," babbles a silly socialite in *A Book of Common Prayer*. Asked about her husband at a cocktail party, Charlotte replies: "He runs guns. I wish they had caviar."

It's a world not entirely unfamiliar to Didion and Dunne. Today, for instance, they are having lunch at Ma Maison, one of L.A.'s most fashionable restaurants. George Cukor is there, as are Jackie Bisset, Dustin Hoffman, and the Jack Lemmons. There are nods and greetings all around as the Dunnes and Carl Bernstein walk to their table. "The same old faces," says Bernstein looking around. "This place never changes."

"No," says Didion. "Time stands still here."

The Dunnes and Bernstein talk about writing as writers will: how many pages a day constitute a good day's work; where the ideal place to write would be. Dunne, who, as his friend Calvin Trillin puts it, is a "creative gossip," regales the others with stories, which Didion occasionally embroiders. The Dunnes' work on screenplays has made them regulars on the local dinner-party–screening circuit, and they are regulars, too, in *The Hollywood Reporter*'s society column "The Great Life."

Collaborators on all their screenplays, the Dunnes regard writing for the movies not so much as a creative effort but as a respite from the solitary rigors of fiction and reportage, and they have worked on a dozen films, including dramatizations of *Play It As It Lays*, *The Panic in Needle Park*, and *A Star Is Born*.

They are currently finishing a screenplay of Dunne's best-selling novel *True Confessions*. That project completed, Didion will go back to work on her next novel, *Angel Visits*. The title, she explains, comes from a Victorian expression meaning "pleasant visits of short duration." Although the book started off as an extended dinner party in which the lives of three generations of a family are revealed, Didion says that the narrative of the book continues to change as she works on it.

When she is in the midst of a book, Didion works at a typewriter in her office from eleven in the morning until four or five in the afternoon. Before cooking dinner, she sits down with a drink and her day's work, penciling in sentences, crossing out others.

"Order and control are terribly important to me," says Didion as she sits on a couch in her den, fingering a tiny green pillbox. "I would love to just have control over my own body—to stop the pain, to stop my hand from shaking. If I were five feet ten and had a clear gaze and a good strong frame, I would not have such a maniacal desire for control because I would have it."

If control is elusive, order at least is provided by a multitude of domestic tasks Didion enjoys: making her own pastry, polishing the silver, taking her orchids to the greenhouse for repotting, preparing dinner parties, helping Q. with her vocabulary. In Didion's novels, the women, too, practice little rituals—improvised regimens relied upon in lieu of any greater order. Even while she is wildly driving the highways, Maria "tried always to let the [gas station] attendant notice her putting the [Coke] bottle in the rack, a show of thoughtful responsibility."

There is in such gestures a means of warding off what Didion has called "the unspeakable peril of the everyday." A means of keeping man's frail civilization roadmarked from the wilderness (the coyotes by the interstate, the snakes in the playpen; the fires and winds of California) that for Didion is always lurking just outside the house. "All the time we were living at the beach [in Trancas] I wanted a house like this," she says of their two-story Colonial home. "I wanted a house with a center-hall plan with the living room on your right and the dining hall on your left when you come in. I imagined if I had this house, a piece of order and peace would fall into my life, but order and peace did not fall into my life. Living in a two-story house doesn't take away the risks."

June 1979

NADINE GORDIMER

. . .

IN EIGHT NOVELS AND SEVEN COLLECTIONS OF SHORT stories, Nadine Gordimer has charted the physical, emotional, and political geography of contemporary South Africa. It is a place peopled by stubborn colonials, well-meaning liberals, disillusioned blacks, and importunate revolutionaries, a place blessed with extraordinary physical beauty and scarred by moral illiteracy. For Gordimer, this country, so filled with promise and fear, is home, and her work remains a kind of spiritual guide to its complicated fate.

A small woman with a strong voice and clear vision, Gordimer speaks with the same unsentimental precision that animates her stories. While much of her work emerges as an indictment of apartheid, her prose is rarely didactic; rather, her method is to observe, carefully and closely, the consequences that politics has on the lives of individuals. "To read that seven or eight times as much money is spent on the education of a white child is upsetting," she says, "but then one goes on to read about oil production or something else. But if someone writes a story about the life of a black child and a white child, you'll understand the implications, the ramifications of those issues in a way the bare facts will never do."

For Gordimer's characters, South Africa's peculiar form of institutionalized discrimination is not merely a political issue, but a fact of daily existence, met on intimate and personal terms. It is a situation, as her heroes in *A World of Strangers* and *Burger's Daughter* discover, that demands continual commitment and that renders an inviolate private life, separate from the problems of the country, virtually impossible—a situation that makes nearly everyone feel estranged, as though they were foreigners in their own country.

"This extraordinary political situation, which I was born into, is a kind of mold that impresses itself on every child," she says. "A child is born and its head is pressed into shape by its mother's birth canal, and I think the society you're a part of also impresses itself forever on your mind. In South Africa, I think it's produced all sorts of distortions—we're all distorted to one degree or another, black and white."

These distortions, as well as the decencies that survive in such a society, have been chronicled in Gordimer's fiction during the last thirty-five years. And taken chronologically, her work not only reflects her own evolving political consciousness and maturation as an artist—an early lyricism has given way to an increased preoccupation with topical issues—but it also charts social changes in South Africa itself.

For instance, Gordimer's first collection, published in 1952, includes a story about a young white girl whose first encounter with a black man elicits fear of assault and rape; another concerns a black servant who humbly laments her place in life. Such characters, Gordimer acknowledges, "could never have occurred in my later writing—I've become much more radical and perhaps that has interested me in subjects that are more radical as well." Her latest collection, *A Soldier's Embrace*, features stories dealing with the difficulties of love between white men and black women, and the ending of a revolutionary movement in compromise and betrayed ideals.

Although most of the stories focus on relations between the races, Gordimer points out that South Africa's fierce segregation makes for a certain "compartmentalization of experience" that limits the vision of any writer, white or black. The white author, she once wrote, "belongs to an elite, and, from the day he is born to the day he is buried in his segregated cemetery, cannot share the potential of experience of the fifteen million on the other side of the color bar. I believe that white writers will have less and less to write about as their inside view of the total society they live in becomes more and more restricted."

With the recent dissolution of PEN's South African chapter, the separation between white and black writers has become more marked than ever. Though PEN had been functioning since 1978 as a biracial organization with progressive goals, Gordimer notes that its black members found themselves in an increasingly awkward situation. On the one hand, they were harassed by the police, who warned them not to associate with white writers; on the other, they were chastised by militant colleagues, who argued for a united black front excluding whites.

"I find it totally understandable," Gordimer says of the black writers' decision to form a new all-black group called the African Writers Association. "They said, 'We feel our place is with our own people.' It came after the Soweto uprisings of 'seventy-six and 'seventy-seven, and there was this feeling among the youngest generation that blacks were going to have to liberate themselves, that the whites just hadn't been able to deliver the goods. It wasn't personal—you could have white friends, but you just didn't belong to organizations with white members.

"And yet, the curious thing about South Africa is that while you have segregated organizations, segregated education, segregated everything, at the same time, in the towns and cities and, of course, on the farms, people are, so to speak, rubbing up against each other. So on the conscious level you have the separation which racial laws have imposed all too successfully; but on the subconscious level, where a writer works, I realized we know each other very well. In conversation, you learn to read between the lines, and between the lines there is this very close knowledge of one another—you know, the kind of dissimulation that goes on between whites and blacks, the lies and excuses we make to one another.

"Suppose a black comes to a white man for something—a job, a recommendation, even a passport. You may as a black person feel very resentful about having to ask a white person for something, but in the end you come along with swallowed pride. Suppose two hypothetical responses on the part of the white man: He could say, 'I'd like very much to help you, but I can't in this case.' What he's really saying is, 'I can't be bothered,' and the black person knows it. In another case, the black person may be unsuitable for the job, but the white person won't say that because he's afraid of appearing to be racist. So he writes a false letter of recommendation—which he wouldn't do for a white person. And both of them know it. The best relationships are where you know someone well enough to acknowledge the lying situation. There are relationships of friendship and loyalty in this situation. They aren't enough to bring about change—they're outside the power structure, but the fact that in spite of everything, there's the possibility of understanding is cause, I think, for hope."

Gordimer herself grew up on "the soft side of the color bar." The daughter of a Jewish watchmaker who had emigrated from Lithuania and his English wife, she grew up in a small gold-mining town outside Johannesburg. She attended an all-white school, was enrolled in all-white dancing classes, and saw movies at an all-white cinema.

"As a child, you don't ask why," she says. "I came from the average sort of white family, and you accepted the fact you could go places that a black child couldn't, the same way you accepted the fact that the sun comes up every morning. It's only later, round about adolescence, that you begin to have doubts about the fact you always have nice clothes and they always seem to wear castoffs. You begin to realize it isn't the same as the sun coming up in the morning. It's not God-ordained; it's man-ordained."

The system of apartheid with which she grew up, Gordimer believes, will not "postdate my life." In fact, in her latest novel, *July's People*, the revolution has already come: the cities are burning, the airports have been taken over by guerrillas, and whites, who have overstayed their time, are fleeing for their lives.

"*July's People* is really the night thoughts of the present," she says. "It's about the sort of things you think when you first wake up in the morning. In many ways, it's there already—the possibilities are there. We saw, in 1975, streams of white colonial Portuguese coming into South Africa from Mozambique, refrigerators and Magic Mixers piled in their cars. And look at what's happened in Rhodesia. When these things are happening, you can hardly call *July's People* a futuristic novel."

"The worst problem, really, is how little you can do about it," she goes on. "It's a very strange situation: in South Africa, to perpetuate discrimination is to be a law-abiding citizen, and to want to smash it, that is to be a criminal. How can you bring about constitutional change in a country where only the white minority has the vote? We were taught in school that we belong to Western democracy, but how can you have a democracy in a country where the majority can't vote? One discovers the lies one lives with all the time."

For all her misgivings about South Africa's present and future, however, Gordimer—who lives in Johannesburg with her husband and children—says she has no plans to leave. Her reasons are similar, perhaps, to those of a character in *A Guest of Honor*, whose "raison d'être was to stay there in opposition, just be there, obstinately, even if he couldn't do much to change things." To write about South Africa while continuing to live there is, for her, a means of testifying, a way of refusing to accept the sad policies of her homeland.

"I was born there," she says. "And it's my situation—by that, I mean it's something I feel I have to deal with. I'm not criticizing people who feel it's best to leave—many people have no other choice—but in my case, I feel the truth of something Jean-Paul Sartre once said, that to go into exile is to lose your place in the world."

December 1981

MILAN KUNDERA

. . .

I T   W A S   D U R I N G   T H E   S T A L I N I S T   E R A   O F   T H E   L A T E
forties, when he was a student in Czechoslovakia, that Milan Kundera says
he first learned the value of humor. He learned he could recognize a
person who was not a Stalinist by his laughter—the ability to laugh was
a sign that someone could be trusted, for it signified irreverence, a refusal
to take history and its policemen seriously. Ever since then, he says, he
has been "terrified by a world that is losing its sense of humor."

"The spirit of totalitarianism is the spirit of absolute seriousness," he
says. "To take things seriously is to believe absolutely what those in
authority want you to believe. He who begins to doubt—he who does not
take things seriously—is either badly regarded or banned or hanged up.
And that means humor isn't only something which makes small pleasures
to us, but it is an attitude of tolerance, too. A small smile is the sign of
a certain attitude, a certain flexibility."

Kundera, who has been living as an emigré in France for the last six
years, learned firsthand about the brutalities of a society without humor.
Since the 1968 Soviet invasion of Czechoslovakia, his books—which refuse
to dignify either the authorities or their solemnity—have been removed
from Czechoslovak libraries and his plays banned from theaters. When his
most recent novel, *The Book of Laughter and Forgetting,* was published in

France in 1979, the Czechoslovak government tried to erase the last vestiges of his nationality: It revoked his citizenship.

By turns amusing and grave, introspective and exuberant, Kundera speaks in Czech and French with a few sentences of recently learned English thrown in for good measure; his wife, Vera, serves as his English translator. As Kundera is quick to point out, he does not see himself as a dissident writer, and his books, for all their controversy, tend to focus more directly on erotic and psychological matters than on matters of political import. They are regarded as "subversive," he says, only insofar as they raise questions of moral and social ambiguity—something that is not encouraged by the Czechoslovak authorities.

"I am a hedonist rather than a politician," he says, "but in modern history, it is not easy to be a hedonist. A writer doesn't want to be subversive—he doesn't want to beat the regime; his own ambition is to discover something that has never been said or seen before. But in a totalitarian regime, whatever is not conventional is regarded as subversive. As for eroticism, in this regime where a man cannot express his liberty in the public life, he is all the more concentrated on his private life—on his loves and his pleasures. That's why Prague under the Communists was a huge erotic paradise. It was one area where people could express their ambition, their vanities."

If much of Kundera's fiction seems concerned with sexual politics, with the shifting alliances between men and women, it also gives the reader a compelling picture of the ironic, even absurd, conditions of life in a totalitarian regime. In *The Book of Laughter and Forgetting,* a man named Clementis lends his hat to a party leader, as they stand posing for a picture; years later, having fallen out of official favor, Clementis is airbrushed out of the photograph; all that remains of him is his hat, sitting on somebody else's head. In a short story in *Laughable Loves,* a young man feigns religious fervor in order to seduce a pious girl; his sexual ploy ends up getting him in trouble with the state's atheistic leaders.

Playfully mixing history with philosophy and fantasy, Kundera creates a world in which routine expectations are undercut, ideals and reason mocked. It is a world similar in many respects to Kafka's—a world, as Kundera notes, seen from the point of view of a small country that has been a victim of history.

"Small countries like Czechoslovakia could never adore the cult of history," he explains. "One cannot imagine Hegel, for instance, coming from Prague. On the other hand, in Russia, both the authorities and the dissidents regard history as something comprehensible, and they take it very seriously. They are convinced they are part of a grand, positive evolution; or they are convinced they live in a great tragedy—either way, they are convinced they are to live in greatness. The point of view of Central Europe is quite opposite. For us, there is no historical mission; rather, one sees the grotesque side of history. Our obsession isn't with a grand future, but with the possibility of our end and the end of Europe."

In terms of culture, Kundera points out, Czechoslovakia has never been part of Russian-dominated Eastern Europe, but belongs instead to Central Europe, with its legacy of Freud's psychoanalysis, Schoenberg's dodecaphony, and the novels of Kafka and Hasek. The occupation of Czechoslovakia, he believes, is as much a cultural disaster as it is a political one: By proscribing Czechoslovak writers and inhibiting artistic expression, the Soviet Union is trying to implement what he calls "organized forgetting"—they are intent on erasing Czechoslovak traditions and replacing them with their own. "It is memory which forms and determines the identity of an individual or a nation," he says. "I developed this paradox—that the fright of death isn't the fear of losing your future, but the fright of losing your past."

Clearly Kundera's own work represents an attempt to preserve a private history, his memories of a country he will probably never return to. The son of a well-known pianist, Kundera was born in Brno, Czechoslovakia; in the wake of World War II, he enlisted in the Communist Party, which represented for him, as it did for so many of the bright young people of the day, "the expression of maximum nonconformity." "All the Czech avant-garde were Communists," he has said, "all the people I admired, the painters and writers. There was a certain beauty and poetry to the revolution."

He was quickly disabused of these ideals, however. Expelled from the party in 1948, he spent several years working as a laborer and jazz musician, and eventually ended up teaching at the Prague Institute for Advanced Cinematographic Studies. Although it seemed, for a while, that a new era of "socialism with a human face" might be possible in Czechoslovakia—*The Joke*, Kundera's satirical novel about life under Stalinism, was published during a period of increased freedom in 1967—these hopes quickly expired with the Soviet invasion of '68.

While his novels have resulted in the revoking of his Czechoslovak citizenship, they have made Kundera something of an intellectual celebrity in the West, where he has even been featured in *Vogue* magazine. It is an irony he savors. In the West, he notes, where artists can become rich and famous, art is often taken for granted as entertainment; in the East, where art remains "the one domain where you can express yourself with relative liberty," it carries "a social importance that is much greater."

"There is another thing I've become persuaded of as well," he continues. "I am convinced that a great novel is always linked with historical events that throw man into situations which demask him. And I think that today on our planet there are two such places—Central Europe and Latin America. I find a lot of significance in the fact that these are also two regions where the novel is extremely alive. Unexpected and new political situations enable us to pose all sorts of metaphysical and anthropological questions."

In his own case, Kundera says, Czechoslovakia's recent history has compelled him to reexamine his relationship with his former country and its relationship with the rest of Europe. "It was naturally very sad to leave," he says. "Whenever you leave something and know you cannot go back, it is sad, and when the town you leave is as beautiful as Prague is, it is especially sad. On the other hand, the Prague which was once a cosmopolitan city no longer exists, Europe no longer exists in Prague, and I, who live in Paris, am perhaps less of an emigré from the real Prague than the people who remain behind. What makes Europe Europe is a certain conception of culture, born in the Renaissance and which is based on the individual. That conception of European culture is dead and dead forever in Prague—and the importance of that tragic event isn't local but European. Seeing that, I know the end of Europe is possible, and that changes your vision of the world—it makes you see the enormous fragility of our culture."

After several years in Rennes and several years in Paris, Kundera now considers France his home. He has made a new life for himself in the Paris intellectual community and says he has no plans to return to Czechoslovakia—"even if one day it becomes absolutely free." France, after all, has given him a special vantage point from which to view his former home: its traditions of rationalism and classicism provide a fitting counterpoint to the Baroque traditions of Prague; and its language, he says, has enriched his native tongue.

And yet Kundera remains a man who cannot forget. Even though he writes essays and letters in French, he continues to write all his fiction in Czech and to set all his stories in the city of his youth. "I always write of Prague, but Prague has become for me a kind of imaginary country," he says. "To write a novel, you must be true to your obsessions, your ideas, and your imagination, and these are things with roots in your childhood. It is the images from your childhood and youth which form the imaginary country of your novels, and this imaginary country, in my case, is named Prague."

Since finishing *The Book of Laughter and Forgetting*, Kundera has started another novel—tentatively concerned with Goethe and concerned with "the confrontation of Prague and the world." The book, he says half in jest, will be his last.

"I believe you must write each book as though it were the last," he says. "It is an illusion for the writer to write the sum total of what he knows, but you must never put anything aside for the next book. I have always had the impression that the book I am working on will be my epilogue, that I will write no more. But I cannot stop—I am condemned to go on."

January 1982

NORMAN MAILER

. . .

"THERE WAS THAT LAW OF LIFE," NORMAN MAILER wrote in *The Deer Park*, "so cruel and so just which demanded that one must grow or else pay more for remaining the same." Clearly it is a sentiment taken to heart by the author himself. Now fifty-nine, Mailer has fashioned a career in which he has continually reinvented a style and a self, using his own personality as a kind of index to discover how the world has changed. The polite young Brooklyn-born, Harvard-educated author of *The Naked and the Dead* evolved, through the fifties and hectic sixties, into the blustering protagonist of *The Armies of the Night*—"warrior, presumptive general, champion of obscenity, embattled aging enfant terrible of the literary world"—and surfaced again in the less flamboyant seventies as a "modest and half-invisible Aquarius." Indeed, the self-portrait that emerges in Mailer's new collection of short work and interviews, *Pieces and Pontifications*, is that of a writer who has traded his egocentric concerns of the past for a new objectivity, his prodigality of emotion and rhetoric for more modest satisfactions.

"By the end of the sixties and into the seventies," Mailer said in a recent interview, "I felt more and more that I was no longer interesting as a subject to myself. In a way, I was no longer perceiving things through myself. I was beginning to look at the world more objectively, and I think my work turned around a bit in other directions."

Given the shape of his own career, he tends to think of his life in terms of decades, and those decades are as distinct to him as "separate countries; the difference between the forties and fifties is the difference between France and England." The forties were a "simple time, a time when I knew what I was doing." He married his first wife, went off to war, and then wrote his first novel, *The Naked and the Dead.* The book was hailed by one critic as "the greatest war novel produced in this century," and the consequences of that early success were to be profound. Not only did his new celebrity cut him off from his own past, but it also made the sort of detached, novelistic observation of the American scene that Mailer then aspired to more difficult to practice. The observer had become the observed, and he soon learned, as he wrote in *The Armies of the Night,* to "live in the sarcophagus of his image."

"I think," Mailer says, "for anyone who's become an author early and has had a good deal of success, as Capote did and Vidal did and Styron did and I did, it's not automatic or easy afterward to look upon other people with a simple interest because generally speaking they're more interested in us than we are in them. This has nothing to do with character, but with the social situation—I am more interested in Marlon Brando than he is interested in me—and it has an immense impact when you're young and relatively shy. You become a mirror and the only way you can perceive events is through the mirror of your self."

So for the next two decades Mailer tried on and discarded a variety of roles, including Greenwich Village bohemian, talk-show guest, filmmaker, self-proclaimed hipster, and would-be politician. During the fifties, he willfully collided with all that was conventional, experimenting with drugs and alcohol and what he once called "the psychology of the orgy." By the sixties, his public inventories of his life had calcified into a kind of legend; he had succeeded in creating a life that personified a popular image of the decade itself.

Certainly, such forays into public life as running for mayor of New York City and marching on the Pentagon provided Mailer with raw experience to write about, and they also helped him to understand "how the world works." The tireless self-dramatization, the courting of public exposure and ridicule—the need, as he writes in the preface of his new collection, to "be there to speak to one's time"—also seemed to act as a sort of "psychic housekeeping," a means of testing his convictions in the open marketplace.

"If you want to know why I do these things," Mailer says, "I do them for myself. I'm old enough now as a writer to enjoy old lines of mine and there's a line in *The Deer Park* I like—'Experience when it is not communicated to another must wither within and be worse than lost'—and I think that's true. I think that when we keep inside us something we think is true and don't speak out, it does bad things to us."

Still, if the rewards of leading so public a life have been considerable, the costs have been high as well. "You're in the position," he says, "of a poor, good-looking kid who decides he's not strong enough, not tough enough, to get all the women he wants in the whole world. So he decides to become a boxer, and he goes into the ring and becomes tougher and tougher and tougher, and by the time he's at the top and gotten really tough, he's also so ugly that the women still won't look at him. So you're out in the world and you learn a great deal as a writer, but it's also very punishing."

"Take running for office," he goes on. "On the one hand, I learned an awful lot about the political process, so I'm not so paranoid about it as I was and, parenthetically, I also ended up with a little more respect for politicians. But in the course of learning this, I ended up making eight speeches a day for three months, and I'm sure I did something to my spontaneous gifts of oratory forever—which has to bear some reflection on your power to form sentences in the loneliness of the room in which you do your work. You know, I'm possibly a less polished writer as a result of running for office and making all those damn impromptu speeches. It ages the brain a little."

Of course, time spent making speeches or advocating causes or going to parties is time spent away from the typewriter; and whether or not the seriousness of one's work is actually affected by such nonliterary diversions, the public's perception of the author often is.

"The price that you do pay," he says, "is that it's harder for people to take you seriously—they're afraid to. They say, 'What is that fool, that flake, going to do next?' and they feel somewhat vulnerable if they like your work. [Today] buying a hardcover book is a sacramental act, and when people have to pay that much money for something, they have to have a certain respect, even a touch of awe, for the author. And if you're unsavory in public life and everyone knows your name, you're not going to sell thousands of hardcover books. The people who sell lots of hardcover books are usually not in the public eye—Saul Bellow, John Updike, John Cheever—and very few people can break that law. Capote's broken it successfully. Vidal's broken it successfully. But I certainly haven't."

Whether it was the literary and psychic consequences of maintaining his self-generated myth, the fact that he felt increasingly out of step with the seventies (a period, he says, characterized by "the lack of ideas that anyone was even remotely willing to die for") or simply a weariness with self-scrutiny, Mailer began to turn away from himself as a subject. Biographies of Marilyn Monroe, Muhammad Ali, Henry Miller, and Gary Gilmore replaced autobiography. And the famous Mailer narrators—the "psychic outlaw," the "generous but very spoiled boy," the "criminally egomaniacal" writer—gradually disappeared.

"Writing is a way of using up anything that's good and bad in you about a subject," Mailer says. "It's supposed to be famously known, for instance, that pornographers end up impotent. It's probably a myth that has a certain amount of practical application. If you work a muscle hard, it tends to develop; but if you overwork it, it can break down. I think something of the same sort is true of the psyche. If you force an aspect of the imagination, it can come to the point where it ceases to return anything at all, and I think I probably got to that point by the time I wrote *Of a Fire on the Moon.* I liked the book in a lot of ways, but I didn't like my own person in it—I felt I was highly unnecessary. And in *The Prisoner of Sex,* I felt my attempt to do something with my own personal relation to things was the least thought-out aspect of the book. I felt I had used up myself as a reference, though I tried once more in 1974 with *The Fight,* and that was wholly feeble."

"What actually happened," he continues, "is that I began to get interested in other people, and this sounds like an extraordinary remark for a novelist to make, but in truth we really write novels out of two impulses. One is to understand ourselves better as we write, and the other is to present what we know about others. And more often it's impossible to truly comprehend others until one's plumbed the bottom of certain obsessions about oneself."

Alternately charming and combative, earnest and sly, Mailer is well practiced in the subtle arts of literary gamesmanship, and he adds that there was also a certain amount of calculation in his adoption of a more objective style. Piqued by critics who have tried to pigeonhole his work, he says he has tended to "start off in a new direction" with every major book, and in that respect, *The Executioner's Song* was written partly tongue in cheek.

"By the time I started that book," he explains, "I'd probably been nettled by people saying, 'He can write about nothing but himself.' 'He can't write objectively.' 'He can't write simply.' *The Executioner's Song* was my way of saying, 'Hey, look, it's very easy to write simply, it's very easy to write objectively; if you know how to write, you can write anything and you can write in any style.' Style is merely a reflection of deeper talents that one hopes to possess."

As Mailer sees it, the finest fiction can intensify "the moral consciousness of people," and for many years he argued that "a writer of the largest dimension can alter the nerves and marrow of a nation." During the seventies, however, he "lost all the easy optimism about how quickly one could affect things in the world as a writer." In part, this was a reflection of his sense that he was growing older, that "the audience was further away, that I was no longer speaking to my own time," and in part a reflection of his belief that today's cultural milieu has diminished the importance of the novelist.

"They're all highly accomplished and skillful and talented and artful," Mailer says of such contemporaries as John Updike and Saul Bellow, "and they're craftsmen to a degree that Hemingway and Faulkner weren't. But I don't think they're as great because greatness doesn't just depend on the author; it also depends on the time. If someone who writes in the equivalent of a Hemingway style came along today, it wouldn't move people as profoundly—their senses are too dulled by TV and their higher senses are too diverted by film. In fact, if I were coming along at this point, either rightly or wrongly, I might be more attracted to writing films or directing films than writing novels."

With such doubts about a novelist's possible influence, Mailer says that during the seventies he started to withdraw from the world. "As you get older," he says, "you realize that what's important is to do one's work and do one's best work and be serious about it. It's not that you're retreating completely—you're just saying, 'It's too much, I abdicate, I resign, I will cultivate my own garden.' You say, 'I will work on that garden on the assumption I will produce an herb that will change all that is before us.' In other words, instead of seeing yourself as the embattled artist, you begin to see yourself as the alchemical artist. Art as magic rather than art as war."

The particular garden Mailer is referring to is his Egyptian novel, which he has been working on since 1972. Part of a trilogy—the second part is to take place in the future; the third will have a contemporary setting—the book is set in the reign of Ramses IX, a pharaoh who lived around 1130 B.C., and for half its length is told from the point of view of a six-year-old boy. Unlike most of his work, Mailer says, the novel "has nothing to say about America today"; rather, his intent is "to create a consciousness that's so different from our own that we read it in wonder as if we were reading about Martians."

It is nearly two decades since Mailer first began to talk about writing a "big" novel, and the stakes and expectations for this new book are high. He has described it as a "novel which Dostoyevsky and Marx; Joyce and Freud; Stendhal, Tolstoy, Proust, and Spengler; Faulkner, and even moldering old Hemingway, might come to read," and says it is sure to affect his literary reputation. "Unless it is very, very good indeed," he says, "it will be like having spent ten years with the wrong woman. I think if you spend ten years on a book and the book is not good, you lose just as much as any man or woman spends being married to the wrong mate. You lose a piece of your life."

Why has it taken Mailer so long to complete the novel? Why has he taken time out for *The Executioner's Song* and the odd journalistic assignment? Family responsibilities and financial pressures—alimony and children's tuition, the aftermath of five previous marriages—have been factors: "When you're young your only problems were your own neuroses; as you get older, those problems are economic, familial—you have responsibilities instead of neuroses." In addition, there are the special problems faced by established authors late in their careers. The youthful need to tell one's story, the drive of early ambition, the joy of "scoring rich allusions"—these incentives gradually dissipate with time, and, as Mailer notes, "a writer who's been around for thirty to forty years is, in a certain way, a battered case."

"That particular insensitivity you have to build about yourself in relation to reviews doesn't do you much good as a writer," he says. "So anyone who has kept working has found ways of renewing his desire to write. And we no more question it than we question our sexual desire. You don't say, 'Why do I have sexual desire?' You're quite content to have it.

"What gets easier is, because one's been through that literary mill so many times, the fears are less and one's professionalism increases over the years. By professionalism I mean the ability to work on a bad day. There's nothing glorious about being a professional. As you become a professional, you become more dogged. You almost have to relinquish the upper reaches of the mind to do your stint of work each day, because being a professional means being able to endure a certain amount of drudgery and the higher reaches of the mind are not enthralled by dull work."

In Mailer's own case, he says that most of the ideas he possesses today (his theories about violence and God and art, for instance, as well as his vision of America as a spiritually impoverished Cancer Gulch) developed during the fifties, when he found himself opposing the dull repressive mores of the times. Today, it seems, he is engaged in "less of an exploration and more of an occupation of territories I reconnoitered years ago."

"What happens is you become the hat on your own head," he says. "You're not having the pleasure of enjoying your own mind the way you used to when you were young, but you have the product of your mind to work with. You know, I ran into Henry Kissinger years ago and I asked him if he enjoyed the intellectual stimulation of the work, and he said in effect, 'I am working with the ideas that I formed at Harvard years ago. I haven't had a real idea since I've been on this; I just work with the old ideas.' I certainly know what he means now—I think there are just so many ideas you can have in your life and once you have them, you have to develop them."

Along with this determination to consolidate the past, there appears to be, on Mailer's part, a new chastening of ambition, a diminution, however slight, of expectations. In a 1963 interview he spoke of "a vast guerrilla war going on for the mind of man." "The stakes are huge," he observed. "Will we spoil the best secrets of life or help to free a new kind of man? It's intoxicating to think of that. There's something rich waiting if one of us is brave enough and good enough to get there." Today he is a more cautious man, less assured of the possibility of coming up with a "vision that would comprehend everything."

"My ambition," he says now, "would not be any longer to try to reach Americans with a book the way Hemingway could reach them with a book, because I believe that's beyond my powers. Hemingway's style affected whole generations of us, the way a roomful of men is affected when a beautiful woman walks through—their night is turned for better or for worse. Hemingway's style had an ability to hit young writers in the gut, and they just weren't the same after that. That would not be my ambition—I don't have that kind of talent. But to give up the ambition entirely is another matter. No, I won't give it up entirely."

June 1982

MARY McCARTHY

. . .

IT IS EASY TO PICTURE MARY McCARTHY AT HOME in France—that "unsentimental country," as she once wrote, "where icy reason had its temples." The classicism and chilly intellectualism of Paris mirror her own rational turn of mind; just as the city's magisterial architecture, its fine restaurants and couture clothing seem to have been designed with her high-brow aestheticism in mind.

This winter, however, cracks are beginning to show in the city's proud façade: a sudden, unprecedented snowstorm has paralyzed traffic, and a succession of strikes has further demoralized Parisians already drained from a year of terrorism and violence. Last September, in fact, six people were killed—and another sixty wounded—when a bomb exploded in front of a discount department store named Tati in the Rue de Rennes. McCarthy and her husband James West live across the street.

Although McCarthy says she still has nightmares about terrorists, her modest apartment seems a perfect refuge of civility and order—a place where intellectual discourse and literary gossip are the order of the day. With its stiffly upholstered furniture, the living room is not exactly comfortable, but it's lovely to look at, all the same. Pale pink tulips, reflected in the fireplace mirror, and a pot of Japanese azaleas echo the pink in the William Morris wallpaper; and everywhere small, pretty objects—butterflies frozen in glass, a tiny brass umbrella, and a persimmon carved from ivory—catch the visitor's eye.

From her perch on a pink chaise longue, McCarthy—dressed in a handsome blue-and-white outfit designed for her by a woman "who's somewhere between *haute couture* and your little dressmaker around the corner"—serves tea and spice cake, and presides over the afternoon. The gaminelike beauty she possessed in her youth has given way to a more stately mien, but her conversation remains animated by the same mixture of girlish charm and intellectual brio shared by all her heroines.

Over the years, McCarthy has written tirelessly about her own life, busily mythologizing herself in the process of inventing a gallery of alter egos. As she readily points out, she is Meg in *The Company She Keeps*—the clever Vassar girl, "a princess among the trolls." She is also Martha, "the bohemian lady" in *A Charmed Life*, whose compulsion "to tell the truth" continually gets her into trouble. She is Kay, *The Group*'s iconoclast and scoffer. And she is Rosamund, the ardent and willfully noble aesthete in *Birds of America*, who is trying "to reform from being a 'hopeless romantic.' "

A more factual portrait of the author was provided by *Memories of a Catholic Girlhood* (1957), McCarthy's closely observed memoir of her Dickensian youth; and with the publication of *How I Grew*—the first volume of McCarthy's autobiography—the self-portrait of the young Mary McCarthy will be complete. At least two more volumes are planned, and when it's finished, the autobiography will minutely document McCarthy's own life—*and* more than five decades of intellectual life in America.

At seventy-four, McCarthy has written nineteen books, achieving recognition as a novelist, critic, journalist, and cultural historian. Taken together, her books attest to a classical, all-around literary career; and they also provide a topical mirror of American life as it has changed over the last half century. In a narrow sense, the books chronicle the follies and preoccupations of McCarthy's own liberal intellectual set, and yet they also open out onto rather more generic issues—sexual freedom in the thirties; radicalism in the forties and fifties, Vietnam and the social upheavals of the sixties; Watergate and terrorism in the seventies. Whatever the subject, the voice is consistent. The point of view is moral (at times, moralistic); the angle of vision, feminine; the tone, logical and cool.

Unlike the works of Rahv or Wilson, McCarthy's criticism does not demonstrate a shared set of radical attitudes toward politics or books, but instead comprises an anthology of reactions to various phenomena—literary, social, and personal. At worst, there is a tendency to squeeze out shrill one-liners at the expense of larger truths (of *The Iceman Cometh*, she wrote, O'Neill "is probably the only man in the world who is still laughing at the iceman joke"); but at its best, McCarthy's essays—and her superb cultural history *The Stones of Florence*—display a keen intelligence and freshness of perception, coupled with common sense and an old-fashioned sense of social responsibility.

"I see her in the Voltairean enlightenment tradition of rational argument," says Karl Miller, the editor of *The London Review of Books*. "Her distinctiveness in America relates to her being some sort of European intellectual, but at the same time, she's rather thoroughly American—someone who is bright and optimistic and practical. She's an improver, who believes things can get better."

Though McCarthy has by no means confined her gadfly activities to the printed page—she even tried to organize a protest to the Vietnam War, based on tax refusal—her social utopianism has been blunted in recent years. "Through the Vietnam period one had certain hopes," she says. "Not that I personally counted on being so instrumental, but that certain beliefs I cared about and groups I cared about had a chance at least of bringing about a better, more interesting course of history."

"I would say now," she goes on, "that I don't think I've had the slightest effect on public behavior. Maybe lyric poets want to have some effect on one particular person. But quite a few people have written me, telling me how I've changed their lives, and while that takes the edge off the feeling that your life's been in vain, it wouldn't disprove the point I was making. That is, if X wrote me saying I've changed his life—what difference would that make?"

As a young girl growing up in the Pacific Northwest, McCarthy had an image of herself "starring, shining somehow," and in the years since, she has constructed one of the most annotated of literary lives. Robert Lowell addressed her as "our Diana, rash to awkwardness," blurting "ice-clear" sentences above the "mundane gossip/and still more mundane virtue" of her colleagues. In *Pictures from an Institution*, Randall Jarrell reputedly drew a wicked fictional portrait of her as Gertrude, a ferocious lady novelist who "has not yet arrived even at that elementary forbearance upon which human society is based." And Norman Mailer simply dubbed her "our First Lady of Letters"—"our saint, our umpire, our lit arbiter, our broadsword, our Barrymore (Ethel), our Dame (dowager), our mistress (Head), our Joan of Arc."

Biographies and memoirs about the New York intellectuals who came of age during the thirties are flecked with references to McCarthy, and central to both the encomiums and attacks is an image of combativeness and radical dissent. William Barrett saw her as "a Valkyrie maiden, riding her steed into the circle, amid thunder and lightning, and out again, bearing the body of some dead hero across her saddle—herself unscathed and headed promptly for her typewriter." And Alfred Kazin portrayed her as the owner of "a wholly destructive critical mind." She had, he wrote, an "unerring ability to spot the hidden weakness or inconsistency in any literary effort and every person. To this weakness she instinctively leaped with cries of pleasure—surprised that her victim, as he lay torn and bleeding, did not applaud her perspicacity."

What was it about McCarthy that inspired such attention? In large part, of course, it was her fiercely adversarial literary and political stands: the vitriolic theater columns she wrote during the thirties and forties for *Partisan Review;* the public skirmishes with Philip Rahv, Diana Trilling, and Lillian Hellman; her impassioned pronouncements on Watergate and Vietnam. She defended Hannah Arendt and William Burroughs when it was easy to assail them; and attacked J. D. Salinger, Kenneth Tynan, and Arthur Miller when others were celebrating their achievements.

To this day, McCarthy appears astonished that everyone does not share her own lofty standards, knowledge—or even her expertise at spelling; and she addresses most any subject at hand with directness and precision. She tells a visitor in detail about the three recent operations she's had for hydrocephalus (otherwise known as "water on the brain"). She casually names various real-life models for characters in her fiction (the bright young woman journalist in *Cannibals and Missionaries* was based on Renata Adler; the senator in that novel on Eugene McCarthy). And she is equally candid about her confrontation with the late Lillian Hellman: "I still feel disgusted by the amount of lying that didn't stop," she says bluntly, adding, "I wanted it to go to trial—so I was disappointed when she died."

The thing about McCarthy's pronouncements is that they are delivered with a distinctive style and flash, and, as Elizabeth Hardwick has noted, this "romantic singularity" has helped her to "step free of the mundane, the governessy, the threat of earnestness and dryness." Indeed, when McCarthy first appeared on the literary scene, she must have seemed like some sort of Shavian heroine—this would-be actress, who used her theatrical instincts to call attention to herself, and who, as William Barrett recalled, intended "to hold her own with men—both intellectually and sexually."

Here, after all, was a woman writer who not only carried on public affairs—and this was the circumspect thirties, remember—but who also proceeded to use them as material for her fiction. Her short story "The Man in the Brooks Brothers Shirt"—which chronicled a casual one-night stand on a train—created an uproar when it appeared in 1941; and *The Group*—which included an almost clinical chapter on diaphragms—became a much talked-about bestseller in 1963.

Thanks to such outspokenness, McCarthy has been held up as an early exemplar of feminist ideals, but she, herself, has little patience with the women's movement, which she sees as "related to the loss of function by women in the domestic sphere." She believes that women have "given away their domestic pride to machines"—washing machines, vacuum cleaners, TV dinners—and as a result have lost their source of self-respect. "I don't care for the whole self-pity business," she adds. "I don't like things that are based on envy, and I'm not such a fool to think that relations between any two persons who live together can be divided up in absolute equality. It's impossible—somebody has to give more."

McCarthy's independent-minded heroines all share a dependence on men ("the mind was powerless to save her," thinks Meg in *The Company She Keeps*. "Only a man . . .") and the author freely acknowledges the large role that men—as mentors, husbands, and friends—have played in her own life. It was Philip Rahv, then an editor of *Partisan Review* and her live-in boyfriend, who helped her get her first literary job—writing theater reviews for the magazine (the other editors figured she must know something about the theater, since she'd once been married to an actor). And it was her second husband, Edmund Wilson, who got her started writing fiction—he put her in a room, she recalls, and admonished her to stay there until she'd finished a story. The result was "Cruel and Barbarous Treatment," the first chapter of *The Company She Keeps*.

At home, in fact, McCarthy seems less the acid-tongued sibyl portrayed by her colleagues, than a pleasant, convent-educated homemaker, cheerfully nattering on in her low, Julia Child voice about the succession problems at *The New Yorker,* and the infidelities of a prominent American writer. Her writings have always demonstrated an ability to mix up the personal and the didactic, the cerebral and the frivolously feminine; and in conversation, too, she moves fluently from discussions of Kantian ethics to analyses of Fanny Farmer.

McCarthy's sentences tend to be as symmetrical—and as Latinate—as those in her prose, but she also speaks with girlish enthusiasm, exclaiming excitedly, like an avid crossword-puzzle addict, over bits of found knowledge and news. The correct pronunciation of Kierkegaard; the exact definition of a kind of embroidery stitch; the alternate name for a chaise longue—all are pieces of information to be pinned down, then happily filed away, until the proper moment arrives, when they may be displayed for the edification of others. Once noted, nothing is forgotten. To this day, McCarthy remembers everything, from the sort of breakfast buns her young son once used to eat at a certain coffee shop, to the wicked limericks Edmund Wilson liked to compose about other writers ("the next one on the list is Malcolm Cowley / Who edited *The New Republic* so foully . . .").

Friends say McCarthy has mellowed over the years—in large measure, they say, as a result of her twenty-five-year-long marriage to James West, a former director of information for the Organization for Economic Cooperation and Development. In Paris, the Wests maintain a busy schedule—cocktail parties, dinners, outings to look at museums and cathedrals; and life at their summer house in Maine is apparently just as social. In McCarthy's hands, even casual events become occasions—"She's the only person I know who gives really nice picnics," says her old friend Stephen Spender—and holidays and birthdays also merit special attention. In such respects, notes her brother, the actor Kevin McCarthy, she has succeeded in "reconstituting" the life they once had with their parents.

As McCarthy has recalled, their parents radiated romance and style: The former Tess Preston was reputed to have been "the most beautiful woman in Seattle," and her husband, Roy McCarthy, possessed a wild, extravagant charm. Life with them seemed, in retrospect at least, a sweet idyll with May baskets and valentines, picnics in the spring and fancy snowmen in the winter—and then it abruptly ended. Both Roy and Tess McCarthy died during the great flu epidemic of 1918, and Mary and her three brothers were summarily sent to live with their great-aunt Margaret and her husband, Myers. It was a harsh and incomprehensible exile, for if their previous life had been Edenic, this new one in Minneapolis often verged on the horrific. The children were made to stand outside for three hours at a time in the winter snow. And they were often beaten with a razor strop—in one case, McCarthy recalls being beaten for receiving a school prize, lest she become "stuck-up."

Although McCarthy's grandfather would later take her away to live with him in Seattle, the years in Minneapolis would leave an indelible imprint. They would make her aware of the possibility of starting over—of inventing a self, as an orphan, out of the raw materials of will and imagination. And they would also make her aware of "the idea of justice"—an idea, she says, that informs nearly everything she's ever written.

"I think the whole thing that happened to us as children really did give rise to these questions," she says. "Not only the sort of divine justice that took our parents away from us and set us down among these awful people, but also the difference between our lives with our parents—which was so spoiled and delicious—and the life in that dreadful house in Minneapolis. And then the fact that I made my escape, while my brothers were left behind. There was certainly a great deal of injustice there—that I was the lucky one."

As her brother Kevin sees it, their experience as children had another, related effect as well: It turned them into critics. "I always thought," he says, "that Mary was busy criticizing the great mistakes that were made back then, trying to set the record straight. It's trying to make things nice again, seeking to regain paradise. And in doing so, you have to show how things are wrong, how they went awry."

"I would think a kind of detachment happens," he goes on. "Something goes so wrong it silences you. But at the same time, there's a tremendous amount of anger. And I think Mary's stifled anger and my stifled anger have a lot to do with who we are and how we've conducted our lives. We had to suppress these things, and it manifested itself by finding fault with things. I think Mary, through her talent, has released a lot of that—using the tools of language."

His sister is less given to looking at their lives in such psychological terms. Having been psychoanalyzed once, she says she is highly suspicious of Freud, for she feels that his theories lead to a kind of emotional determinism, in which will and intellect are diminished. When it is pointed out that all her novels involve groups of one sort or another—closed communities of bohemian artists, academics, etc.—she acknowledges that some underlying longing for family definition might, just might, have something to do with it. But she would prefer to think of the phenomenon as a manifestation of her "political utopianism—the search for an ideal, or, if you like, the Augustinian City of God." "I don't like these biographical explanations," she says. "I like to think things come out of the mind. That is, to me, a sort of reduction: If you say, 'Well, you wanted a family'—so your idealistic, utopian politics just come to that."

It is winter, and the streets and sidewalks of Annandale-on-Hudson—a small river town a hundred miles north of Manhattan—are icy. Clutching a vinyl airline bag containing a paperback copy of *Candide* and a book of notes, McCarthy slowly makes her way up the slippery steps to her class at Bard College.

English 244—"The Place of Ideas in Fiction"—meets on Tuesdays in this attic room. Parkas and knapsacks drape the Formica chairs, Styrofoam cups of coffee decorate the table, and over the green blackboard hangs a crayon-lettered sign that reads, "Welcome to a Subgenious Den." At ten thirty, this is the first class of the day for most of the students, and many of them seem sleepy—or maybe just unprepared or bored. At least, they do not respond with much enthusiasm to McCarthy's questions about *Candide*—"What do you think the message of the book is?" "Have any of you read any Leibnitz?" "What do you think of the Anabaptists?" None of the students have even heard of the Anabaptists, but one girl wants to know if McCarthy's read William Goldman—"he wrote the movies *Magic* and *Butch Cassidy and the Sundance Kid.*"

Although McCarthy eagerly accepted Bard's offer of a teaching chair last year, she is now somewhat dismayed by the prospect of dealing with these students who seem "almost totally ignorant of the whole period spanned by my life, to say nothing of what happened before." One day, she recalls, she asked them about Solzhenitsyn. "Some of them did know about the *Gulag Archipelago* as a title, but when I said, 'What do you think the gulag archipelago is,' they said they thought it was a group of islands off the coast of Japan. It's really very, very disheartening. It's as if they were on some piece of the planet that had broken off, just revolving, turning all by itself—unwitting of either geography or history."

Given her hectic writing and lecturing schedule, one wonders why McCarthy took on the additional responsibility of teaching—particularly now, in the wake of her recent illness. Like many things in her life, it seems largely a matter of will and drive—a sense of duty to her own credo of self-reliance. "I remember Lizzie [Hardwick] and me saying to each other—this was perhaps twenty-five years ago—that we never woke up in the morning without a feeling of intense repentance and a resolve to be better. I don't do that anymore—or almost never. But I do have this idea of improvement—if not in one's powers, at least in one's vision, in one's understanding. I suppose it's all tied up with the American belief in progress. Not that I have that as an idea, but I certainly have it in my personal life. I couldn't live without feeling I know more than I did yesterday."

Certainly these imperatives to better oneself lend a certain puritanical quality to McCarthy's life. Though she and West covet such niceties as an antique Mercedes convertible, though they insist on buying the *best* bottled water, the *best* meat and fish, these luxuries are less frivolous indulgences than eccentric manifestations of her nostalgia for a vanished way of life, and her obsessive insistence on high standards. In other respects, their apartment in Paris is modest, even spartan—there are no time-saving appliances in the kitchen, no television, no word processor or electric typewriter. When McCarthy is writing, she takes only ten or fifteen minutes for lunch, and she spends her free time studying German.

In a sense, there have always been two sides to McCarthy. In both *How I Grew* and *Memories of a Catholic Girlhood*, there is a die-hard, impetuous romantic, who worships Byron and writes outlandish stories about suicide and prostitution. And there is the self-conscious, persevering puritan, who wants to win a pink ribbon at school for good conduct. The first wants to become a famous actress; the second pictures herself as a Carmelite nun.

Failing to win sufficient attention by being a good student, the young Mary will determine "to do it by badness"—she will pretend to lose her faith (and in so doing, actually misplace it). She will lose her virginity at fourteen, renounce her family's bourgeois roots, and become a "wayward modern girl." In becoming a writer, however, she will also develop that other side of her nature—the rational, objective self; and like Flaubert and so many other reformed romantics, she will come to distrust her wilder impulses, attempt to submit them to her perfectionist drive.

"I've often thought," she says, "that I have very little will in terms of abstentions, restraining, though that's been very much developed in me in later years. But when I was young, assertion of the will was not a force for self-control, but a force almost to throw off self-control. I think the only way one can overcome these rather self-destructive drives—to drink too much, talk too much, stay up too late—is by the formation of habits.

"Of course one's tastes also change a bit—one is no longer tempted by certain things that were temptations in the past. For example, I was terribly tempted by detective stories when I was young, and I'd swear off them as though I were swearing off drink. Now, I don't think I've read one in twenty-five years and I have no inclination to read one. Nor do

I have an inclination toward light reading. I enjoy things that are harder more."

Curiously enough, this very same impulse informs McCarthy's writing career. On the whole, her essays and journalism possess an organic assurance—a style, a voice, an originality—that is missing in the fiction, and McCarthy herself says she finds "that writing anything from a book review to a book about Watergate is easier than writing one chapter of fiction." "That may mean that I have no natural talent for fiction," she says, "it must mean that, or that it isn't at least as accessible to me as the other. But I prefer, in the end, writing fiction because you're creating something that wasn't there before. That's where the real joy is. That's where you're really contributing something to the world's treasure."

Indeed McCarthy's fiction has the distinct feel of being a willed creation. With the exception of her first book, *The Company She Keeps*—which melded autobiography and a highly personal voice to produce a wonderfully immediate series of interconnected stories—the novels are all somewhat didactic in conception. Each one, she says, began with an idea: *Birds of America*, a sentimental study of an idealistic boy's coming of age, was meant to "be a novel about the idea of equality and its relation to nature"; *The Groves of Academe*, a brittle portrait of a Machiavellian academic and his sniveling colleagues, was supposed to raise the question, "Where is the justice for an impossible person?"; and even *The Group*, that gossipy chronicle of eight Vassar girls, was conceived as "a history of the loss of faith in progress."

Their execution tended to be equally schematic. "At a given point— usually after the first chapter or second, and again after the third," says McCarthy, "I would stop and write a letter to myself asking questions— that is, Why has this happened? What is the point? and so on. Writing questions and trying to answer them, and on the basis of the answers, going on to write the next chapter."

The problem with this approach is that the narratives grow increasingly mannered; the voice, more and more detached; and the insistent topicality of the books begins to feel dated. In his review of *The Group*, Norman Mailer concluded that McCarthy was really "an engineer manqué in literature." And Hilton Kramer, reviewing *Birds of America*, was even harsher: "The truth is—dare one say it?—that Mary McCarthy cannot write a novel. She lacks the essential fictional gift. She cannot imagine others. Missing from the powerful arsenal of her literary talents is some fundamental mimetic sympathy."

No doubt writing fiction initially provided McCarthy with a means of remaking her own tempestuous past, just as the comic detachment that flavors all her work provided a useful psychological defense. And yet, as McCarthy herself points out, that detachment has also proven to be something of a limitation. "Laughter is the great antidote for self-pity," she writes in *How I Grew.* "Maybe a specific for the malady, yet probably it does tend to dry one's feelings out a little, as if exposing them to a vigorous wind. So that something must be subtracted from the compensation I seem to have received for injuries sustained. There is no dampness in my emotions, and some moisture, I think, is needed, to produce the deeper, the tragic, notes."

If McCarthy hoped, in writing fiction, to transcend the facts of her own past, she would also find that such escape was difficult—if not impossible—for someone of her temperament and talent. Although she says she hopes her fiction has moved in the direction of "greater objectivity" over the years, the novels still form a sort of ongoing biography. *The Group* was inspired by her own schoolmates at Vassar, and the character Kay, she says now, was actually a composite of herself and a friend by the name of Kay. "Maybe it was an impossible fusion," she suggests, "to take as a heroine someone you didn't like, and then to try to appliqué your own experiences—including your husband—onto her. Perhaps that was the real trouble with the book."

The Company She Keeps, of course, recounted many of the adventures McCarthy had in New York—in the years following her divorce from her first husband, the actor Harold Cooper Johnsrud: the desultory love affairs, the makeshift jobs, the dabbling in Trotskyite politics.

Like the heroine of that book, McCarthy says she was an essentially "nonpolitical person" who fell, quite by accident, into the middle of one of that period's great ideological debates. She was at a cocktail party in 1936, she recalls, when she was casually asked two questions: Did she think Trotsky had a right to asylum and did she think he had a right to a hearing? Without thinking much about it, she answered yes to both questions. The next day, she says, "I got a letter from something calling itself The Committee for the Defense of Leon Trotsky, and there was my name on the letterhead. No one had ever asked me to sign anything, and I was furious.

"I was just about to call the committee to tell them to take my name off that list, when I began to hear that a number of people—including Freda Kirchwey, the editor of *The Nation,* and God knows who else—had dropped off the list. And as soon as I heard that, naturally, I turned completely around and felt very glad I hadn't asked them to take my name off because I would have had to be in the company of people like that."

She began going to Trotskyite meetings, and in order to be able to debate Stalinist friends, she began reading more and more literature on the subject. Even so, she recalls, "the *PR* boys"—that is, Philip Rahv and company—"were always afraid I'd commit some awful bourgeois error."

Similarly, when Edmund Wilson—who was regarded by the *Partisan Review* editors as an eminent elder statesman—asked McCarthy out to dinner, "the boys," she recalls, worried that she would embarrass them all "by having the wrong literary opinions."

They needn't have worried—Wilson, who was then forty-two, soon asked the twenty-five-year-old McCarthy to marry him. McCarthy was living at the time with Rahv, but she says they "were fighting all the time." "It was class and race warfare," she says. "Mostly class. His family were shopkeepers mostly; mine were mostly lawyers." She says he used to read her "lists of achievements by Jews"—and that he tried to read the New Testament, on her behalf.

"I told Wilson I'd live with him," she recalls, "but I did not want to get married. Still, I couldn't have married Rahv—he'd never gotten around to getting a divorce from his wife, and I guess I felt guilty. I felt somehow, since I'd gone to bed with Wilson, that I should marry him. It was wrong, of course—I wasn't in love with him, and I was kind of in love with Rahv, and in retrospect, Philip and I probably had a lot more in common."

In the wake of her grandfather's death that winter, however, McCarthy says she found herself increasingly drawn to Wilson's promises of quiet domesticity. As she recalls, "With Wilson, there was the feeling I was going back to my own people. The next thing I knew, I was sitting next to this stranger on a train to get married."

The marriage would last seven years, and several years later, in her novel *A Charmed Life*, McCarthy would draw a nasty portrait of Wilson, turning him into a loud, unattractive intellectual named Miles Murphy, who "wanted to be another Goethe and had ended up as a rolling stone." Wilson shrugged it off lightly, unlike Rahv, who reacted to McCarthy's teasing portrait of him in *The Oasis* with a lawsuit (later dropped).

"You could not treat your life-history as though it were an inferior novel and dismiss it with a snubbing phrase," reflects the heroine Meg in *The Company She Keeps*. "It had after all been like that. Her peculiar tragedy (if she had one) was that her temperament was unable to assimilate her experience; the raw melodrama of those early years was a kind of daily affront to her skeptical, prosaic intelligence." It is an outlook common to many of McCarthy's heroines, and one suspects that their creator, too, shares this unwillingness to trust in fate, this desire to make sense of life through rules, definitions, explanations, this need to control disorder through intelligence and logic.

McCarthy's own life, after all, seems to have had more than its share of accidents and chance occurrences: the deaths of her parents, her "escape" from Minneapolis with her grandfather; her accidental tumble into Trotskyite politics, her precipitous marriage to Wilson. Had her parents lived, she once observed, they would have been "a united Catholic family, rather middle class and wholesome"—and she might very well have ended up "married to an Irish lawyer and playing golf and bridge, making occasional retreats and subscribing to a Catholic book club."

In *The Company She Keeps*, Meg dreams of having a "brilliant career"—she dreams of becoming "a great writer, an actress, an ambassador's gifted wife"—and as her autobiography makes clear, McCarthy not only cherished similar dreams herself, but she also succeeded in using her will and intellect to become that imagined person. After years of feeling like an outsider—the orphan in a strange household, the girl from the Far West at Vassar, the "bourgeois" theater critic at *Partisan Review*—she now seems, in Meg's (and Chaucer's) words, "my own woman well at ease."

Though she contemplates no further novels, McCarthy says she hopes one day to write a study of Gothic architecture. In the meantime, there are at least two more volumes of the autobiography to complete, and these days, she finds, the past is very much present. "You're thinking about it not only when you're writing, but in between—at night in bed, early in the morning. You're thinking over this material, again and again, and it's a little . . . not painful exactly, but on the border of painful."

What sort of self-assessment is she making? "Not too favorable," she says slowly. "But then it'd be awful if one formed a favorable assessment of oneself."

April 1987

V . S . N A I P A U L

. . .

In V. S. Naipaul's stories, there is always an area of darkness just beyond the edge of town: colonists arrive, empires rise and collapse, and a new, not-so-brave world emerges; but always the bush remains. It is a dark vision, and a vision shaped by the author's own familiarity with the margins of society. "It came from living in the bush," he says. "It came from a fear of being swallowed up by the bush, a fear of the people of the bush, and it's a fear I haven't altogether lost. They are the enemies of the civilization which I cherish."

By "the bush," Naipaul is referring to ignorance and obscurity, but he is also referring to his native Trinidad, where his grandfather, a Brahmin from Uttar Pradesh, India, had come as an indentured worker. Now, at the age of forty-eight, Vidiadhar Surajprasad Naipaul has presumably left all that behind, although a deep residue of anxiety remains. Polite, self-conscious, and ascetic, he wears the tweeds and flannels of an English country gentleman. He has won every major literary award in Britain, and has reportedly been nominated several times for a Nobel Prize.

In both his fiction and his essays, Naipaul has focused on what he calls "half-made societies"; places, as he wrote in his last novel, where "the West is packing its boxes, waiting for the helicopters." The West Indies (*The Middle Passage*), India (*A Wounded Civilization*), Africa (*A Bend in the River)*, and South America *(The Return of Eva Perón)* have all been meticulously examined in his spare, unforgiving prose, and he is now working on a nonfiction book about Islam, based on recent travels to Iran.

His meditations on that country, characteristically enough, display a profound suspicion of ideology. "All the awakening has to do with money—it doesn't have to do with any new spiritual development," he says of the revolution there. "Money has awakened people who have been on the margin a long time. Money has also opened their eyes to their deficiencies. Money has filled them with a kind of shame, therefore. Take away the money, and they'll become quiet as mice again." As he sees it, the current stirrings in the Islamic world spring not so much from a distrust of the West, as from a kind of envy coupled with "rage at their own incompetence, a delayed recognition of backwardness."

In Naipaul's remarks, as in his books, there is no moralizing, no positing of good and evil. Things fall apart, but history simply proceeds. His distrust of the colonizers, it seems, is commensurate only with his distrust of the colonized. He rejects as a "fairy tale" the notion of a bright new world made up of young, emerging nations just as thoroughly as he rejects nostalgia for the vanished world of empire. If he shows some sympathy for the casualties of history, his harshest words are reserved for those "revolutionaries who visit centers of revolution with return air tickets," those casual ideologues who export rhetoric.

"Certain subjects are so holy that it becomes an act of virtue to lie," he says of the liberal fashions of the day. "Never say 'bush people,' never say 'backward country,' never say 'boring people,' never say 'uneducated.' But turn away from what is disagreeable and what happens in the end is that you encourage the chaps *there* to start lying about themselves too. So they lie because it's what is expected of them. Soon everyone begins to lie."

Such opinions have obviously done little to endear Naipaul to the liberal establishment, and critics both here and in England have increasingly tried to portray him as a reactionary. They have chastised him for not upholding a popular, optimistic vision of the Third World, but the author maintains he is "not a spokesman for anything."

On the face of it, some of Naipaul's opinions expressed in conversation might seem to confirm his critics' suspicions. He is, as he wrote once in an essay, an unrepentant "snob." Expressed in his perfect Oxbridge speech is a disdain for his native Trinidad and other "primitive" societies, and there is also an intolerance with those who fail to appreciate his work.

"I can't be interested in people who don't like what I write because if you don't like what I write, you're disliking me," he says. "I can't see a Monkey—you can use a capital *M*, that's an affectionate word for the generality—reading my work. No, my books aren't read in Trinidad now—drumbeating is a higher activity, a more satisfying activity."

Acerbic as he sounds, though, Naipaul is hardly a simple elitist; his sharp perceptions are deeply rooted in and validated by his own history. "I do not have the tenderness more secure people can have toward bush people," he explains. "I feel threatened by them. My attitude and the attitude of people like me is quite different from the people who live outside the bush or who just go camping in the bush on weekends."

As a young man in Trinidad, Naipaul developed a fierce alienation and he became determined to escape the boredom he felt there. "These people live purely physical lives, which I find contemptible," he says. "It makes them interesting only to chaps in universities who want to do compassionate studies about brutes." This attitude would give his writing a distinctive tone of exile as well as a detachment, but it would have personal consequences as well. As he wrote in his semiautobiographical novel, *A House for Mr. Biswas*, "his satirical sense kept him aloof. At first this was only a pose, an imitation of his father. But satire led to contempt . . . [that] became part of his nature. It led to inadequacies, to self-awareness and a lasting loneliness."

Writing became, for the young Naipaul, a means by which he could at once leave behind his past and examine it through the distance of art. Yet becoming an author, he says, was harder; it was a willed act of self-creation. He did not feel that he possessed any particular talent for the vocation, nor that he had anything pressing to say. Rather, he wanted to pay homage to the life of his father, who had worked as a reporter on a local paper. And he wanted to be famous. "From eighteen to twenty-three, this ludicrous ambition filled me up with despair," he says. "I had nothing to say, but I had to learn how to write. I had nothing else to do. No other hope, no other opening."

Though his earliest novels, such as *The Suffrage of Elvira* and *Miguel Street*, use irony to great comic effect, the vision darkens, perceptibly, in more recent works. "I have nothing to be gloomy about," says Naipaul, trying to be optimistic. "It's hard to think of a more interesting age or a better age. More people now have possibilities, more people now feel themselves to be men. Perhaps my gloom has something to do with how my brain sits in my head. It also comes from the nature of the profession—

writing is a very solitary business, you know, and the actual spending of so much time writing must affect the person. It's odd, isn't it—the profession can change the man and then that becomes part of the subject."

After he finishes his book on Islam, Naipaul says, he wants to take a rest. He wants to "yield to cliché," to let the newspapers and television define his subjects for a while. "I'll become a Monkey," he says, laughing. "I intend to go torpid for several months and then it will probably well up again—all the vital fluids. Perhaps that's why I've found writing so hard—I've probably been fighting the Monkey side of my nature. But it's something I've done for so long now—I feel confident I will go on."

December 1980

PHILIP ROTH

. . .

IN PHILIP ROTH'S LATEST BOOK, *ZUCKERMAN Unbound*, an earnest young student of literature writes an extravagantly comic novel about sexual liberation and finds, to his horror, that he has achieved not the literary honor he always dreamed of, but a kind of awful notoriety. Nathan Zuckerman is accosted by strangers, gossiped about on talk shows, accused of "depicting Jews in a peep show atmosphere of total perversion," mistaken for his hero, Carnovsky, and pictured on the cover of *Life* magazine. In short, he experiences the same kind of fame his creator, Roth, experienced a decade ago with the publication of *Portnoy's Complaint*.

In Roth's own case, he once recalled, he heard Jacqueline Susann tell Johnny Carson that she wouldn't mind meeting the author of *Portnoy*, but that she didn't want to shake his hand. Columnists remarked on his new status as a millionaire and incorrectly identified him as an escort of Barbra Streisand and Jacqueline Onassis; rabbis assailed him for writing an anti-Semitic book, and *Life* magazine hailed him as the author of a "wild blue shocker." In *Zuckerman*, as in so many of his previous novels, Roth has again made his own life and vocation the subject of his art, reinventing his life and giving it the resonance of literary myth.

Neil Klugman in *Goodbye, Columbus*, Gabe Wallach in *Letting Go*,

Alexander Portnoy in *Portnoy's Complaint*, Peter Tarnopol in *My Life as a Man*, David Kepesh in *The Professor of Desire*, and Nathan Zuckerman in *The Ghost Writer* and *Zuckerman Unbound*—all are versions of the same Rothian hero. Bright, sensitive, and painfully self-conscious, these protected children of lower-middle-class Jews are torn between duty and desire, boyish needs and manly aspirations, family loyalties and aesthetic obligations. They feel put upon by predatory women and overbearing parents, and they suffer further assaults from their own guilt-ridden consciences.

"I think one has one's set of characters, one's set of predicaments, one's set of preoccupations and obsessions," says Roth. "You hope they aren't narrow, but if they are, they are. You just go with what's strong in you. Like a pitcher—a great pitcher has maybe ten pitches in him."

Yet just as Zuckerman is dismayed to find people confusing him with Carnovsky, so is Roth averse to readers drawing parallels between his life and those of his fictional creations. To do so belittles the importance of a novelist's imagination, and it soils the stance of moral seriousness that Roth, like Zuckerman, so deeply cherishes.

"Yes, I had fame like Zuckerman's with *Portnoy's Complaint*," he says. "But it was not nearly so interesting and focused and pointed and lovely and shaped as this. I don't have a younger brother, as Zuckerman does; my father didn't die; no one tried to kidnap my mother, but I thought, What if?

"I was looking for things that would crystallize a vague and hazy experience. I think of writing as acting, as performing and pretending. Why make Zuckerman my age? Because I know what it means to be of that generation. Why have Zuckerman write that kind of book? Because I know about that kind of book and its consequences. But it's language and moral sensibility that transform raw experience into fiction. It generally takes about ten years to catch up on experience—for it to fade away as experience and to reassert itself as a product of the imagination. But the experience is only the ground that you set your feet on. It isn't that it happened to you. You want to make words out of things you've seen. Those who convert literature into gossip don't get what reading's all about."

Reticent about his life, though eager to talk about Truth and Art and Fiction, Roth, at the age of forty-eight, still displays the professorial manner he acquired as a young graduate student, serving a literary apprenticeship to the old masters Henry James and Gustave Flaubert. Like the hero of *My Life as a Man*, who speaks of "the decorousness, the orderliness, the underlying sobriety, that 'responsible' manner that I continue to affect," he is sensitive about his "Good Name."

Only with close friends does Roth also display his talent for verbal improvisation and mimicry, and his manic wit—gifts developed as a child listening to such borscht-belt comedians as Henny Youngman. Yet it is these two inimical sensibilities together—the one willfully civilized, the other wildly comic; one, tender and sentimental; the other, satiric and Rabelaisian—that form the animating forces of Roth's fiction, accounting for what he has called the curious "zigzag" of his career.

Certainly his early work, from *Goodbye, Columbus*, which won him a National Book Award at the age of twenty-six, to *When She Was Good*, a studied account of a midwestern Joan of Arc bent on a moral crusade, reflected a preoccupation with civility and the duties of adulthood. The prose was refined, even fastidious, and it was informed by an earnest morality. At the time, Roth, who had grown up in Newark the son of an insurance salesman, tended to regard fiction as "something like a religious calling"—an elevated notion, he once wrote, that "dovetailed nicely in my case with a penchant for ethical striving that I had absorbed as a Jewish child."

He approached his chosen vocation with high ideals and modest expectations. "My expectation was that I would always have to teach at a university to earn a living," he recalls. "Nor did I particularly just want to be a writer. There is a studious side of me that likes to read and teach, and back then, thirty-eight hundred dollars a year was quite enough for me to live on."

By the mid-sixties, however, things had changed. Roth had spent several years in psychoanalysis; he had been scarred by a bad marriage, not unlike the one depicted in *My Life as a Man;* and he had begun to hunger after the success he saw such friends as John Updike and William Styron achieving.

Having declared himself for "the art of Tolstoy, James, Flaubert, and Mann"—"whose appeal was as much in their heroic literary integrity as in their work"—Roth believed he had sealed himself "off from being a morally unacceptable person." Instead, he found himself being criticized as "self-hating," tasteless, and anti-Semitic; and he soon set himself the rather odd goal, as he wrote in *Reading Myself and Others*, "of becoming the writer some Jewish critics had been telling me I was all along: irresponsible, conscience-less, unserious."

The result, of course, was *Portnoy,* which used to outrageous effect the raw, impassioned humor Roth's friends had been enjoying in private for years—humor that would be pushed to even greater extremes in *The Breast, Our Gang,* and *The Great American Novel.* The theme of *Portnoy,* appropriately enough, was the throwing-off of duty, its hero's determined and futile attempt to free himself from responsibility and guilt.

With *Portnoy,* Roth got the success he'd wanted, and he got it in spades. "It was beginning to come writers' way in the sixties," he says. "Aside from Hemingway and Faulkner, ordinary writers didn't become celebrities that way before. Then in the mid-sixties Mary McCarthy published *The Group,* and she wound up on the cover of *Time.* Mary McCarthy, of all people. The crucial ingredients are sex and money—sex as a subject, money as an outcome. They make the writer accessible to the public as something more than a writer because they have a sensational aspect."

Roth says he was initially pleased with his sudden fame, then bewildered, and finally alarmed. Unlike his hero Zuckerman, he did not stay in New York, but escaped his new-found celebrity by moving first to Yaddo, the writers' colony, and later to an old farmhouse in Connecticut, where he still spends half of every year. Like Lonoff, the reclusive author he portrayed in *The Ghost Writer,* Roth has become "deeply skeptical of the public world" and now leads a willfully quiet life. His days are spent "turning sentences around"; his evenings in reading novels, underlining important passages just the way he did when he was a graduate student at the University of Chicago many years ago.

"The concentration of writing requires silence," he says. "For me, large blocks of silence. It's like hearing a faint Morse code—a faint signal is being given, and I need quiet to pick it up. Besides, what do I need the city for? A little bit goes a long way. One week in New York will take care of me for a year."

These days, Roth spends several months a year in London and he also travels frequently to Eastern Europe to talk with local writers. His interest, he says, derives from a sense of "temperamental and literary kinship" and from a profound appreciation of the differences between their lives and his.

"I was struck by what happens to a celebrated writer there and what happens to a celebrated writer here," he says, comparing the consequences of his writing a book like *Portnoy* in the United States with the consequences of, say, his friend Milan Kundera's writing a book in Czechoslovakia. "The difference was in freedom and the differences from my point of view were almost comically vivid: In my situation, everything goes and nothing matters; in their situation, nothing goes and everything matters. Every word they write has endless implications, whereas in the States, one often doesn't have the sense of making an impact at all."

There is to these remarks a certain wistful longing, as though Roth regrets the gaudy consequences of his own literary success. In *Zuckerman Unbound,* the hero experiences a similar feeling: his fame has cut him off from his family, his past, and his early expectations. All that remains to be done is to continue writing. As another Rothian hero remarks, "Literature got me into this and literature is gonna have to get me out."

May 1981

WILLIAM STYRON

. . .

As he struggles to write his first novel, Stingo, the young hero of *Sophie's Choice,* dreams of becoming "a writer— a writer with the same ardor and the soaring wings of the Melville or the Flaubert or the Tolstoy or the Fitzgerald who had the power to rip my heart out and keep a part of it and who each night, separately and together, were summoning me to their incomparable vocation."

Stingo, as many readers will realize, is a fictional version of his creator—a portrait of the author as a young man, innocent of history and hungry for artistry and fame. William Styron, who is fifty-seven, has now spent some three decades working at that vocation. Like Stingo, he wrote a precocious first novel *(Lie Down in Darkness)* about a young southern girl and her familial legacy of guilt. Like Stingo, he followed that achievement with a short novel *(The Long March)* about his adventures in the war—"a taut, searing book eviscerating the military in a tragicomedy of the absurd." And, like Stingo, he also wrote a lengthy historical novel *(The Confessions of Nat Turner)*, chronicling the life of "that tragic Negro firebrand." Yet, while a middle-aged Stingo talks of the "pooping-out of ego and ambition," Styron says that, after writing four books, he feels no diminution of powers, only a pleasant "placation of devouring ambition."

"I feel I'm at a good point," he says. "I feel healthier than I did years ago when I was drinking a lot, and I think I can write with somewhat more ease than I could long ago. Looking back, I think I see a growth and maturation—certainly in my style. I don't feel at all ashamed of *Lie Down in Darkness*—except for one or two floridly derivative passages. What I'm saying is I think the style of a book like *Sophie's Choice* shows a kind of serenity that my earlier work does not have—it's the quality of not calling attention to one's own language. It was also very, very good to feel such a sense of having written a book that sort of worked on all the levels one wished it to work on."

Although Styron regards *Sophie's Choice* as essentially a story about "the awakening of a young man from innocence into revelation," it is also the story of Sophie, the beautiful but haunted survivor of Auschwitz, whom young Stingo befriends. It is a complicated story about innocence and evil, memory and desire, a story about the ways in which the past intrudes relentlessly upon the present, and like Styron's previous novels, it touches upon other ambitious themes. This penchant for creating novels with large canvases apparently stems from a suspicion that his own life, in Styron's words, "has been rather ordinary—vast areas of it are just not dramatic or interesting enough to write about," and it stems, too, from his philosophical sympathy with Melville's dictum that "to write a mighty book, you need a mighty theme."

"I think too many writers in recent years have been boring or insignificant because they haven't sought themes commensurate with their imaginations," he says. "There's nothing wrong with the material of middle-class life—that's been the bread and butter of contemporary writing for centuries—but, again, I think one has to either establish a new theme around it or in some way invigorate this raw material. I think Updike does it rather well. At his best, he's probably our best internist of middle-class life, its delights and diseases. But he's an immensely gifted writer, and I think others who have attempted this have come back with the same old tired stories."

There is, Styron believes, "some sort of poetic apprehension, an excitement, that comes when you're writing about the most important things within your command." His own novels tend to focus on one recurrent theme, namely "the catastrophic propensity on the part of human beings to attempt to dominate one another." Combined with a southerner's acute sense of history, this theme tends to result in a vision that is both tragic and fatalistic.

A baroque taste for violence frequently informs Styron's novels—

murder, suicide, and rape are recurrent motifs—and, for all their differences, his heroes remain alike in one respect: all of them are victims, casualties of history and society, as well as of their own weaknesses and failings.

"There doesn't seem to be any rational order in existence," Styron says. "This is certainly not an original view, but it seems to me that human beings are a hair's breadth away from catastrophe at all times—both personally and on a larger historical level, and this, perhaps, is why I've written the sort of books I have. I mean, I was never a slave nor was I at Auschwitz, but somehow these two modes of existence sort of grabbed me and became a kind of metaphor for what I believe a great deal of life is about. Why is it that the human animal, unlike other creations in the framework of nature, is the only entity capable of destroying itself and its fellows? It seems to me that evil plainly is an attribute only of the human being and that with rhythmic regularity it creates horrendous situations in which it threatens to destroy itself in the form of wars, political despotism, fascism, or slavery.

"This theme has really found me. Why, I don't know. Perhaps it's a result of being in World War II—being a fairly sensitive boy of eighteen and finding myself in a war which, however just it might have been, nonetheless threatened to kill me. I think something like that, which affected many men of my generation, caused me to wonder about human domination, about the forces in history that simply wipe you out. You're suddenly a cipher—you find yourself on some hideous atoll in the Pacific, and if you're unlucky you get a bullet through your head. And within the microcosm of the Marine Corps itself you're just a mound of dust in terms of free will, and I think this fact of being utterly helpless enlarges one's sensitivity to the idea of evil."

Just as Styron's preoccupation with evil stems from a particular episode in his life, his books, however ambitious, also remain grounded in distinctly autobiographical concerns. In writing about Stingo in *Sophie's Choice*—"a fairly complicated and bedeviled person with a comical gift which saves him from his own miseries"—he says he was trying to rediscover his own past. With Nat Turner, he tried to reinvent the slave leader in his own image as a means of fulfilling "the moral imperative of every white southerner—to come to know the Negro."

"He was indeed a reflection of me, and I don't apologize to the blacks for that at all, because I think that any character of substance in a literary work is a product of the author's personality. I think that by turning my own residual southern racial crotchets around—in effect, trying to view white men like me from Nat Turner's point of view—I was able to work out a lot of possible racial bigotries."

For Styron, in fact, writing represents a kind of therapy, a way of coming to terms with life through self-analysis: "I look back on the characters in my books—and there are so many who are neurotic, unable to cope, frustrated, and obsessed—as an attempt to get rid of my own frustrations and obsessions." It was Styron's first novel, *Lie Down in Darkness*—the story of Peyton Loftis's struggles with a heavy-drinking father and domineering mother—that explored, perhaps most intimately, his personal dilemmas. Although he once spoke of modeling Peyton on a friend who committed suicide, he now points out that her plight was based more on his own adolescent gropings and struggles with "a step-mother who was as close to the wicked-stepmother image as one can possibly imagine."

"Now that my father and stepmother are both gone, I think I can speak without hesitation," he says. "*Lie Down in Darkness* is a book which is really a mirror of the family life I myself put up with. Plainly, in writing this, I had brought resources of what I hoped was art to the whole thing. I wanted to be a writer, I was dying to write a book, and I saw, even then, the necessity of embedding this in a sociological framework—to show a small town in the South in all its variety, to show the kind of rootless upper-middle-class country-club life I'd seen. So I put it on a larger canvas, but the basic torment between Peyton and her family was really a projection of my own sense of alienation from my own tiny family. That is, my father, whom I really loved, and this strange woman who had just come on the scene and who—I think I'm speaking as objectively as I can—was really trying to make my life a hell."

"The book was a form of self-psychoanalysis, which freed me of any need to go to a shrink," he continues. "I was never in despair like Peyton, but at the age of twenty-two, when I started that book, I remember being in a wildly unhappy state of neurotic angst. I had very few underpinnings. My emotional life was in upheaval. I'd lost what little faith I had in religion. I was just adrift, and the only thing that allowed me any kind of anchor was the idea of creating a work of literature which somehow would be a thing of beauty in the old-fashioned sense of the word and would also be a kind of freeing for me of these terrible conflicts that were in my soul. And by the time I got to the end of that tunnel I was a relatively happy young man."

Since then, Styron has found that writing helps him "keep an equilibrium," and he has shaped his life around his work. For the last twenty-eight years, he and his wife Rose have lived quietly in rural Connecticut. Although they occasionally see such neighbors as Philip Roth and Arthur Miller, Styron says, "I don't feel myself caught up in the New York literary life or, God forbid, the academic literary life, which is my idea of living death."

Pinned to the wall of his study is a quotation from Flaubert—"Be regular and orderly in your life like a bourgeois, so that you may be violent and original in your work"—and these days Styron spends most afternoons in this room, working on his next book, a long novel about the Marine Corps, set during the Korean War. He has already written some fifty thousand words and is planning a field trip to Nicaragua this winter to gather further background material. Somewhat reminiscent of Conrad's *Lord Jim*, the novel focuses on the spiritual plight of a brave and intellectually gifted marine colonel who is obsessed by memories of an atrocity he committed in Nicaragua years before. The book, says Styron, is intended to be a kind of "parable of the United States' nosy involvement in places like Latin America."

While the book once posed considerable difficulties—he put it aside to work on *Sophie's Choice*—Styron says that writing in general has actually become somewhat easier over the years. "I think that you no longer agonize, like Flaubert, over *le mot juste*. You still want to write a felicitous sentence, but it's not going to kill you if it's not the most beautiful thing in Christendom. So you're satisfied, not with second best but with the best you can do."

What's more, Styron says he no longer worries whether his next novel will exceed or approximate the success of his previous ones, for he thinks of writing not as "a series of mountain peaks, but as a plateau with a series of indentations. . . . It's a rolling landscape, rather than one of these theatrical Wagnerian dramas with peak after peak, one being higher or bigger."

Given the achievement of such authors as Faulkner, Fitzgerald, and Hemingway, Styron says he thinks it took his own postwar generation "longer to get out from under the shadow of its predecessors than probably any other literary generation. We were intimidated by the grandeur of these people, and I think we were unduly worried about our own abilities to cope."

When *Lie Down in Darkness* first appeared, many critics discerned "echoes of William Faulkner," and Styron himself acknowledged early debts to the master of Yoknapatawpha County, as well as to Robert Penn Warren and Thomas Wolfe. Those influences have since been submerged in his own narrative style.

"I think I've realized I've achieved a voice," he says. "It may not be as striking as that of some of my predecessors, but who cares? I think that every writer who is serious, who grew up in my generation, has wanted to say, 'Okay, look here, we cannot be epigones for the rest of our lives. We are now grown men. Don't compare us with our predecessors. Read us because we are whoever we are—Styron, Mailer, Updike, Roth, or whoever, and judge us on our own achievement.' And I think we have finally achieved that. I don't think there's been any successor to Faulkner in terms of sheer protean genius and energy, but I think there have been a significant number of writers of the generation after Faulkner who have written beautifully and well about their times. The point is that in our own way we are as good, and I don't think that's a vainglorious statement. I think the postwar writers have achieved a rather remarkable body of work."

December 1982

JOHN UPDIKE

.   .   .

AN HOUR NORTH OF BOSTON, IN A SUBURB NOT unlike those inhabited by the men and women in his novels and short stories, John Updike lives in an old New England house. Although the study betrays its owner's literary vocation—floor-to-ceiling shelves filled with his own books in a dozen languages, ungainly stacks of galleys waiting to be reviewed, and a National Book Award tucked away in the corner of an unused bar—the eighteenth-century house, with its comfortable blend of tradition and modernity, might belong to any suburban couple. There are antique wing chairs and a nubby, white Design Research sofa in the living room, snapshots of children from two marriages on the walls, and golf clubs on the floor. Indeed, Updike's home testifies to the same virtues of the ordinary and the domestic that he has illumined throughout his fiction.

Gracious and self-deprecating, Updike possesses a boyish charm similar to that radiated by his heroes. The deracinated voice is soft, the smile quick, the conversation imprinted with a slight stutter and an unconscious gift for metaphor. At forty-nine, he has written twenty-five books, and his work, considered as a whole, gives—as he once wrote in an essay on Vladimir Nabokov—"the happy impression of an oeuvre, of a continuous task carried forward variously, of a solid personality, of a plentitude of gifts explored, knowingly."

Endowed with a pictorial imagination and a poet's sensitivity to language, Updike has taken as his subject the American middle class—with all the sweetness and pain attendant upon its rituals of marriage and divorce and child-raising—and defined, with perhaps more precision than any other American author, the mundane crises of contemporary life.

Updike's latest book, *Rabbit Is Rich,* is a sequel of sorts to two earlier "Rabbit" novels: the critically acclaimed *Rabbit Run,* written when he was twenty-eight, and *Rabbit Redux,* which appeared nearly a decade ago. Unlike much of his recent work, the Rabbit books are not set on Boston's sedate North Shore, where Updike currently resides, but in the Pennsylvania of his youth; the hero, Harry "Rabbit" Angstrom, is not an educated, suburban sophisticate, but a former high-school basketball star who now sells cars. While this subject matter is occasionally at odds with Updike's cultivated voice, the novels remain a testament to his belief that "there is a lot worth saying about people who aren't especially beautiful or bright or urban."

Written as a kind of reaction to Jack Kerouac's *On the Road, Rabbit Run* traced not only a young man's desire to flee the constrictions of domestic life, but also the consequences of his flight on those around him. *Rabbit Redux* found Harry ten years older, working as a linotype operator, and terribly confused by the public events of the 1960s—the feminist revolution, the black movement, and the Vietnam War—which intrude upon and shake his comfortable family nest.

The reverberations of those years have faded somewhat by the time Harry surfaces again in *Rabbit Is Rich.* It is 1979, and he has inherited his father-in-law's Toyota agency, joined the local country club, and settled into the comfortable but precarious limbo of middle age; he feels "a strange sort of peace at his time of life like a thrown ball at the top of its arc is for a second still."

There is a certain stillness to this book as well—it is flatter, less vigorous somehow, than its predecessors. Harry's search for an old girlfriend and the child of his she once bore, his decision to move out of his mother-in-law's house, and his realization that his son Nelson is reliving his own mistakes—these bare bones of narrative action make for a feeling of willful circularity. Instead of charting, as he did in the previous books, Rabbit's growth and his struggles against the temper of the times, Updike now seems more interested in delineating his character's state of mind. And in an odd way, this impulse seems appropriate to Harry and his condition: middle age, after all, is a period of consolidation, of stock-taking, of stasis even, and its peculiar tone and texture are here subtly evoked.

It is not a pleasant book, this third Rabbit novel. Updike has always been fascinated by the dark underside of American domestic life, and in *Rabbit Is Rich* his scrutiny focuses on the guilt and resentments shared by husbands and wives, fathers and their children. Both the sex Harry engages in and the language he employs are considerably cruder than before, and this change in his psychic metabolism attests to a certain change in the society around him. As documented by Updike's keen journalistic eye, America has become an ugly, materialistic place—defined by disco music, television shows, and cheap hamburger joints—the controlling metaphors of which are shortages of gas and runaway inflation.

As a trilogy, in fact, Updike's Rabbit novels constitute something of an epic: They chronicle both the maturation of one aging athlete and the evolution of an America through three remarkable decades. In addition, they help define Updike's own philosophy and art, for while Harry bears little immediate resemblance to his decorous creator, the two do share, as the author puts it, certain qualities of "Rabbitness."

"He's about my age, though a year younger," says Updike, who speaks in the same measured, precise prose as his books. "He is very human in that he's a compound of physical urgencies and spiritual illusions. In this, he resembles not only me but, I suspect, many men. Also, I think, like me, he's kind of good-natured and accepting of what happens to him as though it were a sort of letter from above."

What else can Updike say about Rabbitness? He pauses. "A wish to do no harm, as long as it doesn't cost him a great deal to avoid harm, is part of his character. A certain hardness of heart is also true of him; he is kind of callous at times. Yet he also has a great willingness to learn. He, like me, has been taught a lot not only by individual instructors, but by the times. It's been an era of increasing openness, of reconciliation to our bodies."

Indeed, like so many members of his—and his author's—generation, Rabbit is caught on the margins of a changing morality, living in a time when the old pieties and restrictions no longer really hold, when the temptations of a new, hectic sexuality are a constant lure. He is torn between old-fashioned notions of duty and self-sacrifice, and the new imperatives of self-fulfillment. Pulled down by the importunate demands of the flesh and raised up by vague spiritual aspirations, he wants to be both safe and free, and so suffers from guilt even as he yearns for salvation. His heroes, observes Updike, "oscillate in their moods between an enjoyment of the comforts of domesticity and the familial life, and a sense that their essential identity is a solitary one—to be found in flight and loneliness and even in adversity. This seems to be my feeling of what being a male human being involves."

These conflicts, so endemic in Updike's characters, from the Reverend Thomas Marshfield in *A Month of Sundays* to Henry Bech in *Bech: A Book*, are somewhat muted in *Rabbit Is Rich*. Harry has begun to enjoy what his creator calls the "relative happiness and freedom from tension that you might find in your forties." And in terms of his own career and life, Updike, too, seems to have achieved a measure of peace, although that very fact elicits a kind of melancholy, a spiritual discomfort with the quiescence of middle age.

"I have no earthly reason for complaint, really," he says, "though this doesn't necessarily make a contented person. There's a moment in the organism when it's thrust outward into the world and the call to mate and the need to make your mark no longer clamor at you, but the body hasn't quite begun to collapse, so in a strange way it's kind of a happy moment. But while being at peace is probably a pretty good condition for a car salesman, I'm not sure it's a good condition for a writer.

"I look back now to when I was a college student and marvel that that skinny fellow had the courage to throw himself on the world and appoint himself a writer. So I'm pretty content professionally, though I'm at a curious moment, it seems to me, when I must push on. In a certain sense what I once could do, I can't do now, so I have to locate what I can do."

Clearly Updike is not suffering from the sort of writer's block that afflicted the aging hero of *Bech: A Book*. Besides producing nearly a book a year, he regularly contributes stories and book reviews to *The New Yorker*. But he seems, nonetheless, to be plagued by persistent doubts. Having started out as a poet, he now writes little verse at all and foresees the day when he will forsake the short-story form as well.

"There's a crystallization that goes on in a poem, which the young man can bring off, but which the middle-aged man can't," he says. "It saddens me that, for whatever reason, I can't or don't write much of it anymore. Nor do I write as many short stories as I used to, or write them with the same ease—that sense of just being like a piece of ice on a stove. I feel myself being pushed toward the novel as my exclusive métier, in part because I'm no longer as adept at the shorter form as I was.

"It may be a kind of muscular thing that also makes ball players retire at forty," he goes on. "Certainly writing is, among other things, a kind of athletic achievement—just the mental quickness, the ability to combine thoughts simultaneously. Also, I think that any achievement and especially artistic achievement is born partly out of the illusion that what you have to do is important and that you can do it. And one of the powers of youth might be the power of conjuring up this illusion. Once you start to doubt whether something is worth doing, there's a terrible tendency not to do it.

"You have said a certain amount by my age and you have possibly unpacked your bag to a great extent. I say this as a kind of critic, and my being a book reviewer these days may give me this unfertilizing perspective—the possibility there are enough books in this world, enough books by *me* in this world. And yet, I enjoy so much making books, making words march down the page that I'm not really tempted to stop. I'm convinced I can still pull something out of the fire that hasn't been done before."

In the past, some critics have faulted Updike for writing too gracefully, too lyrically—his prose, Norman Mailer once declared, was "precious, overpreened, self-indulgent." Others have taken him to task for failing to write a "big," important novel, a novel commensurate with his talent. Norman Podhoretz, for one, went so far as to assert that "he seems a writer who has very little to say."

Yet while his work has occasionally been uneven—his self-imposed quota of producing a book a year has resulted in such slight, imperfect works as *Marry Me*—Updike has demonstrated an extraordinary range since making his precocious novelistic debut with *The Poorhouse Fair* in 1959. He has moved fluently from fiction to parody, light verse, and children's books, as well as distinguishing himself as one of America's finest critics. And his novels, however limited in canvas, have also been more varied and ambitious than many of his critics have acknowledged.

The Centaur—a tender portrait of a generous, well-meaning schoolteacher who was modeled on Updike's own father—won the 1964 National Book Award for its Joycean infusion of myth into the mundane events of daily life. *Couples* examined the consequences of sin in a post-Fall Eden, attesting to the author's sociological eye and theological vision. *Bech: A Book* projected, with much high-spirited wit, Updike's own writerly concerns onto an unlikely Jewish author. And *The Coup* expanded Updike's fictional territory beyond the small towns of America, conjuring with masterful detail the imaginary African kingdom of Kush and its imperial leader, President Elleloû.

What these works share, of course, is a durable autobiographical impulse that surfaces in certain dominant motifs and preoccupations. Whether it is Rabbit feeling so surrounded by the dead that "he feels for the living around him, the camaraderie of survivors," or Henry Bech feeling like "a fleck of dust condemned to know it is a fleck of dust," or President Elleloû looking up at the stars and lamenting that "we will be forgotten, all of us forgotten," Updike's characters are all afflicted by existential intimations of their own mortality. That fear is at once terrifying and restorative: It threatens to make everything they do meaningless and futile, but it also sends them running back to God. This theme, like so many others in his work, is rooted in Updike's own life.

Raised a Lutheran by churchgoing parents, Updike experienced a kind of philosophical panic during his late twenties. "It was the fear of dying," he recalls. "Although I was in no immediate danger, I realized one day I would indeed die, and in light of this fact, everything took on a kind of greasy sheen of hopelessness. I had little children at the time. I was in the prime of life. I was a young married man on the rise, living in a pleasant small town, and I went around caked with terror. I remember building my little girl a dollhouse about this time, and hammering those pieces of plywood together in my basement made it seem somehow that I was hanging on with my fingernails to a side of a cliff."

He began reading Karl Barth and Søren Kierkegaard. These writers gave him a kind of solace and they renewed his faith. "They convinced me that this was the human condition," says Updike, "and that we could leap our way out of it. And once you take this highly intellectually unhealthy leap into faith, the world becomes accessible again. This realization's helped me to be creative and do my job or at least fill the shoes of a human being—shoes that maybe other people don't find so hard to fill. Not that the dread ever disappears—it's like you keep giving yourself anesthetic, but the toothache is still there, and if you miss a shot, it might return."

No doubt some of those fears were nurtured by Updike's childhood during the Depression. A cherished only child, John Hoyer Updike grew up in Shillington, a small Pennsylvania town that has since been romanticized as a kind of enchanted place in his Olinger stories. In actuality, it was a somewhat precarious existence. His father supported the family on a schoolteacher's annual salary of $1,740 and Updike now recalls "an air of being refugees, an undercurrent of hysteria."

"Work was sacred," he says. "The specter of actual starvation and social humiliation was very real then. My father was an awfully good man in terms of fulfilling his responsibilities. He went off to work, day after day, sick or well, even though he didn't much really like teaching. I had his example of self-sacrifice before me constantly and maybe felt somehow that he had done enough self-sacrificing for the two of us. And so I've not tried to live his life, even though I feel all those generations of Protestant righteousness."

For the young Updike, reading—especially P. G. Wodehouse—and drawing provided an escape from the drabness of the world around him, and his mother, an aspiring writer herself, encouraged his artistic aspirations. The arrival of a *New Yorker* gift subscription settled matters once and for all: Updike decided that more than anything he wanted to work for that wonderful magazine in Manhattan.

Talent and great good fortune combined to fulfill those ambitions with remarkable celerity. In 1950, a full scholarship brought Updike to Harvard, where he studied English literature, worked for the *Lampoon,* and met and married a fine-arts major named Mary Pennington. After graduation, they left for England, and John enrolled at the Ruskin School of Drawing and Fine Art in Oxford—an experience that would help sharpen his pictorial eye. When they returned to the States a year later, it was with John's assurance of a job at *The New Yorker* as a "Talk of the Town" reporter.

Inspired by J. D. Salinger, Updike already had greater aspirations: Each day, before sitting down at his desk to compose pieces about such matters as the pigeons in Bryant Park or cocktail hour at the Biltmore, he would write three pages of a first novel that was to be titled *Home.* Although he would abandon this project after six hundred pages, Updike felt convinced that he had found a vocation, that he possessed something special and luminous worth saying.

He soon found, however, that it was difficult to become a novelist in New York. The very intensity of the city made "writing fiction based on little more than your own experience and witnessing seem a little foolish," and he was also convinced, he says, that "an American bard ought to immerse himself in an America more typical than New York City." So in 1957, after only two years at *The New Yorker,* twenty-five-year-old John Updike and his family moved to Ipswich, Massachusetts.

There, the Updikes raised their four children—Elizabeth, David, Michael, and Miranda—and pursued a low-key existence, rarely venturing into Boston, much less New York. They attended church almost every Sunday, and on alternate Wednesdays played recorders with a group of friends. Updike joined the building committee for the local church, as well as the town's Democratic committee. In time, such activities were chronicled in his *New Yorker* stories, although the most sustained and certainly most controversial portrait of Ipswich would appear in *Couples,* his 1968 novel about Tarbox, a fictional community where adultery is the favorite pastime.

By the early 1970s, Updike's own marriage was foundering. He moved to Boston as a "divorcing bachelor" in 1974, and some three years later married the former Martha Bernhard, an old friend and neighbor in Ipswich. Instead of returning to Ipswich, the new couple, accompanied by Martha's three children from her former marriage, moved to nearby Georgetown.

The divorce and the attendant circumstances, Updike acknowledges, were traumatic, and the experience underscores just how concerned his fiction is with marriage and betrayal, love and sex and guilt. "There are prices paid for our strayings from the social net," he says. "We're tightly enough packed that if one thing moves or falls out of place, there's a jostling felt all down the line, and someone suffers even if it's not you. You can perceive that your own wealth and happiness are in some sense carved from the hides of people who are less wealthy and happy, that your own sexual happiness is often carved from the hides of people who wind up as losers. So there's a temptation in front of my characters to remain absolutely quiet and not be guilty of anything—shame over aggression. And in my own life, I guess, I tend to be quiet, although I haven't been uniformly so."

"Divorce is a great guilty-making thing, of course, especially when it's your idea," he goes on. "The only consolation on this moral level is that it is your idea and that you are, in a sense, carrying out something—you are acting, and there is a way in which it is better to act and take the blame than to act hopeless and complain. I think that one way or the other, we make those around us pay, and maybe in my case and in many others, divorce for all of the immediate sorrows around it is kinder than not."

His divorce, like the joys and problems of his first marriage, was meticulously chronicled by Updike in a series of *New Yorker* stories about an attractive young couple named the Maples. They also left New York to live in a Boston suburb, had four children, quarreled and reconciled, and finally obtained one of the first no-fault divorces in the state of Massachusetts. Although Updike himself has been the subject of fictional scrutiny—both his mother and his eldest son, David, have published quasi-autobiographical stories in *The New Yorker*—one wonders what sort of consequences his closely autobiographical work has had on those he loves.

"I suspect there's some pain in living with me and reading my undoubtedly distorted and self-serving version of events that are somewhat real," he says. "But I've been surrounded—from my parents to my wives to my children—by forbearing and tactful people who haven't complained too loudly. And, in all cases, it seemed to me that my value to those nearest me was generated by my being a writer, and it was essential to my being a writer that I be fairly honest."

These days, Updike feels, just being a writer has become something of a full-time occupation. Whereas in the past, he could spend his mornings writing and devote his afternoons to being a householder and a citizen, he now finds that the duties of being a prominent author take more and more of his time. Trips to New York to see editors and other writers are more frequent these days than in the past ("Being a writer is a little like being a tiger, in that it takes a lot of landscape to support you, but it's good to see other tigers now and then just to know your stripes aren't the only stripes around"). And Updike, like Bech, finds that success has bred a host of distractions. He is asked to serve on prize committees, speak at universities, and support all manner of important causes—activities he regards with a measure of distrust.

"It was a trend ten years ago," he says, "for writers to speak up for the oppressed, for draftees, for the ghetto poor. And every cause in itself can be argued for, and many can be embraced as a citizen. Still, it seems to me quite corrupting for a writer to think of himself as a spokesman or a savior. All these other good things you could be doing are to the eventual neglect of the one indubitably good thing you could be doing—writing your best stuff and doing it honestly and irresponsibly even. We owe nobody anything, but we owe the reader the best book we can produce."

October 1981

GORE VIDAL

. . .

IN GORE VIDAL'S BOOKS THERE IS A PERVASIVE
cynicism, a tone of tart disillusion. Politicians, whether in Rome or Washington, plot and swindle; people couple and uncouple carelessly in search
of pleasure; and the world proceeds stupidly toward an ignominious end.
The satire, as critics have pointed out, is glib and frequently artful, but the
vision remains a cold one, admitting little hope and even less charity. Like
his prose, Vidal's conversation also possesses an air of erudite exasperation;
his sentences are not only footnoted with classical allusions, but are also
punctuated by sighs and yawns. He is afflicted, it seems, by a kind of
spiritual fatigue, and he does little to hide it.

Having had successful careers as a playwright (*The Best Man, Visit to
a Small Planet,*), scenarist (*Ben Hur,* and Tennessee Williams's *Suddenly,
Last Summer*) and critic, Vidal has just made another addition to his
already considerable oeuvre as a novelist—*Creation,* a historical epic set
in the fifth century B.C. According to Vidal, this seventeenth novel of his
will probably be his last.

"Working on this book, I thought, death can only be an improvement
over what it felt like," he says. "I ended the world in my last book *Kalki*
and, having ended the world, I've now gone back to the origins of all our
systems of thought. There is also a whole new television generation which

has grown up and since I'm dedicated to the written culture, I find that rather dismaying. It's like being one of the greatest living makers of stained-glass windows and the age of faith has ended. I'm at the top of a very tiny heap."

The younger generation is hardly the only thing Vidal finds dismaying these days; he is dismissive, in fact, of nearly everything. And since everything is relative in his world view—there is no such thing, he believes, as good or evil—he feels that he alone serves as the arbiter of truth. As he sees it, Christianity is "a perfect religion for slaves," the family is an "outdated" notion; critics who have disliked his novels are "dummies," and writers like Herman Melville who deal with high romantic ideals are "endlessly corny."

Changing seats three times so that a photographer can shoot his "good" side, Vidal arranges his face—a face he once described as that of one of Rome's "later, briefer emperors"—in a mirror, turns sharply to a visitor and offers another observation. "I suppose you'll call me a narcissist," he says. "Well, a narcissist is someone better looking than you are."

Over the years, this Vidalian spleen has frequently been vented on politics and politicians, and the current state of affairs inspires further putdowns. "There is no new administration," he says simply. "There's a permanent governing class. Every four years they put on one of these TV spectacles and they pretend it makes a difference whether it's Reagan or Bush or Kennedy. But the country is still owned by the Chase Manhattan Bank and CBS. And they're out to make a police state. The welfare will be turned off and there will be rioting and they want to protect what they've got."

If such statements produce curious echoes of the sixties, it is not altogether surprising. Vidal has not voted since 1964, and for many years, has lived abroad, at La Rondinaia (the Swallow's Nest), his Italian estate in Ravello. As a newly registered resident of Los Angeles, however, the novelist is now contemplating a run for the Senate from California in 1982. He would run on an "anti-Pentagon, anti-CIA, anti-American Empire" platform, he says, and if elected would attempt to change the Constitution and institute a parliamentary system. He says he thinks he has a chance of being elected.

As Vidal now tells it, he shares the populist views of his grandfather, the late Senator Thomas Pryor Gore of Oklahoma, and he believes that if he can talk to enough people, a majority will accept his views. "I tend to a kind of majoritarianism," he says. "Get the liberals going on that—

they're terrified of majority rule. I say if you have to trust something, you might as well trust the people at large."

Although he says he does not remember any remarks to the contrary— "I'm rather startled by my consistency," he says—his opinions have evidently undergone something of a change. In *Views from a Window,* a collection of his own quotations of which he was co-editor last year, he said: "I do not admire 'the people' as such. No one really does. Their folk wisdom is usually false, their instincts predatory. Even their sense of survival—so highly developed in the individual—goes berserk in the mass. A crowd is a fool. But then, crowds don't govern. In fact only in America do we pretend to worship the majority, reverently listening to the herd as it Gallups this way and that."

Populist or not in politics, Vidal remains a decided elitist when it comes to matters of fiction. As he has elegantly argued in many essays, he believes that most modern American writing falls into one of two categories: plastic exercises in academic fiction or tedious studies of bourgeois behavior. He regards both as portentous signs of the novel's fall and decline. "I'm not interested in the middle-class, middle-brow novel, which is ninety percent of what's being done now," he says. "It seems to me that that sort of thing is done so much better by soap operas and movies like *Kramer vs. Kramer.* These books are always teaching morals in a very crude way—identity crises, mature relationships, sacrificing all for love. It's very difficult for a writer like myself who doesn't share these prejudices."

Vidal's own novels—from *The City and the Pillar* and *Myra Breckenridge,* to such historical novels as *Julian* and *Burr*—tend to be concerned with death, power, corruption, and the willful throwing-off of convention. To the author, they make up a kind of elaborate *Dunciad;* like Alexander Pope, he says, he has the task of mocking the follies of others. Frequently the satire is colored with misanthropy. Vidal now believes that "people are all peddling something false," that mankind itself is "running lemminglike into the sea." Overpopulation, pollution, and shortages of energy and food—these are recited by him with a kind of relish, for they serve as confirmations of his own pessimism. He is, as he says, "a crisis person."

In fact, while Vidal usually opts for the observer's detachment, he does not exempt himself from the entropy he sees around him. *Creation* took six years to write, and the experience, he says, left him convinced that his ability to work was beginning to break down. At the age of fifty-five, he says he now thinks about death all the time and feels he is "pretty near the end." He has recently found that he derives a kind of energy from crowds, and he plans to spend the next year lecturing and campaigning. "Some writers take to drink," he explains, "others take to audiences."

"I'm not selling anything," he adds. "Most people who are rich or famous are trying to sell themselves to be loved. I don't care whether I'm loved or not. *I'm* the one keeping the score."

March 1981

EUDORA WELTY

. . .

On Sundays in Jackson, Mississippi, when her family used to take afternoon drives along the banks of the Pearl River, ten-year-old Eudora Welty would climb into the front seat of the Studebaker between her parents, give them a look of impatient expectation, and say in a small voice, "Start talking, please." She loved to listen to them talk, and it was that affection for stories, that southern tradition of conversational art, she believes, that first gave her the ability to write.

"Place—and time, too—make the framework of any story," says Welty, speaking in a soft drawl. "The more I see other cities, I realize how I've stayed in one place, how it's become a source of all the information that stirs the imagination." Although her first attempts at writing, made while she was a freshman in college, were set in Paris—one story began, "Monsieur Boule inserted a delicate dagger into Mademoiselle's left side and departed with a poised immediacy"—she says she soon realized that her subject matter lay not in the seeming glamour of distant places, but in the people she knew at home.

Some of Welty's work—most notably *The Optimist's Daughter*, which won a 1973 Pulitzer Prize—evokes the clash between the civilities of the old gentry and the crass vitality of the new, but her writing remains largely devoid of topical, political references. Like Chekhov, she is preoccupied with the enduring past and its effect on individuals. Hers is a sensibility shaped by a time when one could still tell which county a person came from just by his accent, when even those who left for school or work or love always came home at Christmas.

"Time is very important to the South because it has dealt with us," she says. "We have suffered and learned and progressed through it, and there's a sense of continuity there that speaks to any writer. It gives a person a sense of dramatic narrative because you can watch things happen through generations or through a family."

Welty herself is actually only a first-generation Mississippian—her mother came from West Virginia, her father from Ohio. That fact "made me realize there were many ways of looking at things," she says, recalling that people used to occasionally call her father a Yankee. And while she is quick to point out that that circumstance never made her feel alienated, she does observe that "I have often had in my stories an outsider or a stranger who tries to break into a circle—I think it was a way to reveal character."

Certainly Welty is no outsider in Jackson today. Having never married, she continues to live in the big red-brick house where she grew up. "It's really too big for one person," she says, since the death of her parents and her two brothers. "But I like keeping it because my family built it and no one's ever lived in it but us." She spends her free time gardening and painting, serves on the board of an amateur theater, works for the Society for the Prevention of Blindness, and takes a vigorous interest in local politics. It is a quiet life, she says, and a private one. She has vowed, in fact, to burn all her correspondence, arguing that it is a writer's work, not his life, that matters.

When it comes to the actual process of writing, Welty is thoroughly practical. She writes when she has something to say, and says she can write anywhere—sitting in a hotel room or even the front seat of a car. Rarely does she agonize. "It's not that I don't work hard," she says. "But it's so marvelous to develop an idea, and while you're in the midst of a story, so many things in your daily life seem to apply to it—you see something on the bus and think how you can use it. The story's like a magnet and without it, you'd never notice all these things. I even love to revise: It's like a piece of work I can put on the table and make better, the same way I can make something with my hands."

Welty reworks her stories using scissors and pins to put paragraphs and thoughts in their proper place, but once finished, rarely bothers to reread them. She simply goes on to the next story. Her first collection, *A Curtain of Green, and Other Stories,* published in 1941, was peopled with such "grotesques" as a spinster who drowns herself in a rain barrel and a clubfooted man, and she now observes that "in the beginning I tended to exaggerate some outward thing to show a character's inward condition." Although she still builds a character from the inside out—much like a Method actor, starting with an emotion and adding degrees of visual detail—she no longer relies on such easy symbolism. Her novel *Losing Battles,* published in 1970, chronicled the plight of a poor Mississippi family almost entirely through dialogue.

That dialogue, along with ideas for some of her characters, often comes from stories Welty's mother used to tell her, from local newspaper clippings ("During the last cold spell, Miss So-and-So's forty jars of preserves exploded"), and from the tales and gossip that constitute a kind of local art form in Jackson. "There's a love of company and a relish of human idiosyncrasy for its own sake there," she says. "I remember Robert Penn Warren was at my house one day, and we just sat around after dinner and, as he was leaving, he said, 'I have never laughed so hard—not a serious word all evening!' Now that's rather southern—that even big intellects love conversation for its own sake."

"I rather enjoy life," she goes on, "but you can't live in the South and not be conscious of that history. There's a general memory of death and devastation on the premises—it's a knowledge of history, really. Maybe it's bound to change, but I still feel there is a southern character—a view, an outlook, a leaning toward certain forms of life—that will persist for a time anyway."

June 1980

ELIE WIESEL

. . .

''HE HAS THE LOOK OF LAZARUS ABOUT HIM,''
wrote François Mauriac of his friend Elie Wiesel, and Wiesel, a survivor
of two Nazi concentration camps, has indeed returned from the dead with
a story to tell, a story he has spent his adult life recounting. Like all writers,
he is a witness, attempting to preserve history with his words. And yet
in his case, the experience was so horrific, the consequences so enormous
that the author says he is caught in a "dialectical conflict" between the
need to recount and the futility of all explanation.

"On one hand, we must testify," he says. "If I survived, it must be for
some reason: I must do something with my life. It is too serious to play
games with anymore because in my place someone else could have been
saved. And so I speak for that person. On the other hand, I know I cannot.
The war, my experience, transcends language—it is impossible to trans-
mit. I know one thing no one else will know except those others who have
been there. When we left that war, when we left that world, we did not
talk about it—it is too personal, too intimate. But it is always present. I
know whatever I do, whatever I write, is always against the background
of that event."

At heart, in fact, all Wiesel's stories are "pilgrimages to the past,"
examinations of the uses to which memory may be put. The guilt survi-

vors felt on being chosen to go on living, their responsibility to the dead, and their anger at a God who could let such a thing happen—these issues have all been chronicled by Wiesel. There are no answers in his work, only questions.

Sometimes the protagonist relives the horrors of the camps *(Night)*, sometimes he returns to his homeland *(Beyond the Wall)* or journeys to Israel *(A Beggar in Jerusalem)*, but the story always remains anchored in the facts of Wiesel's own life. For the author, writing serves both as a kind of expiation and as "a protest to God," a means of trying to understand something that defies both reason and imagination. It is an existential act, he says, an act of defiance, made in the face of the void.

Born in Sighet, a small town in the Carpathian mountains of Rumania, Wiesel grew up in a Hasidic community, studying the Talmud and the mysteries of the cabala. It was a highly focused life devoted to study and prayer, a life devoted to God. Then, one day in 1945, the fifteen-year-old boy, his parents, and his three sisters were placed on a cattle train and taken to a place they had never heard of. The place was Auschwitz.

"If anyone had told us where we really were going, many of us would have fled to the mountains," says Wiesel. "That's what hurt—that no one told us. We were so isolated: the rest of the world knew, but we didn't even know what the word *Auschwitz* meant. The first day there, I was walking with my father and a man came up to tell us what was going on, and I remember saying to my father, 'It is impossible. We live in the twentieth century, not the Middle Ages—people cannot be silent.' People were silent."

Wiesel and his two older sisters were the only members of the family to survive; his father was killed before his eyes. Also killed were the child's faith in a benevolent God, his trust in a beneficent universe. The war utterly changed the world as he knew it, he says, and it also altered the shape and direction of his own life.

"If it hadn't been for the war, I would not have written probably," says Wiesel. "I would have become a teacher of the Talmud. I would be obsessed and concerned with my little Jewish world, my religious needs. After the war, I became more tolerant of people. Before, I didn't know any non-Jews. If I had to walk by a church, I would change sidewalks so as not to walk in front of it. My fear of the other was a wall. Without the war, I would never have questioned any of my beliefs. I wouldn't have been involved in action. The event made me realize the urgency of personal commitment."

It took many years for Wiesel to write about the war, and in 1956, when the highly autobiographical *Night* was completed, he had difficulty finding an American publisher. "They said too morbid, too sad," he recalls. "No one wanted to hear about it. People felt ashamed and embarrassed. They did not want to be reminded." Since then the Holocaust has become a widely documented phenomenon: it was the subject of a controversial television series, and more recently, the focus of a Broadway play. It is a development that Wiesel finds disturbing.

"Twenty years ago they ignored the truth by refusing to listen," he says. "Now they ignore it by trivializing it. I am all for the survivors to speak out—I believe it is testimony that must be heard, for I am utterly convinced that if our generation forgets, there will be no next generation. But this is not something you play with; it's not a fashion or a fad."

It was fear "of doing what I did not want others to do," adds Wiesel, that led to his decision in 1970 to no longer write directly about the war. "I wanted to maintain its sacred dimension," he says. "I would still like to tremble when I pronounce the word *Auschwitz.*" Although he still believes that everything "should be related" to the Holocaust, he has since turned to such subjects as the Hasidic movement, the Bible, and the plight of Jews in the Soviet Union. The last was the subject of a nonfiction book, *The Jews of Silence,* and a play titled *Zalmen, or the Madness of God,* and it is also the subject of his eighteenth book, *The Testament.*

As Wiesel points out, many Russian Jews started out believing that "Communism would be Messianism without God," and they worked to advance the revolution. Unfortunately, he says, their vision of a promised land was not to be, and Stalin's own anti-Semitism was revealed all too clearly during his last days, when he ordered the rounding up of Jewish intellectuals. On August 12, 1952, dozens of Jewish poets and writers were executed, vanishing without a trace.

To Wiesel, who has been studying the problems of Russian Jews since a visit to the Soviet Union in 1965, the fault lies in the very nature of Communism itself. "It's a distorted utopia," he says. "It preaches a prophetic international state where everyone is the same. But it is the individuality of a person that must be preserved. Communism would solve the Jewish question by making the Jews disappear—not necessarily by killing them, but by assimilating them. When Stalin realized that Jews refuse to assimilate, he decided to use other methods."

In writing about Russian Jews, as in writing about the Holocaust, says Wiesel, he holds no hope of remaking history, no real hope of changing attitudes. "Once upon a time I was convinced it must be possible to shake people up," he says softly. "Now I don't think it's possible. I write because I must, and if I still scream, it is to prevent the others from changing me." And so he spends his days in a room overlooking Central Park, turning his anger and his pain into words. Over his typewriter hangs a black-and-white photograph of a small wooden house. It is a picture of the house where he was born, and it serves, he says, as a reminder of the vanished world of his childhood, "a world where everything was possible."

"I am pessimistic now," he says. "I am pessimistic because I don't trust history. But at the same time, I am optimistic. Out of despair, one creates. What else can one do? There is no good reason to go on living, but you must go on living. There is no good reason to bring a child into this world but you must have children to give the world a new innocence, a new reason to aspire toward innocence. As Camus said, in a world of unhappiness, you must create happiness."

April 1981

DIRECTORS

. . .

INGMAR BERGMAN

. . .

IT IS A CHILLY, DESOLATE PLACE, THIS ISLAND FÅRÖ. During the summer, tourists come here, bringing with them the laughter of children and the sun, but spring comes late to the island, and even in May, reminders of winter remain. A Baltic wind that twists the evergreens into the shape of bonsai trees blows in from the sea, and in the early morning hours, a damp, insidious fog settles over the beaches, draining the landscape of color and turning everything gray.

For Ingmar Bergman, who has had a house on Fårö since 1966, the island represents more than the landscape of his imagination, more than a familiar setting for his movies. It represents, he says, the one place where he feels safe and secure, the one place in the world where he actually feels at home.

At sixty-four, Bergman possesses the face of a mandarin. Though his pale gray-green eyes can quickly turn cold and suspicious, there is a twinkly childlike brightness to his features and he is capable of expressing a warm bonhomie. These days, in fact, he seems particularly happy to play the role of benevolent paterfamilias—both in the studio and at home on the island; and this new prodigality of spirit is reflected in his latest film, *Fanny and Alexander*—a film that depicts the possibilities and joys of family life as well as its familiar perils. The movie, says Bergman, represents "the sum total of my life as a filmmaker"; he insists it is the last one he intends to make.

"Making *Fanny and Alexander* was such joy that I thought that feeling will never come back," he says. "I will try to explain. When I was at university many years ago, we were all in love with this extremely beautiful girl. She said no to all of us, and we didn't understand. She had had a love affair with a prince from Egypt and, for her, everything after this love affair had to be a failure. So she rejected all our proposals. I would like to say the same thing. The time with *Fanny and Alexander* was so wonderful that I decided it was time to stop. I have had my prince of Egypt.

"To make another picture and have it feel gray and heavy and difficult with lots of problems—that would be very sad. And I have seen many of my colleagues get older and older and more and more dusty until suddenly they are thrown out, and they cannot get money for their next picture and must go around with their hats in their hands. That is something I do not want—better to stop now when everything is perfect."

A testament to the remarkable alchemy of life and art, Bergman's movies form a kind of ongoing autobiography, and *Fanny and Alexander* represents, at once, a nostalgic reinvention of the director's own childhood and a mature summation of his work. All the familiar Bergman themes and motifs are here—the humiliation of the artist, the hell and paradise of marriage, the search for love and faith—but they are infused, this time, with a new tenderness and compassion. "It's a big, dark, beautiful, generous family chronicle," writes *The New York Times*'s film critic Vincent Canby, "which touches on many of the themes from earlier films, while introducing something that, in Bergman, might pass for serenity. It moves between the worlds of reality and imagination with the effortlessness characteristic of great fiction."

Indeed, *Fanny and Alexander* possesses a generosity of vision reminiscent of Shakespeare's later comedies, for in summing up his life's work, Bergman seems to have achieved a measure of distance from and acceptance of his own past. "Perhaps it is an illusion, but I have the feeling I can see wider and understand more," he says. "It's like climbing a mountain. The higher you get, the more tired and breathless you become, but your view becomes much more extensive."

For those who have followed the director's career, this movie—so rich in allusions to previous works—provides a kind of index, a Rosetta Stone, to his entire oeuvre. And yet the movie is also more accessible, more straightforward, in narrative and form than many of his earlier films, providing the simple delights of a Proustian-flavored fairy tale of good and evil, innocence and knowledge.

Since establishing himself in the mid–1950s with *Smiles of a Summer Night*, *The Seventh Seal*, and *Wild Strawberries*, Bergman has earned critical acclaim as one of the world's foremost auteurs. Translating the tragic, introspective vision of Strindberg from the theater to the screen, he brought a new seriousness to the form—and he also demonstrated the medium's ability to probe philosophical issues and delineate interior states of mind.

During a career that spans some four decades, he has made some fifty movies, and while those movies portray worlds as disparate as the allegorical realm of *The Seventh Seal* and the banal domestic one of *Scenes from a Marriage*, they share an imaginative geography. Faith is tenuous in Bergman's landscape, communication, elusive; and self-knowledge, illusory. God is either silent (as in *Winter Light*) or malevolent (as in *The Silence*), and Bergman's characters find themselves ruled, instead, by the capricious ghosts and demons of the unconscious.

More persuasively than any other director, Bergman has mapped out the geometry of the individual psyche—its secret yearnings and its susceptibility to memory and desire. And in a sense, his determination to focus on existential matters rather than on larger social and political issues mirrors perfectly the attitude of his native country. Neutral in two world wars and virtually free of crime and most other social ills, Sweden lacks the sort of problems that lend themselves to conventional dramatic representation; its dramas are interior ones, hidden deep beneath the bright, clean surface of social engineering.

In chronicling his own anxieties and fears, Bergman has found a parable for both Sweden's peculiar afflictions of the spirit and those of the modern world. The Sweden he has portrayed in such movies as *Face to Face* and *Scenes from a Marriage* is a country where nearly everyone owns a summer house and drives a Volvo, a country where everything, on the surface at least, is orderly and serene. But Bergman's Sweden is not the paradise envisioned by idealistic social architects. Rather, it is a country given to atavistic rhythms and quickly shifting moods; a country of short, brilliant summers and long depressing winters, a country where even the most sophisticated city dwellers live much the way their ancestors did on farms—isolated and trapped within their homes. Here, a Calvinistic sense of fate endures, the one vestige of an age when this most secular of nations still believed. Here, money and technology have wiped out poverty and hunger, yet have failed to lower the suicide rate or alleviate despair. Here, the meliorative ideal founders on the rock of human nature.

Bergman's home is located far from the modern planned communities of suburban Sweden, far from the conveniences of mass transportation. To get to Fårö, you must first fly from Stockholm to Visby, an ancient walled city of medieval churches and ruined choirs. From Visby, there is an hour's drive across Gotland—a rocky island whose flat horizon is broken only by the steeples of abandoned churches, as numerous as telephone poles, stretching to the ocean. A ferry ride across a cold, windy bay follows, and then another drive across the sparsely populated island of Fårö itself, past ramshackle farmhouses and fishermen's shacks, through sheep pastures and pine groves to the director's isolated house: a low frame structure that stands perched like a lighthouse on the very edge of the sea.

The same color as the shale stones that cover the beach, the house seems almost a part of the landscape—gray, stark, and inhospitable. Inside, though, the wall-to-wall carpeting and sleek Scandinavian modern furniture lend a sense of happy, if somewhat contrived, normalcy and cheer. There are crayon drawings by Bergman's grandchildren on the study wall, and stacks of family photo albums on the table. The prevailing impression is that of a pleasant, middle-class model home; a room of screening equipment and an opulent television set are the only luxuries on display.

Dressed in an old flannel shirt, a worn cardigan, and a little red woolen ski hat, Bergman, at first glance, might be one of the island's farmers. Alternately animated and introspective, he speaks English slowly, almost cautiously, but becomes enthusiastic when it comes to showing a visitor around his grounds. He prepares his own lunch with aplomb, and drives his green Volvo station wagon along Fårö's narrow gravel roads with careful expertise.

Still, there is a calculated quality to his casualness. Although he says he hates meeting people he doesn't know, he immediately throws an arm over the shoulders of a visiting stranger, and he punctuates his conversation with declarations of his sincerity and good will. One has the sense that this is learned behavior of sorts—the gestures of a lonely and self-preoccupied man who wants very much to be liked, a man who has worked with actors all his life and who is keenly aware of performances and masks.

As the director himself acknowledges, his bluff exterior belies a wealth of dualities. Bergman is a self-professed agnostic who is deeply superstitious; a puritan who has married five times and carried on highly publicized liaisons with his leading ladies; a stickler for details (he has been known to send a telegram to change an appointment by ten minutes) who spends hours at a time daydreaming. "I am very much aware of my own double self," he says. "The well-known one is very under control; everything is planned and very secure. The unknown one can be very unpleasant. I think this side is responsible for all the creative work—he is in touch with the child. He is not rational; he is impulsive and extremely emotional. Perhaps it is not even a 'he,' but a 'she.'"

In his movies, Bergman has frequently taken this double self—the intuitive, feminine side and the masculine, analytic one—and split it into two characters: the worldly squire and the ascetic knight in *The Seventh Seal*, the artist Vogler and his adversary Vergerus in *The Magician*, the silent actress and the gregarious nurse in *Persona*.

In the case of *Fanny and Alexander*, he has taken the mirror of his personality and broken it into shards, each one reflecting a different facet of his character: the grandmother, "an old professional, who has lived a lot and is very surprised, though without bitterness, to find that suddenly she is old"; Isak Jacobi, the old Jewish antique dealer who possesses the powers of magic; Gustav Adolf, the loud, boisterous uncle who loves the company of women; the dour bishop, who tries to bend everyone to his will; the mother, Emilie, who as an actress "wears a thousand masks"; and, of course, the movie's ten-year-old hero—dreamy, secretive Alexander.

Besides ransacking his own life, Bergman mines the lives of his colleagues and friends for ideas and information. Just as many of his artist heroes display certain parasitical tendencies—the novelist in *Through a Glass Darkly*, for instance, watches his daughter's nervous breakdown with clinical fascination—he, too, is a voyeur, constantly watching others and taking mental notes. Introduced to a stranger, he asks all sorts of personal questions—a tactic that reflects both defensiveness and genuine curiosity—and he evidently does the same with friends. "If I would tell him I have a cancer and was going to die, he would be extremely sorry, but also extremely curious," says Harry Schein, the former director of the Swedish Film Institute and one of Bergman's confidants. "He's interested in the unhappiness of his friends. He dwells on it—he can get material. We often have long phone calls, and if he asks, 'How are you?' and I say,

'Fine,' he would be extremely disappointed. A human being in pain—he can learn much more."

Indeed, Bergman is highly dependent on his observations of others to give him a sense of ordinary life. Although the theater (which demands the interpretation of another writer's work) and the island Fårö (which gives the famous director a measure of anonymity) help reduce his myopia, one feels that he still shares, with many of his characters, a difficulty in reaching outside himself.

Preoccupied with his own emotions, he is constantly annotating his own conversation—"I know this sounds naïve," he will say, or, "I'm trying to be honest"—and from time to time, he will issue public statements about his films, as though he fears being misunderstood. There are open letters to his cast, subsequently published on op-ed pages, and there are published versions of his scripts, complete with detailed descriptions of characters and motivation. Bergman says he has never been in analysis, but he employs the language of psychiatry with ease, and like others employed in the business of self-dissection, he likes to refer to himself in the third person, as "Ingmar."

Bergman has carefully nurtured his intuition, protecting it like a rare plant from the harsh light and noise of the outside world, and the private realm he inhabits resembles the one so often depicted in his movies—a dreamlike place, where fantasy and reality, the conscious and unconscious, overlap and merge.

"It's difficult to explain," he says, "but the other morning I woke up here on the island and came into my study. I was sitting here looking out at the sea, and suddenly I had a very strong feeling that on my left side was my mother. I knew she was there. I was not dreaming. It was just the feeling that she was here, communicating with me. And then the sun came up, and after ten minutes or twelve minutes, this feeling went away."

Heightened by the intensely personal nature of his movies, Bergman's self-absorption is also the result of a strangely isolated life. As a child, brought up by strict Lutheran parents, he felt lonely and inept at communicating with his peers; since the age of twenty, he has lived almost entirely within the self-enclosed world of the theater and film studio. "My only talent," says a character in *Fanny and Alexander*, echoing the director's own point of view, "is that I love this little world inside the thick walls of this playhouse. . . . Outside is the big world, and sometimes the little world succeeds for a moment in reflecting the big world, so that we understand it better. Or is it perhaps that we give the people who come here the chance of forgetting for a while . . . the harsh world outside. Our theater is a small room of orderliness, routine, conscientiousness, and love."

No doubt the decision to live within this little world, safe from the confusions of history, was partly a conscious one—the result of Bergman's one youthful, and devastating, step into politics. Sent abroad for the first time at the age of sixteen—as an exchange student—he lived with a clergyman's family in Germany. The year was 1934, and he soon found himself swept up in the country's burgeoning enthusiasm for Hitler. He attended a Nazi rally in Weimar and listened to the clergyman deliver sermons based on *Mein Kampf.* "We were absolute virgins politically and we found it marvelous," he recalls now. "We were infected." By the time he returned home to Sweden, he says he had become a "little pro-German fanatic."

Years later, when he saw pictures of the concentration camps, he felt enormous guilt and shame. "I understood I had made a great mistake," he says, "and since then political thinking has scared me to death." For years, he did not read political books or editorials, and he declined to vote. Instead, he told himself that self-knowledge was the most one could hope for, that anything more smacked of hubris and pretension.

It was a position similar to that expressed by Emilie in *Fanny and Alexander.* "All I bother about is myself," she says. "I don't bother about reality either. It is colorless and uninteresting; it doesn't concern me. Wars and revolutions and epidemics and poverty and injustices and volcanic eruptions mean nothing to me unless in one way or another they affect the part I am just playing."

The two Bergman movies that do venture, albeit tentatively, into the realm of politics are actually rooted in his guilt about the war. Set in 1923, *The Serpent's Egg* attempts to examine the seeds of the Nazi evil, and *Shame,* Bergman has said, originated in a question he once asked himself— "How would I have behaved during the Nazi period if Sweden had been occupied and if I'd held some position of responsibility or been connected with some institution?"

It is the politics of relationships and the sociology of the psyche that is really Bergman's concern. Marriage and the perils of domestic life (*Thirst, Scenes from a Marriage, From the Life of the Marionettes, Fanny and Alexander*), the deceptions of love (*Summer with Monika, Smiles of a Summer Night*), the artist and his persecution by society (*The Magician, Sawdust and Tinsel,* the *Hour of the Wolf* trilogy: *Hour of the Wolf, Shame,* and

The Passion of Anna), the difficulties of faith *(The Seventh Seal, Winter Light)*, and the psychological complexities of the soul *(Persona, Cries and Whispers)*—these are the preoccupations that recur throughout his work and they all are rooted in personal dilemmas and the director's own nightmares and dreams.

Most of his films, Bergman has said, have grown "like a snowball" out of some small flake of experience or memory. He has found that filmmaking has a therapeutic effect and, in many cases, he has subjected a particular obsession to this process of analysis and catharsis. "I have been working all the time," he says, "and it's like a flood going through the landscape of your soul. It's good because it takes away a lot. It's cleansing. If I hadn't been at work all the time, I would have been a lunatic."

The Seventh Seal, which portrayed a medieval knight's confrontation with death in a plague-ridden land, helped him overcome his own fear of dying. *Wild Strawberries*, which depicted an aging man's reassessment of his barren existence, was made "as a rundown of my earlier life, a searching, final test." *Face to Face*, which chronicled a successful woman's descent into madness, helped him give his own angst "a name and address. In this way it [was] deprived of its nimbus and alarm." And *Fanny and Alexander*, he says, has helped him come to terms with the terrors and joys of his own childhood.

For Bergman, that childhood remains remarkably palpable. He thinks of himself as something of a child, and whenever he goes to the studio, he has the sense that he is a little boy again—the same little boy who, after breakfast, would go upstairs to his room, take out his toy theater, and put on Strindberg plays.

"I have maintained open channels with my childhood," he says. "I think it may be that way with many artists. Sometimes in the night, when I am on the limit between sleeping and being awake, I can just go through a door into my childhood and everything is as it was—with lights, smells, sounds, and people. . . . I remember the silent street where my grandmother lived, the sudden aggressivity of the grown-up world, the terror of the unknown, and the fear from the tension between my father and mother."

His childhood, Bergman has said, shaped his imagination and, for him, the past is always present. The world of the church that he grew up in as the son of a minister imprinted his mind with a religious vocabulary and peopled it with images of demons and saints. And his relationship with his parents shaped his view of the sexes with Freudian clarity and force. While he feared his stern, authoritarian father, he unabashedly adored his mother ("I was in love with her," he says. "I knew what she liked and disliked and I used to try to find ways to win her love"), and to this day he believes that "women are more intuitive than men—they have their emotional life more intact."

It is an attitude reflected in his films: The female characters are usually endowed with strength, patience, and an instinctive wisdom, while the men tend to be selfish, stupid, or somehow incomplete—either self-indulgent artists, eager to sacrifice their loved ones on the altar of their art, or stony intellectuals, intolerant of others' frailties and fears.

Certainly this is true of the men and women in *Fanny and Alexander*. The male characters are all buffoons of sorts: One uncle is a lecherous old man; another, a self-pitying failure; and the stepfather is another of Bergman's obnoxious moralizers, determined to impose his values on everyone else. Most of the women, on the other hand—from the gracious grandmother to the long-suffering mother—represent a panoply of virtues. Sensual, resilient, and open to their emotions, they love and humor their men, combining in their passion the devotion of a mother and a mistress.

In *Fanny and Alexander*, Bergman has drawn on memories of his grandmother's house, and he has turned the world of his childhood into a fairy tale set at the turn of the century. The early scenes portray, with almost Dickensian festivity, the daily life of a bourgeois family named Ekdahl who run a theater in a small Swedish town. When their father dies, however, Alexander and his sister, Fanny, find their happy little world shattered from within: Their mother remarries, and her new husband, the bishop, institutes an icy, puritanical regime.

Alexander, clearly, is a portrait of the artist as a young boy. Like Alexander, Bergman used to spend hours playing with a magic lantern; like Alexander, he had difficulty distinguishing between fantasy and truth; and like Alexander, he was punished for this "lying." The scene of humiliation in which the bishop whips Alexander and locks him in a closet was based on the director's own experience, and similar confrontations between a young hero and a father figure, between an overly sensitive artist and an unfeeling intellectual, surface again and again in his work.

That repressive atmosphere at home endowed Bergman with both a need to connect with others and an appreciation of how people use power to manipulate one another—emotions that eventually led him to work in theater and film.

"I think I have just one obsession—to touch other human beings," he says. "That desire for contact, I think, was the reason why I came to this profession, because as a child I was very shy and very lonely and very afraid of other people. Of course, it was not only this very beautiful reason, but it was also a longing for power, for manipulating other people. I think that's a disease every director has—a kind of professional illness."

According to his colleagues, that desire to manipulate people often extends beyond the studio. "With his friends, with his actors, he plays the authority figure," observes Jorn Donner, the producer of *Fanny and Alexander.* "In a sense, he has become the father he hated. He can become very jealous, say, if one of the actors in his film works in the theater in the evening. And he tries to influence their professional life. He says, 'You should do that, you should not do this.' In Sweden, he has enormous power—he has made careers and indirectly probably destroyed them— and so people tend to listen."

Insecure and suspicious, Bergman not only values control over others, but over his own life as well. He says that as a young man who already had had three marriages and five children, he realized his "life was a terrible flop," and he decided, then and there, that "if I cannot be perfect in my life, I will be perfect in my profession."

"You can't direct reality," he says, "and that sometimes makes me very insecure and scared. But when you direct a picture, you can decide everything. You can do everything you want, you can control every little detail. It's always handmade."

Acutely aware that this control afforded by art is illusory, Bergman has portrayed the artist in such movies as *The Magician* and the *Hour of the Wolf* trilogy as both charlatan and saint: someone guilty of lies and deceit, but also capable of performing miracles—"the one impossible trick" of making a ball stand still in the air. In *Persona,* the actress Elisabet Vogler chooses to become mute, arguing that her art has no meaning; and Bergman himself believes that the narrative order provided by art is really a placebo taken in lieu of anything better.

For Bergman, faith, like art, offers the consolations of order and redemption, and his movies all address man's spiritual dilemma, his inability to reconcile the needs of the flesh with the immortal longings of the soul. Such titles as *The Seventh Seal* and *Face to Face* come from biblical quotations, and the movies themselves are filled with similar allusions. In conversation, the director is fond of quoting O'Neill's dictum that all great art deals with man's relation to God. He says he is fascinated by the human capacity for "unmotivated cruelty"—a kind of original sin that cannot be explained by reason.

With *Winter Light,* made in 1962, a fundamental change occurs. While such earlier films as *The Seventh Seal* and *The Virgin Spring* were animated by an anguished search for God, *Winter Light*—which depicts a minister's own loss of faith—implies that whatever answers there are to be found are to be found here on earth.

The philosophical shift, Bergman explains, came during a short hospital stay. Coming out of the anesthesia, he realized he was no longer scared of death, and that the question of God had suddenly disappeared. Since then, his movies have all articulated a wary humanism in which human love holds the one promise of salvation.

In most cases, though, that ideal love eludes Bergman's characters. Instead, love turns out to be a dangerous emotion that either reinforces their loneliness or brings contagion with another's neuroses. It is as though Bergman, in accepting a world bereft of God—a world in which human beings are responsible for everything—had also resigned himself to a kind of purgatory on earth. Only recently, with such films as *The Magic Flute* and now, *Fanny and Alexander,* does he seem to have embraced the possibility of communion, the possibility of human happiness here on a God-abandoned earth.

"When Ingmar was younger, there was a bitterness to his films," says Harry Schein. "With *Fanny and Alexander,* there's a greater sense of harmony. I think Ingmar has it personally as well. In many ways, I feel he still lives a very difficult life—he talks of angst, of that anxiety where you wake up in the middle of the night—but superficially he seems more harmonic. On the surface, he is nice and charming and almost civilized." Certainly, a change in demeanor and in style of life has gradually occurred. The Bergman of the 1950s, who was establishing himself as a director, was an angry young man, an inventor of bohemian poses. Having repudiated the bourgeois values of his parents—he left home, after coming to blows with his father—the director reveled in the roles of novice existentialist and temperamental artist. He read Sartre and Camus and took to signing his letters with the insignia of a little devil. He appeared at rehearsals and filming sessions wearing a beret and scruffy beard, and his cast became accustomed to his fits of melancholy temper: he tore telephones out of walls and once threw a chair through a studio's glass control booth.

"I was very cruel to actors and to other people," says Bergman now. "I think I was a very, very unpleasant young man. If I met the young Ingmar today, I think I would say, 'You are very talented and I will see if I can help you, but I don't think I want anything else to do with you.'

I don't say I'm pleasant now, but I think I changed slowly in my fifties. At least I hope I've changed."

The change, it seems, came partly as an act of self-preservation. As a young man, Bergman notes, "I was a package of emotions on two legs—my life was completely chaotic." Since then, observes Jorn Donner, "Ingmar has been trying to fight the bohemianism in himself by leading a well-ordered life. When you think you are a bohemian or a lazy person, you have to fight that and impose a discipline—it's a little puritanical. He is very much the bourgeois today: he likes to see Ingrid and himself as the proprietors of a small French restaurant—you can't get more bourgeois than that."

His wife, Ingrid—a pleasant woman with a kind face who bears, Bergman notes, a remarkable resemblance to his own mother—has helped him establish cordial relations with his eight children from previous marriages and liaisons, and every July the children and four grandchildren come to Fårö to celebrate the director's birthday.

Bergman's daily schedule seems equally well ordered, if not a bit fanatical in its precision. He gets up every morning at eight and writes from nine until noon. Lunch—which for the last fifteen years or so has consisted of berries and sour milk—is followed by two more hours of work and a nap at three. Before dinner, he takes a walk and after dinner watches television—he is especially fond of "Dallas"—or a movie from his large 16-millimeter collection.

Like Jenny Isaksson, the psychiatrist in *Face to Face* who suffers a nervous breakdown, Bergman has cultivated neatness and efficiency as a means of containing his anxieties and fears. The surface calm bears a disturbing resemblance to that of Sweden's; beneath it, he says, he remains "extremely neurotic." "Ingmar, at the slightest provocation, will produce a nervous breakdown," says his agent, Paul Kohner. "He has a delicate disposition."

He will always be one of those people who closes doors behind him, says Bergman—someone who insists on an aisle seat in movie theaters. He will always knock wood when things are going well, and he will always suffer from a delicate stomach and bad dreams. "I have a lot of tics and phobias," he says. "I hate to travel. I hate to go to festivals. I hate it when somebody goes close behind me. I'm scared of the darkness. I hate open doors. It has to do with some primitive feeling of insecurity. I can't control it, but I know where my phobias are and how they work."

Although he maintains that he is unneurotic about his profession ("I look at my pictures and stage productions as furniture, as something for people to use," he says. "I can say, 'This chair is good, this one is very bad' "), Bergman is, nonetheless, compulsive about his work, and he acknowledges that he has frequently used it as a way of escape.

"When I was younger, it was a way of avoiding things," he says. "I would say, 'I have no time now to discuss it.' Or, 'When the picture is concluded, then I will think it over.' Or, 'I will cry when I have had my last shooting day.' Always when a picture opened, I was at work on the next picture, so when something was unsuccessful or a flop, I just had no time to think about it."

Even if *Fanny and Alexander* is his last feature film, Bergman hardly plans to abandon his hectic schedule. He will continue to work in television—the medium that originally produced *Scenes from a Marriage* and *Face to Face*—and will continue to stage operas and plays. He has adapted Molière's *School for Wives* for television, and plans to stage *King Lear* for Stockholm's Royal Dramatic Theater.

It was during a rehearsal of Strindberg's *Dance of Death* at the Royal Dramatic Theater in 1976 that Bergman was arrested, in a highly publicized incident, for tax evasion. The charges were later dropped—the Swedish government subsequently issued a formal apology—but the director exiled himself from Sweden and moved to Munich.

"It was sad when we went away," he says. "I said to Ingrid, 'There are only two solutions or possibilities. It will kill me or stimulate me.' Looking back now, I think it was, in a way, a very stimulating and fantastic experience." At the time, though, the experience caused Bergman enormous trauma, leading to a nervous breakdown. It not only seemed a fulfillment of all his worst fears of humiliation, but it also meant leaving the country he loved.

"I am so one-hundred-percent Swedish," he explains. "Someone has said a Swede is like a bottle of ketchup—nothing and nothing and then all at once—splat. I think I'm a little like that. And I think I'm Swedish because I like to live here on this island. You can't imagine the loneliness and isolation in this country. In that way, I'm very Swedish—I don't dislike to be alone. Before I married Ingrid, I lived in this house for sixteen months. An old woman came three hours a day at four and made dinner for me and she cleaned up and at seven she went away. And that was the only company I had. I lived like that week after week, month after month, and in a way I liked it very much."

Although he had made a pleasant enough life for himself in Munich,

Bergman desperately missed his home on Fårö, and one summer day in 1977, he remembered how the lilacs in his garden used to explode into blossom during that one week in June. That evening, he and his wife took a plane to Stockholm. They took another plane to Visby, then drove a car back to their house on Fårö. "The night was clear," he recalls, "and there was no darkness, and we got here at midnight and were sitting outside the old house, looking and smelling the flowers. The next day we went back to Munich. That in a way is very strange, but somehow very Swedish."

Bergman is spending his summers again on Fårö, and after fulfilling some theater commitments in Munich, he says he will return to Sweden for good. "For a long time, I didn't want to come home," he says, "but now in a few years I think I will return. I think it's time for Ingmar to go home."

June 1983

DAVID BYRNE

. . .

IN THE OPENING SCENES OF DAVID BYRNE'S NEW movie, *True Stories,* shots of a flat Texas landscape give way to images of a town named Virgil; the images of small-town shops, industrial plants, and prefab houses to cameos of some of Virgil's leading citizens: a genial plant worker named Louis Fyne, who's taken out television advertisements in his search for the perfect wife; Kay and Earl Culver, a happily married couple who haven't spoken to one another in decades; Miss Rollings, the Laziest Woman in the World, who hasn't left her television or bed in years; as well as neighbors introduced only as the Cute Woman, the Computer Guy, and the Preacher.

Inspired by people in tabloid newspaper stories, these characters may initially strike us as unlikely eccentrics, trapped in banal, suburban lives, but as reimagined by the director and his collaborators, they gradually emerge as "people like us"—people whose sympathetic depiction attests to a new feeling of acceptance, even a sense of belonging, on Byrne's own part.

"I guess I've gotten to like people more," he says quietly. "I don't feel so separate anymore. I feel more confident we have the same likes and dislikes, the same concerns, and it makes me feel less shy. I think I used to feel other people's lives and mine were so different that we could do our business, but not have that much more to say. Now I sort of feel I can go up to people in small towns and talk in a nice way, and not feel I'm a total foreigner."

While he's probably best known as the lead singer, songwriter, and guitarist of the rock group Talking Heads, Byrne has long evinced an interest in other art forms—in addition to designing award-winning videos, he's collaborated on stage pieces with Robert Wilson and Twyla Tharp—and in *True Stories*, he's brought those disparate talents together to create a portrait of a town through music, words, and images. The result is a fictional world that's at once ordinary and surreal; a world as immediately resonant as Sherwood Anderson's Winesburg, Ohio, or Edgar Lee Masters's Spoon River.

It's a brand-new town, this Virgil, one of those seemingly interchangeable towns that have sprouted in the suburbs of the New West, full of fast-food joints and housing developments and dominated by a huge industrial plant. The people here spend their days working on the local assembly line or hanging out at the mall; their evenings, watching television or going to nearby clubs. Their kids daydream to the sound of rock-and-roll, and they, too, like to fantasize about their lives, reinventing themselves in the images of people glimpsed in the movies and TV: Rambo and Prince, Burt Reynolds and Elvis.

Still, few of the clichés about middle America and the alienation of contemporary society seem to hold here. Unlike Sam Shepard's West or Joan Didion's West, Byrne's is not a deracinated frontier, co-opted by materialism and brave new values. Rather, it remains a place of possibilities, a land of alternatives and freedom, where both individuality and a sense of community can thrive. Indeed, as filmed by Byrne, the tacky, brightly colored buildings of Virgil and the surrounding desert landscape take on a kind of minimalist elegance that contributes to the picture's heightened, almost hypernatural, sense of reality.

"The whole thing sort of represented a challenge to me to try to appreciate something very different from what I grew up with," says Byrne, recalling his own childhood in an old section of Baltimore. "It was the idea that something could be very different physically, but that people could still live as sort of a community."

"A lot of the people we met in Texas didn't have a lot of connection with each other," he goes on, "but none of them seemed to feel alienated. They seemed to respond to mass culture in a very individual way—like, they'd take a prefabricated house and do something odd with it on the inside. So rather than causing them to be alienated, this fast-food stuff seemed to bounce off them. I guess I was sort of proposing that there are these other possibilities. And maybe it was also a little bit of someone from New York imagining these little pockets of Utopia out there."

Such a sanguine observation on Byrne's part may initially startle long-time followers of Talking Heads. Many of the group's earlier songs, one recalls, talked about alienation, in arch, formalistic terms: questions of identity and the presentation of self predominated, and the mood of contemporary angst was underlined by the chilly, hard-driving beat of the music. "Psycho Killer" (1977), Byrne's very first song, depicted a mad-man's descent into paranoia with wit and mock hysteria ("I'm tense and nervous and I can't relax. / I can't sleep 'cause my bed's on fire. / Don't touch me I'm a real live wire"). "No Compassion" (1977) portrayed a misanthrope, impatient with the world about him ("Other people's prob-lems, they overwhelm my mind. / Compassion is a virtue, but I don't have the time").

As for "The Big Country" (1978), it addressed many of the same issues as *True Stories,* but from the vantage point of a detached observer, whose sour-grapes disdain of the ordinary colors what he sees out an airplane window: "Places to park by the fac'tries and buildings. / Restaurants and bars for later in the evening. / Then we come to the farmlands, and the undeveloped areas. / And I have learned how these things work to-gether. / I see the parkway that passes through them all. / And I have learned how to look at these things and I say, / I wouldn't live there if you paid me."

In *True Stories,* Byrne again casts himself in the role of observer—he plays the Narrator, a nerdy visitor from the East, dressed up in a Sears Roebuck cowboy suit, bought in "the naïve belief that everybody in Texas wears cowboy clothes." And yet, there's nothing condescending or judg-mental about this outsider: As he drives about town in a bright red convertible, introducing us to various characters, he seems an earnest fellow, the sort of good-natured chap Jimmy Stewart might have played for Frank Capra.

"Sometimes it's just a question of suspending judgment," says Byrne. "It's a way of finding a way out of a contemporary bind where you seem to get into a rut of putting things down and being nostalgic for the good old days and in general complaining about the emptiness of modern life. I wasn't so much proposing a solution or an answer in this movie, as making some kind of attempt to be more open."

In a sense, that same quality of openness—a willingness to sympathize with and even embrace new points of view—also informs the gradual evolution of the Talking Heads' music. When the band—originally made up of Byrne, Chris Frantz (on drums), Tina Weymouth (on bass), and, later, Jerry Harrison (on guitar and keyboards)—first began playing at CBGB's a decade ago, the band had a decidedly minimalist aesthetic. Many of the songs, Byrne now recalls, were really "more like sketches for songs—just the barest framework; we didn't allow ourselves dramatic tricks or the musical equivalent of that, like building to a dramatic climax or using sensuous rhythms." And the band's performance style was similarly ascetic: avoiding all the usual rock-and-roll pyrotechnics, the Heads tended to stand stiffly on stage, dressed simply in T-shirts and jeans— there were no lighting effects, no sexy gestures, no attempts whatsoever to give the audience the sense of a "show."

"When we started the band, we pretty much stripped everything down to basics," says Byrne. "We were skeptical of even accepting little things like the idea that a stage performance is a performance—that what you might wear on stage is different from what you wear off stage. When you're young, you do stuff as a reaction to everything else, and it's highly critical—so often what you end up with is kind of a pared-down version of everything. Even if you don't know exactly what you are, at least you think you know everything you're not.

"In retrospect, I think that was good—if you start off trying to use all these different elements without understanding how they work in your own work, it can become too much to handle. Later, maybe, you can accept things—not because they've just been handed down to you, but because they've become part of your own history."

Over the years, the band's music gradually began to grow denser and more richly textured, as new influences (including West African poly-rhythms and American funk rhythms) were assimilated and new group members added. It's a development echoed by the very structure of *Stop Making Sense,* the band's 1984 concert film, which gradually builds from shots of Byrne alone on stage into an elaborately staged production, with half a dozen sidemen, carefully designed slide shows, and even costumes (in the form of Byrne's famous "big suit").

At the same time that the band's concert style was taking shape, notes Byrne, his own writing was beginning to accommodate elements he'd previously eschewed. For instance, following his work with the English producer-composer Brian Eno on *Remain in Light* (work that involved the dismantling and rearrangement of traditional song structures), he says he found he could "accept more traditional song structures again." The interlocking polyrhythms used on that record (which, in traditional African society, play an important role in promoting social harmony and a sense of shared purpose) would also leave their mark, musically and philosophically, on Byrne's work. A stark, almost mechanistic view of modern life, echoed by the music's rigorous structuralism, would increasingly give way to a recognition of the limits of rationalism ("stop making sense"), and also to a more generous vision of the world, in which the community becomes more important than the isolated individual. In fact, while the apparent simplicity of songs from *True Stories* and the Heads' last album, *Little Creatures,* may well recall some of the band's earliest efforts, their tone of benevolence and playful innocence also indicates a deeper philosophical shift.

"The structure of the songs used to be very intellectual," says Byrne. "It's not so apparent now—the thought behind it's more natural, like it just came out. With the earlier songs, I was reading a lot of books about systems theory and stuff—it was a time when artists were adopting elements of that kind of thinking. In the last ten years, I've accepted there are kind of hidden structures holding things together, but I don't feel the need to make sense of them all.

"There was a period in my writing where sometimes I felt I had to reflect my own ideas, but often stuff seemed to work best when I felt I was speaking from the point of view of some character—where I was proposing a point of view, rather than saying, 'This is what I believe.' "

"Once in a Lifetime," for instance, was written from the perspective of a bourgeois suburbanite; "Television Man," from that of a TV addict; and "And She Was," from that of a woman who believes she can float. In the future, Byrne says he hopes to take this approach even further by taking "other people's lives and setting them to music"—perhaps even writing songs based on actual transcripts of people talking.

Art, as Byrne sees it, can "filter real stuff or present it from a particular angle so it appears to function like a metaphor for something else"; and he's frequently used bits of reality as found material in his work. The song "Once in a Lifetime" grew out of preachers' sermons he'd been listening to on the radio; just as the people in *True Stories* have antecedents in magazine and newspaper stories. The character of Louis Fyne (played by John Goodman) was based on a man in a *Weekly World News* article who planted a "wife wanted" sign on his front lawn; and those of Kay and Earl

Culver (played by Anne McEnroe and Spalding Gray) were inspired by a married couple in another *World News* item, who hadn't spoken to one another in thirty-one years.

The picture, Byrne feels, "gets some of its strength from the sources of all the stuff being revealed. It's nice when people aren't quite so sure what's real and what isn't. It makes it seem that maybe it's possible to look at these towns or these people this way—that it's not something that exists purely in the filmmaker's imagination."

The film began, in fact, with a pile of these news clippings, and some visual ideas that had been floating around in Byrne's head for years (an image of a woman talking in her sleep, another of a luminous glass of milk)—elements that he, Stephen Tobolowsky, and the playwright Beth Henley eventually shaped into a script. Considerable work was done establishing connections between various characters, but Byrne says he found himself dismantling elements of the plot in order to "give the movie a build and flow" that's less dependent on traditional narrative than on a collagelike sequencing of episodes, visual set pieces, and music.

"The process wasn't so very different from the way I'd worked on songs," he says, "and no different from how I'd worked on videos, where I'd draw a lot of storyboards and reorder them till they had a sort of structure that made some sort of sense."

Although Texas, a right-to-work state, was initially chosen as a shooting location for financial reasons, Byrne notes that "after the first trip it was hard to think of the story as taking place anywhere else." Not only did the local people project an independence of spirit that fitted in perfectly with the movie's themes, but they also seemed to possess a larger-than-life vitality that gave their personalities the brightness of "pop-up figures" in a children's book. The desert vistas—all horizon and straight lines—provided what Byrne calls "an existential landscape" that worked to heighten his characters' dilemmas. And the region also gave him a rich, indigenous supply of music (gospel, zydeco, country and western, R & B, and Tex-Mex) that helped inspire the songs.

The songs are meant to "expand on the personalities of the characters," he says, but they're also supposed to serve as "a representative sample of all the music you'd hear in that locale. They're about what each character feels, but also about the community and the feelings of the whole." Indeed the movie's final song, "City of Dreams," becomes both a summation of individual characters' stories, and a hymn to an older dream, the dream of the immigrants who first came to this land where "the dinosaurs did a dance" and "the Indians told a story."

"The Civil War is over," goes the song, "And World War One and Two / If we can live together / The dream it might come true / Underneath the concrete / The dream is still alive / A hundred million lifetimes / A world that never dies / We live in the city of dreams / We drive on the highway of fire / Should we awake / And find it gone / Remember this, our favorite town."

October 1986

BRIAN DE PALMA

. . .

THE OPENING SEQUENCE OF THE NEW FILM *BLOW Out* is immediately recognizable as the work of Brian De Palma: a couple, entwined in each other's arms on the floor, are watched through a window by a man, who, in turn, is watched by another figure, a figure wielding a knife. The knife comes down, and the killer moves on to his next victim, a girl who is taking a shower. The sequence is intended as something of a self-parody—most pointedly, of the director's previous movie, *Dressed to Kill*—and it's also an ironic distillation of motifs dominant in De Palma's recent work, namely illicit sex, voyeurism, and violent murder, all served up with expressionistic horror.

For De Palma, *Blow Out*—a thriller starring John Travolta as a sound technician who witnesses an assassination and its cover-up—represents a summary of techniques and ideas examined in previous works. While its elaborate orchestration of terror and sophisticated cinematic vocabulary echo such formalized works as *Dressed to Kill,* the film's overtones of Watergate and Chappaquiddick recall the director's early political comedies such as *Greetings* and *Hi, Mom!*

As in most of De Palma's films, the action in *Blow Out* is heightened; the vision, stylized. Unlike many directors, De Palma says he has little interest in trying to "Xerox life"; he is preoccupied instead with creating a sort of Grand Guignol world where everything is slightly exaggerated, even surreal, as in a nightmare or a dream.

"That's my sensibility, bizarre as it may be," says De Palma, whose reserved, polite demeanor stands in contrast with the extravagant strangeness of his movies. "And I have a very stylized visual sense which lends itself to that. Obviously, it can't be too bizarre, or people won't identify with it, but life, as I see it, is bizarre to begin with—most of the ideas I do, you can see on the Phil Donahue show." *Sisters* featured a Siamese twin possessed by the evil spirit of her dead sibling; *Carrie,* a vengeful teenager with telekinetic powers; *Phantom of the Paradise,* a deformed rock star; *The Fury,* two more telekinetic adolescents; *Dressed to Kill,* a transsexual murderer; and *Blow Out,* a political henchman who kills young women by garrotte.

If such films have displayed an extra-large measure of violence and sex, says De Palma, it is because sex and violence lend themselves uniquely to the cinematic form. "When you work in an art form, you're very aware of what its primary strengths are," he says. "And I think film is one of the few mediums in which you can deal with sex and violence—you can't really do it on television or on stage. So, they're elements to be explored in film. Whether you want to paint with those colors is up to you. But because of my very sort of formalistic training, I sometimes go for what is the strongest, most vivid color on the palette, which in the case of movies is violence. It plays very strongly, and I can do it very well. I don't think you can work with all these colors on the palette if you start trying to decide if something's a good color or a bad color. Either you do it well or you don't do it well."

Making a film vivid and effective, making it a technically perfect machine that will manipulate the audience's emotions, has always been one of De Palma's goals. Having grown up the son of a Philadelphia surgeon—watching his father perform operations probably contributed to his own *sang-froid* toward violence and blood—the director initially approached moviemaking as a technician, not as an artist.

Like the John Travolta character in *Blow Out,* and the Keith Gordon character in *Dressed to Kill,* he was something of a scientific "whiz-kid" as a student, and he says he assembled his first films the same way he put together his computers, methodically figuring out scenes and camera angles. Among his first low-budget features were *Greetings,* a critically acclaimed comedy about three draft dodgers, one of whom was played by a young Robert De Niro; and its sequel, *Hi, Mom!,* a counterculture send-up of white liberals, black revolutionaries, and practically everything else.

By the early seventies, however, the director had decided that these comedies lacked sufficient structure, and he turned to the suspense form as a vehicle for tight, precise storytelling. It was possible, he found, to touch—and frighten—an audience through images, which appeal to the subconscious, rather than through dialogue and traditional exposition, and he set about mastering a cinematic grammar that would enable him to tell a story *visually*. The main source of that grammar was the late Alfred Hitchcock. From Hitchcock, says De Palma, he learned how to present a sympathetic character that the audience could readily identify with; and he learned how to show everything from that character's point of view.

Although some critics have argued that De Palma's emphasis on visual imagery produces movies that are no more than a series of dazzling set pieces, the director explains that he regards film as a medium more akin to music or dance than literature, that "character and story to me are not the primary focus."

"*Dressed to Kill* is just being totally preoccupied with visual storytelling, where form is content," he says. "You're not interested in any deep philosophical matters there. You're basically expressing all your ideas in visual forms. Now that I've developed this very sophisticated cinematic grammar, though, I'm sort of trying to deal with the content aspects a little more."

That content has frequently been derivative. *Blow Out* is reminiscent of Antonioni's *Blow-Up*—in De Palma's version, the photographer, whose pictures inadvertently document a crime, becomes a sound technician. Like Hitchcock's *Rear Window*, *Sisters* focuses on a bystander who sees a murder through a window; like Hitchcock's *Vertigo*, *Obsession* concerns a man obsessed with the memory of his dead wife, and like Hitchcock's *Psycho*, *Dressed to Kill* features a schizophrenic murderer with a nasty penchant for attacking victims in the shower.

Often there is a good bit of self-conscious and satiric humor at work here: The opening scene of *Blow Out* pokes fun at De Palma's own horror movies, just as the title underlines the resemblance to Antonioni's *Blow-Up*. In addition, De Palma's films are often filled with scenes designed to reinforce the audience's awareness of the medium itself, a Brechtian tactic that emphasizes the filmmaker's, and audience's, role as voyeur. There are movies within the movie in *Murder à la Mod, Sisters,* and *Home Movies,* and there are references to television programs in practically all his films.

Quick to acknowledge that Hitchcock and others *have* had a strong effect on his work, De Palma argues that the demands of a specific genre—in his case, suspense—preclude a wealth of innovation. "Hitchcock found the kind of scenarios that work best," he explains. "So, when you work in the suspense form, you're almost forced to use some of the ideas he pioneered. Hitchcock's like a grammar book, and it's all there to be learned. What matters is how you use that grammar in your own films. For instance, I think I'm much more of a romantic than Hitchcock: I kind of temper my visual imagery with romantic music, emotionality, and slow motion that's much more toward Wagner. It's more sweeping."

For all their derivative elements, De Palma's films purvey a single vision of the world. As a character in *Blow Out* observes, it is a cold, unforgiving world in which one "ends up either crazy or dead." People, for the most part, are manipulators, looking for ways to realize their own selfish ends. The blackmailer in *Blow Out* isn't upset that his victim is accidentally killed; he plans to cash in on the death by selling his pictures for more money than before. Similarly, the reporter who witnesses a murder in *Sisters* hopes to turn the event into a sensational story that will further her career.

For De Palma, paranoia and guilt are just some of the side effects of living in what he sees as a corrupt, materialistic society. Having started his career making low-budget, experimental pictures with Sarah Lawrence students, the director quickly became disillusioned with Hollywood—his first commercial feature, *Get to Know Your Rabbit*, was cut without his permission—and subsequent run-ins with studios over the release of films galvanized his cynicism.

"I have this real sense of the effects of the capitalistic society in which everything is done for the sake of profit," he says. "It's totally attacked the moral fiber, and I'm very interested in how it affects the lives of people who go up against it—*Blow Out* is very much about that. I don't think the system can be changed. It's too strong and powerful—it just engulfs you."

The director's few idealistic characters, in fact, usually end up going mad or adopting the questionable ethics of the people around them. The songwriter in *Phantom of the Paradise* decides to get back at the people who have stolen his music, and in the process becomes a monstrous creature himself. Similarly, Carrie, the persecuted teenager played by Sissy Spacek in the movie of the same name, takes revenge on her enemies, only to bring about a fiery debacle in which she and nearly everyone around her are killed.

Such tales, says De Palma, carry an implicit moral: "Basically, you reap what you sow. If you do evil, you will get evil back." In many cases, that "evil" includes sex, for it is cause, in De Palma's films as in Hitchcock's, for guilt and punishment. Whether the sin is adultery (as committed by the Angie Dickinson character in *Dressed to Kill*) or simply physical passion (as enjoyed by the woman played by Margot Kidder in *Sisters*) sex frequently seems to lead to murder.

"I don't actually think that you're going to be punished for sexual promiscuity," says De Palma, "but I think there's something in us that says, 'I shouldn't have done this because I'll be punished.' I believe that you do pay for your moral transgressions. If you have someone terribly innocent and they get killed, then I think you're making a statement about something else—that the universe is totally absurd, and I don't really believe that. For me, the basic moral underpinnings are there, although I tend to do it a little excessively."

Because his vision tends to be so baroque, De Palma says he plans to base his next movie on a nonfictional event—the 1969 murder of Joseph Yablonski, the United Mine Workers leader, and his family. He plans to ground his stylistic extravagance in reality, the same way he has grounded his own life in a disciplined, domestic routine. Indeed, De Palma's life, like his demeanor, is a low-key one.

"I think a little like Hitchcock," he says. "You can lead a normal, reasoned life; you don't need to be a bizarre person in order to make very stylized, bizarre movies, though that doesn't mean you don't see things that way. It almost helps you to have a very regulated life so you can deal with these kinds of very crazy concepts. You have to work very hard to ground things like Siamese twins and kids with telekinesis in some kind of reality most people can understand."

February 1981

LOUIS MALLE

. . .

TWO YEARS AGO, LOUIS MALLE VISITED ATLANTIC City for the first time, and he felt the shock of recognition an experienced director knows when he sees the perfect visual metaphor. Seen from the Boardwalk, it was a glimpse of elegant old hotels coming down, of shiny new casinos going up, a glimpse of that instant in time when "nothing was finished, when there was no present, only a past and future." For Malle, this image, which was to be registered in his highly praised new film *Atlantic* City, not only captured his sense of America as a culture that has gone directly "from innocence to decadence," but also served as an illustration of that rare "moment of extreme fluidity" that he has examined in film after film.

Whether it is a historical period (France caught between occupation and liberation in *Lacombe, Lucien*) or a turning point in an individual's life (the delicate transition from adolescence to maturity in *Murmur of the Heart*) Malle says he has always been fascinated by those suspended moments "when something is going to happen and things are not going to be the same."

"It's a very acute sense of time and what time does to you," he says, "and a sense that the past is always present. The definition Stendhal used for the novel was of carrying a mirror along a road. I like to think of my work that way—that sense of movement, movement in time."

Since moving here in 1975, Malle has focused on his adopted home: *Atlantic City*, which stars Burt Lancaster as an aging associate of mob hit men, describes the anomie that afflicts old-timers and newcomers in that coastal New Jersey town; and *Pretty Baby*, released in 1978, relates the story of a child prostitute whose coming of age coincides with the closing down of the red-light district in turn-of-the-century New Orleans. In both cases, the films' concern with shifting values reflect Malle's conviction that America embodies the acceleration of history that has taken place in the twentieth century.

"One thing that is fascinating to a European is it seems that American economy and society and even psychology are very much for permanent change," he says in precise, slightly accented English. "It is striking to see the movement of people here from the Northeast to the Southwest, to see buildings go up that will last twenty years and then be torn down, to see objects that are manufactured to be obsolete in five years. There is still a pioneering spirit here, a basic believing in progress that is probably absent in Europe. If you go to the middle of the country, you still find people looking at their lives in terms of the future instead of the past. Nothing is taken for granted here, and life is sort of a permanent struggle—you have to get up every morning and get motivated to continue your ascension, social and financial. Perhaps that's why this country has a greater number of casualties, because there are just a lot of people who cannot cope with it. A lot of people drop out."

Although Malle's camera often focuses on the sleazy—suburban New Jersey with its billboards; a New Orleans whorehouse with velvet curtains and satin banquettes—there is a lyricism to his artistic vision, as though the very tawdiness of the landscape and its people aspired to something more.

His camera, however, remains nonjudgmental. There is a detachment, a European coolness to his approach which instead of seeking easy moral lessons, dwells on the ambiguities of detail. "It's not what you look at, but the way you look at it," says Malle. "Maybe *Atlantic City* expresses a point of view that is slightly different—I think I look at things other people who are more familiar with the scene might pass by."

Wry and articulate, Malle, who is forty-eight, combines the confidence of a professional who is sure of his craft with the introspection of a man who thinks of himself as a chronic outsider. A romantic who believes that art can force people to reconsider their comfortable assumptions, he is also a realist wary of self-indulgence. He says he was well aware of the risks of coming to America to work.

In addition to the difficulties of directing in a foreign language—a factor less pressing in Malle's case, given his fluency in English—he has had to contend with differing audience sensibilities. "I would say mass audiences in this country are more puritanical than in Europe," he says. "And they probably want more to be able to identify with what's going on on the screen. It's really sort of a subtle balance between identification and wish-fulfillment. The key to a number of successful movies recently has been some sort of projection of the American Dream—an ideal vision of a world where life is easier than it is in actuality. It is more difficult to get audiences interested here in hardcore naturalism."

Over the years, though, Malle had made many visits to America, and he says he felt confident that he "knew more about this country than most Europeans." What perhaps surprised him the most about actually working in America was the emphasis on commercial success. "It's probably more difficult working here than in France," he says. "There's very little chance here they'll give a director carte blanche, and if they do it's because your last picture has been tremendously successful at the box office, not because you've made good films. I don't think there is in the language here the equivalent of *artiste maudit*—this romantic character who is an artist and who is never noticed until he is dead.

"During the last twenty years in Europe, film has been recognized as art. I'm not sure this step has been reached here. It's possible in Europe to be a successful artist without necessarily being extremely successful commercially. Here, it's basically much more in the hands of accountants—there is an obsession with the hit, the blockbuster, which means the ultimate goal is for you to come up with a picture that will please everybody. I've always worked the opposite way. I've been more interested in—not in displeasing people, but in disturbing, provoking them. I want to force them to ask questions."

Certainly many of Malle's films have provoked controversy both here and abroad. His second feature, *The Lovers*, which brought him early fame at the age of twenty-six when it won a special prize at the 1958 Venice Film Festival, was condemned by censors for what were then regarded as dangerously explicit sex scenes. *Murmur of the Heart*, the story of a young boy's coming of age, offered a delicate indictment of the bourgeois values of the grown-up world, but achieved notoriety for its depiction of sexual passion between mother and son. Its light, humorous treatment of such subjects as incest, masturbation, and infidelity confirmed, for many Americans at least, the French reputation for naughty sophistication.

A darker and more disturbing image of France surfaced in Malle's next film, *Lacombe, Lucien,* a dispassionately told story about a seventeen-year-old French peasant boy who casually, almost haphazardly, slips into collaboration with the Germans during the final days of World War II. It was a study of the supreme ordinariness of evil, and while it won much critical praise, it was also attacked in France by the Left and the Right.

In retrospect, Malle's oeuvre seems remarkably eclectic, ranging from such somber, closely observed works as *Le Feu Follet*—a study of the last forty-eight hours in a suicide's life—to such extravagently comic exercises as *Zazie dans le Métro,* a sort of slapstick farce about a young girl who goes on a sightseeing tour of the Paris underworld. As the director points out, however, both these films were concerned with the corruption of innocence—a theme in *Lacombe, Lucien* and *Murmur of the Heart* as well.

His women, Malle adds, tend to be the stronger characters; more often than not, they are dreamers, rebelling against the conventions of their lives. Jeanne Moreau, who runs off with her boyfriend in *The Lovers;* Lea Massari, who seduces her son in *Murmur of the Heart;* and Susan Sarandon, who drives off into the sunset with a cache of cocaine-earned money in *Atlantic City*—all are determined individuals, committed to their passions even in defeat.

The director's men, on the other hand, are often adolescents—if not in age, then by temperament. To them, growing up means the loss of innocence and initiation into another world, a world of duplicity and compromise. Maurice Ronet as the suicide victim in *Le Feu Follet*—a film Malle made at the age of thirty, "that very depressing stage when you have to accept you are an adult"—is a dissipated playboy, who has outlived his boyish enthusiasms and wasted his youthful charm. The teenage hero in *Lacombe, Lucien* is undone by his own naïveté, and fourteen-year-old Laurent in *Murmur of the Heart* hovers on the edge of maturity, afraid of facing life alone.

Nearly all of Malle's characters feel alienated and cut off. The hero in his first film *Ascenseur pour l'Echafaud* murders his lover's husband, then is trapped by himself in an elevator; he and his mistress are never even seen together on the screen. *Vie Privée,* a 1962 film starring Brigitte Bardot as a Bardot-like actress, looked at the isolating consequences of fame; *Le Feu Follet* examined the despair of a man who realizes he has never touched or been touched by anybody, even his closest friends; and *Atlantic City* depicts a set of solitary people whose lives are momentarily brightened by chance encounters with strangers.

"It's always sort of resented, this isolation," says Malle. "It's like an evil or a disease or something you don't especially choose to be. I believe the best part of your work has to be unconscious. It's not a conscious preoccupation for me to expose loneliness in my films—it just happens that way. If I end up with a series of characters with a sense of being cut off, it has to do with my own situation. When I was in my teens, I was very much of a loner and not by choice. It was something in my nature and everything I've been doing since has been trying to reconcile myself with other human beings."

The youngest son of a wealthy sugar family, Louis Malle grew up in surroundings similar to those depicted in *Murmur of the Heart.* It was a rigid world, he recalls, a world "with all the advantages of money and education and a lot of hypocrisy." There was a strict Catholic education against which he rebelled—he was thrown out of one school, he says, for arguing about the true existence of Christ—followed by matriculation at the University of Paris, where his parents wanted him to study political science. Malle, however, had already decided that he wanted to make movies and he soon transferred to the Institut des Hautes Etudes Cinématographiques.

Filmmaking, he had discovered, served a sort of therapeutic function. In the first place, his apprenticeship with Jacques Cousteau (Malle co-directed the underwater documentary *The Silent World*) introduced him to individuals far removed from the rarefied world of the haute bourgeoisie and it forced him to interact. "Dealing with Cousteau's people I was suddenly seeing real people," he recalls. "I was this sort of intellectual, abstract-thinking, spoiled rich kid, and they gave me a hard time. They probably saved my life."

What's more, the very process of making films, it seemed to him, provided a way out of his self-absorption: it meant communicating with actors and writers, and it meant turning the lens of self-scrutiny outward to the world at large. "The fact you go out there with a camera forces you into a relationship with the world," he says. "It forces you to look and to listen more than if you didn't have that thing to do. But weirdly enough, as soon as you put observing as your occupation, it forces you to stand outside—it isolates you further. It's taken a long time to make my peace with it—whether it's a documentary or fiction, you feel that you're using people, that you're somehow taking advantage.

"The ritual of putting people together in a film—it reminds me of Mass, which for me is theater. But what's so interesting about movies is it makes every spectator into a voyeur—you are going into one of these big rooms and you are going to see someone else's dreams. There is this sort of interplay between dream and reality. You are essentially alone with the movie and I believe one pleasure of the movie spectacle is almost close to masturbation—it's a very solitary pleasure and permits people to indulge in something that is almost a vice."

That sense of being a voyeur, a surreptitous observer of others, was instilled in Malle during his early years with Cousteau—years when he spent hours filming underwater, "where the gravity is different, where your senses function differently." It was reinforced further in 1968, when he went to India to make his award-winning documentary, *Phantom India,* and found himself filming people who were afraid that the camera would steal their souls.

The experience of working in an alien culture, says Malle, caused him to reexamine all that he had once taken for granted, and it led to an oblique cinematic style increasingly concerned with the shifting, impressionistic nature of reality. "India was a turning point in my life," he says now. "It made me realize there is always a different way of looking at things. I no longer believe, like some people, there are certain truths; I believe there is a truth only at a certain place and a certain moment."

The trip to India had another effect as well. It renewed Malle's sense of artistic purpose, for he had left France feeling "tired of actors, studios, fiction, and Paris." He had begun to feel that his work was becoming staid and repetitious—"if I went on that way, I worried I'd end up becoming part of the Académie Française"—and he felt a growing conflict between his position within the Paris film establishment and his belief that a director should function as a kind of agent provocateur. Ten years later, just prior to coming to America, a similar sense of stagnation had begun to bother him.

Although *Murmur of the Heart* and *Lacombe, Lucien* had won enormous critical acclaim, *Black Moon* (1975)—a surreal parable about an Alice-in-Wonderland–type character—was assailed as obscure, and Malle worried that his work "was becoming a little Byzantine, a little too esoteric." Both *Black Moon* and *Lacombe, Lucien* had been filmed near his home in the distant countryside of southwest France, and the director says he was starting to feel removed from the mainstream of life.

So in 1976, Malle moved to America to start filming *Pretty Baby,* and he has since made a home for himself in this country. "I needed to renew the fire and that's what I did coming here—in my work and in my life," he says. "Living here has given me a sense of threat—in France, I was sort of a prima donna—and I liked this challenge very much. Coming to America, I had this very strong feeling it was like starting from scratch, like going back to your first years when you were young."

June 1981

MARTIN SCORSESE

. . .

WHEN MARTIN SCORSESE FIRST READ THE SCRIPT
for *The King of Comedy* in 1974, he dismissed it as a one-gag film. The story
of an ambitious young comic who kidnaps a famous talk-show host in
order to get himself on television didn't interest him at all. Years passed,
and Scorsese directed, with much acclaim, such movies as *Alice Doesn't
Live Here Anymore, Taxi Driver, New York, New York,* and *Raging Bull.*

When he read the script of *The King of Comedy* again in 1979, he says
he finally understood what it was all about. The film had taken on an
acutely personal meaning, and it would provide him with a means of
taking stock of his own career—for reassessing his early ambition and the
consequences of his more recent success.

In *The King of Comedy* Robert De Niro plays a novice comedian
named Rupert Pupkin who will do just about anything to get Jerry
Langford, a television personality played by Jerry Lewis, to invite him on
his show. Pupkin wheedles, he whines, he makes a complete pest of
himself, and when that doesn't work, he resorts to kidnapping and ran-
som. His ambition is blind and crazy, says Scorsese, and it is based on his
own youthful will to succeed at any price.

"I can identify with Pupkin," he says now. "It's the same way I made
my first pictures with no money and with the constant rejection—going

back and going back and going back until finally, somehow, you get a lucky break. Actually luck doesn't have that much to do with it; it's just this constant battering away at this monolith. Pupkin goes about it the wrong way, but he does have drive. I remember I'd go anyplace, do anything. I'd try to get into screenings, get into any kind of social situation to try to talk up projects. It's important who you meet—after all, if you meet forty or fifty people, the one person who will produce your first film might just be there."

It took almost a decade of struggling—after receiving a master's degree from New York University's film department in 1968, he edited documentaries and made commercials—but Scorsese's hustling paid off. Made in twenty-seven days for $650,000, his third feature, *Mean Streets,* earned acclaim at the 1973 New York Film Festival and helped establish him as one of the country's outstanding new directors—a reputation he would enhance with each successive film.

In retrospect, however, he says that that success incurred heavy personal costs: three marriages fell apart, and his friendships, too, suffered from the pressures of his work. Intense, driven, and passionate in his love of film, Scorsese speaks in rapid staccato sentences—sentences that pile up on each other as though he cannot talk fast enough to express all his thoughts. Though his conversation often erupts into bursts of self-deprecating humor, he possesses the nervous introspection of someone who has always been a loner.

"I wanted to look at what it's like to want something so badly you'd kill for it," he says of *King of Comedy.* "By *kill* I don't mean kill physically, but you can kill the spirit, you can kill relationships, you can kill everything else around you in your life. It does affect personal relationships, and the final line for me at the time was that if I had to make a choice between work and a relationship, the personal relationship would go by the wayside. I don't have regrets—whatever's happened over the years, I think happened for the better—but maybe the reason I made this picture is because I hope I wouldn't think the same way now."

If Rupert Pupkin represents the unaccommodated ambition Scorsese possessed as a young man, the Jerry Langford character provides a kind of metaphor for the fame the director has since achieved. Like Langford, he worries about the demands of others who want to latch on to the coattails of his good fortune, and like Langford, he feels more and more cut off by success.

"In the period of the last three or four years," he says "I've cut off a lot of the people around me—usually they need something, they want something and they think you can give it to them, but you can't. You have to be very, very careful. And while it's nice to be the center of attention, the danger is it may alter your perceptions. The most important thing for a director is his sense of the relationships between people. This social behavior I find fascinating, and very often, if you walk into a room and you're the center of attention, it's harder to pick up on these things. So what you have to do is go to things that are more deeply rooted—things that haven't altered, things that have obsessed you for years, things that you really know."

One of the things that Scorsese has captured most powerfully in his films is a sense of American life—not so much life lived in the mainstream, but life lived on the margins, where the promises of the Dream seem both alluring and elusive. Charlie, the young apprentice hood in *Mean Streets*, wants to make it on his own, but remains indebted to his gangster uncle. Alice, liberated from the past by her husband's death, sets off for Monterey, hoping to make a new life as a singer. And Jake LaMotta in *Raging Bull* also dreams of success without knowing how to husband his talents.

In documenting these characters' lives, Scorsese has created precisely observed worlds. *Mean Streets* gives us a portrait of life on the Lower East Side, as it is played out in the local pool halls and bars; *Alice*, a portrait of blue-collar life amid the motels and diners of the Southwest; and *Taxi Driver*, a portrait of nightlife in New York City, where alienation erupts into violence and despair. But while the director's movies often seem to be making certain social observations—*King of Comedy*, for instance, may be viewed as a kind of comment on America's obsession with celebrity—Scorsese says that those aspects do not really interest him. *Taxi Driver*, he explains, "is much more Dostoyevskian than political"

In fact, Scorsese has consistently been interested in using film as a means of exploring his own behavior and preoccupations. "It's like when you're in therapy and the doctor takes a videotape of a session," he explains. "I'm not videotaping my life, but in a way I am trying to put certain things about myself on canvas. Like I know this guy Travis in *Taxi Driver*, I've had the feelings he's had, and those feelings have to be taken out and explained. I know the feeling of rejection Travis feels, of not being able to make relationships survive. I know the *killing* feeling of really being angry."

The random violence in his movies, the sense that anything can happen, stems in part from the street action the director witnessed as a child growing up in Manhattan. And the sense of being an outsider that so many of his heroes share also has autobiographical roots. The son of a clothes presser, the director grew up in Little Italy, where asthma and a frail physique prevented him from taking part in the macho, street-smart life around him. He spent most of his free time going to the movies, and those movies made him want, more than anything, "to be part of that incredible world of the creation of films." "Films are like having a person around," he says. "And to have films be so much a part of your life that you can't live without them is kind of nice, and I thought that's what I wanted to achieve for other people."

In *Mean Streets,* Scorsese created a dark, vital portrait of life on the Lower East Side—the very life he once felt so excluded from. Although the picture chronicled the attempts of young men trying to make it as small-time gangsters, it was concerned, at heart, with the hero's struggles to reconcile the moral dictates of his conscience with the brutal code of life around him. It raised the question, says Scorsese, of "how does one practice Christian ethics and morals when you're in a world of that sort— can you be a hoodlum and also be a saint?"

The religious themes grew out of Scorsese's own Roman Catholic upbringing and his adolescent determination to become a priest. Although he later dropped out of the seminary and has since become an agnostic—"I lost my faith in the man-made aspects of the religion"—he says he still harbors a "fascination, not necessarily with the Church, but with the teachings and trying to understand what the teachings are about." It's a concern that animates many of his films. In his first feature *Who's That Knocking at My Door?,* a young man attempted to reconcile sexual desire with his Catholic sense of guilt. In *Taxi Driver,* the demented hero's asceticism and isolation turned him into a kind of saint-run-amok; his determination to purge New York of its pimps and prostitutes possessed all the fervor and intensity of the Old Testament God. And in *Raging Bull,* the boxer Jake LaMotta's rise and fall became a mythic tale of suffering and redemption.

Not surprisingly, *Raging Bull* reflected certain spiritual struggles Scorsese was experiencing at the time. It was 1978, and the director had just finished making *New York, New York*—a picture, he says now, that marked the end of his love affair with film. Employing painted backdrops and big musical numbers, the movie had been intended as a kind of homage to the Hollywood films of the forties that Scorsese loved so much, but in shooting the picture, he found that it was "nightmarish" to try to re-create what no longer existed: the "factory" provided by the old studio system was gone, and the visual style of the old movies proved difficult to merge with his own.

To make matters worse, Scorsese was also feeling overextended: while finishing *New York, New York*, he was also working on *The Last Waltz*, another documentary called *American Boy*, and staging Liza Minnelli's Broadway show *The Act*. He was traveling too much and spending too much money, and he had begun to question all his values. "Your values are upside down when the fun begins to take over, and you don't even know where you are," he says. "I think L.A. became too much during that period, too much of a movie-star town, and I realized I didn't belong."

And so, before beginning *Raging Bull*, Scorsese took a ten-day vacation and did a lot of thinking about how confused his life had become. Somehow, in the midst of this, he had a kind of revelation about how to make *Raging Bull*. Having already touched upon the after-effects of success in *New York, New York* (the marriage between the Liza Minnelli and Robert De Niro characters falters when her career takes off and his does not), he says he realized that a similar parable was provided by the story of Jake LaMotta, who won a boxing championship at the expense of his family and self-esteem. "I didn't think *Raging Bull* would be successful," he says. "I thought it would be the end of my career—it was the last statement, and as a last statement, it was about how to live your life."

As it turned out, the movie earned Scorsese critical praise and enabled him to make a stylistic breakthrough. In the past, his films had possessed a nervous, eclectic style. They were filled with references to previous films—the Wizard of Oz homage in *Alice*, the *Star Is Born* allusions in *New York, New York*—and his hectic, expressionistic camerawork often jarred with his tendency to work with actors in a naturalistic, almost documentary, fashion. Largely in reaction to the high stylization of *New York, New York*, he had tried to simplify his technique in *Raging Bull*— the movie was even shot in gritty black and white—and in so doing had managed to integrate all these disparate elements into a cohesive style. In *The King of Comedy*, the director's camera is even more static; it represents, he explains, an effort to simplify things further, to "denude the style" and achieve a new clarity and purity of expression.

In a sense, Scorsese has tried to do the same thing with his life. At the end of 1979, he left Los Angeles and moved back to New York, and he now lives quietly in Lower Manhattan. The apartment has the same empty, antiseptic look of Jerry Langford's apartment in *The King of*

Comedy, and it is filled with the sort of provisional furniture—metal bookcases and cheap metal and rattan chairs—someone acquires in the wake of a divorce. The television set is frequently left on without the sound to give the illusion that someone else is home, and Scorsese says the first thing he does every morning is check the TV listings to see what movies are on.

Although he has remained in touch with such friends as Brian De Palma, Steven Spielberg, and George Lucas, he sees far less of them than he did during the late sixties and early seventies, when they were all starting out together. Most of his time is spent working. At the moment, he is making plans to shoot his next picture based on Nikos Kazantzakis's *The Last Temptation of Christ.*

"It's calmed down a lot," he says. "It may be kind of boring and lonely at times, but it's better for the work and it's better for you as a person. At forty, you do start to think about things differently. When you finally get a lot of things you think you wanted, and it's not what you expected, you wonder what you do really want. The religious thing is probably for me the only way to have some sort of foundation. So you search, and in the process of searching, you may never get anything but you may learn something about yourself, about life.

"I must say, I can understand why people eventually stop making pictures—because to make films in such an impassioned way, you really have to believe in it, you've really got to want to tell that story, and after a while, you may find out that life itself is more important than the filmmaking process. Maybe part of the answer for what the hell we're doing here has to be in the process of living itself, rather than in the work." He pauses, and then laughs. "Of course," he adds, "you're talking to a person who's leaving this Sunday to look for new locations for the next picture."

February 1983

STEVEN SPIELBERG

. . .

As a child growing up in the fifties, Steven Spielberg knew, just knew, that another magical and somehow terrifying world lay just beyond the placid surface of his family's suburban life. Even the tiny crack in his bedroom wall, illuminated by the hallway light, promised all sorts of marvels. "I remember lying there, trying to go to sleep," he says, "and I used to always imagine little Hieronymus Bosch–like creatures inside, peeking out and whispering to me to come into the playground of the crack and be drawn into the unknown there, inside the wall of my home in New Jersey."

To this day, Spielberg says he continues to be fascinated by "what I think is there but cannot see," and that capacity for wonder, combined with a prodigal imagination, has informed nearly all his films, from *Jaws* to *Close Encounters of the Third Kind* to *Raiders of the Lost Ark*.

In his two latest pictures, Spielberg returns to the suburban milieu of his own childhood, but invests that world with the supernatural: *Poltergeist*, which he produced and cowrote, is a darkly imagined horror movie, portraying a family threatened by the vengeful spirits of the dead; while *E.T.*, the story of a ten-year-old boy who befriends an extraterrestrial stranded on earth, is a contemporary fairy tale, offering a vision of innocence and hope.

"*Poltergeist* is what I fear and *E.T.* is what I love," explains Spielberg. "One is about suburban evil and the other is about suburban good. I had different motivations in both instances: In *Poltergeist*, I wanted to terrify and I also wanted to amuse—I tried to mix the laughs and screams together. *Poltergeist* is the darker side of my nature—it's me when I was scaring my younger sisters half to death when we were growing up—and *E.T.* is my optimism about the future and my optimism about what it was like to grow up in Arizona and New Jersey."

A romantic in his approach to movies, Spielberg is less interested in depicting life as it is than in depicting life as it might be—heightened and idealized on the screen. Ghosts *(Poltergeist)*, extraterrestrials *(E.T.)*, UFOs *(Close Encounters)*, and vengeful killer sharks *(Jaws)* populate some of his pictures, while in others, a single incident (a young outlaw couple's decision to retrieve their child in *The Sugarland Express*, for instance, or the appearance of a Japanese submarine off the coast of California in *1941*) triggers an accelerating sequence of events, the sort of wildly improbable events that can happen only in the movies.

"I have a real chemical imbalance between what's real and what's not," says Spielberg. "I tend to side with what isn't real in picking a subject, more than I do with what's really happening out there in the street—enough directors make movies that reflect life as we see it every day. There's no proof UFOs exist or that ghosts exist, but it's always nice to imagine what you think could be there, and the best movies I've ever seen are movies that are slightly above one's normal eye level—something you have to reach up to and suspend your disbelief for.

"I think I'm a movie idealist, who thinks things should always be better than they are. And if they can't be better on a day-to-day basis, then it's easier for me to make them better in a movie."

The sort of movies Spielberg likes to make have the same effect on audiences that the pictures he saw as a young boy had on his youthful imagination: They entertain through constant "stimulus-response, stimulus-response," and they "take people out of their seats to get them involved—through showmanship." As a child, in fact, Spielberg says he never dreamed of becoming a director, he dreamed of becoming "all those heroic people up there on the screen." And to this day, making movies still provides him with vicarious pleasure—a kind of celluloid substitute for all his Walter Mitty dreams.

"In the past," he says, "I've made movies about experiences that I've never had because that way I can explore all those 'what ifs.' You see, I'm all the characters in my movies. I was as much Indiana Jones as Harrison Ford was in *Raiders*, and in *E.T.*, I was E.T.'s eyes. Through the movie, I had to imagine what it would be like to be a creature visiting earth and what life would be like from his perspective."

The real heroes in most of Spielberg's pictures, however, are not aliens like E.T., but people who represent his version of Hitchcock's innocent bystanders. They are "ordinary people," as Dr. Lacombe says in *Close Encounters*, "under extraordinary circumstances"—people like the suburban families in *Close Encounters, E.T.*, and *Poltergeist*, who live in pleasant ranch houses filled with appliances and television sets and refrigerators stocked with beer and Cokes and potato salad.

"They're common, everyday types of people to whom nothing really happens until I come along," says Spielberg. "In the movies I've made, I've tried very, very hard to take the bystander, toughen him up, thereby robbing him of his innocence, in order to combat the forces that are against him. I like contradictions—victims and predators. I love movies where there are opposing forces and they're stronger than the hero and the hero must succeed either by finding a way around or going straight through."

In the case of *E.T.*, Spielberg points out, the opposing force is not a tangible enemy like the shark in *Jaws*, but the grown-up world and its threats. Whereas ten-year-old Elliott wants only to love and be loved by his extraterrestrial friend, this grown-up world, represented by corps of doctors and technicians, wants to preserve E.T. as a specimen of alien life. "I always thought of the adult world as being symbolized by tall people who cast giant shadows," says Spielberg, "people who don't think like kids, but think like professionals. That's dangerous—they might understand E.T. biologically and scientifically, but they'd never ever understand that he had a heart."

Certainly a similar message has long been a favorite theme in children's literature—from J. M. Barrie's *Peter Pan* to Antoine de Saint-Exupéry's *The Little Prince*—and *E.T.* is filled with references to well-known books and films. During one scene, John Williams's score recalls the music used in *The Wizard of Oz* to announce the arrival of the Wicked Witch; and in the movie's penultimate scene, Elliott and his friends soar into the sky on their bicycles in much the way that Peter Pan and Wendy flew off to Never Never Land. But while Spielberg and the writer of the film, Melissa Mathison, were well versed in the genre they were working in—before starting, they screened such movies as *The Night of the Hunter, Bambi, The*

Blue Bird, and *Our Mother's House*—the film also grew out of preoccupations that have animated Spielberg's work from the beginning. Most of his movies, after all, have featured children in pivotal roles. *Sugarland, Close Encounters*, and *Poltergeist* all involve the attempt of a mother to regain custody of her child. And in both *Close Encounters* and *E.T.*, it is a child—and those adults who maintain a childlike openness to the possibility of miracles—who is granted communion with these visitors from outer space and a vision of a more lovely world.

"I've always wanted to do something about kids because I'm still a kid," says Spielberg, who at thirty-four still radiates a boyish enthusiasm and ingenuous charm. "I'm still waiting to get out of my Peter Pan shoes and into my loafers. I think it's easier for me to have a complete conversation from Pac-Man to exobiology with an eleven-year-old than it is to sit down with an adult and discuss Nietzsche and the Falklands. Why? I guess because I'm probably socially irresponsible and way down deep I don't want to look the world in the eye. Actually, I don't mind looking the world in the eye, as long as there's a movie camera between us."

That, of course, is exactly what Spielberg has been doing since he made his first home movie at the age of twelve. The son of a computer specialist and a concert pianist, who were divorced when he was a teenager, Spielberg says he was an awkward child—"the weird, skinny kid with the acne"—who didn't have a lot of friends. His parents moved several times, from Ohio to New Jersey to Arizona to California, uprooting Steven and his three younger sisters, and leaving him with a lasting sense of dislocation.

Movies, the young boy discovered, opened up a new world of possibilities—an exciting world wonderfully different from the suburbs his parents always lived in—and he soon learned that he could express himself more easily with a movie camera than by writing papers or having grownup conversations with his parents. "Movies took the place of crayons and charcoal," he says, "and I was able to represent my life at twenty-four frames a second. I kind of hid in the closet—like Elliott does in the movie. Instead of E.T., I had a movie camera and a small editing table and that was my relationship with films as long as I can remember, really. It hasn't cut me off from life, really, but it's given me a useful tool to explain it back to myself. I see life a lot clearer after the film's developed and I'm in the darkroom, watching it. That's when I really have perspective."

At twelve, he filmed a collision between his Lionel train sets. At thirteen, he earned a Boy Scout merit badge by making a three-minute

8-millimeter film that featured one of his friends robbing a stagecoach and counting the money. And at sixteen, he made *Firelight,* a two-and-a-half-hour science-fiction movie that anticipated *Close Encounters.*

When the young Spielberg was not making movies, he was watching them or watching television shows—"The Honeymooners," "Captain Midnight," "Sky King," "American Bandstand," and "Popeye." Such Disney films as *Bambi, Fantasia,* and *Snow White* nurtured a moralistic sense of good and evil, along with a well-developed sense of terror, and he says he also learned important lessons about storytelling from Frank Capra movies like *A Pocketful of Miracles, Meet John Doe,* and *It's a Wonderful Life.*

While enrolled at California State College in Long Beach, Spielberg spent most of his free time sneaking onto the Universal lot and making his own 16-millimeter films. In 1969, having gotten little response to his work, he decided to shoot something that would prove to industry executives that he "could move a camera and compose nicely and deal with lighting and performances." The result was *Amblin',* a twenty-four-minute short about a pair of hitchhikers, which won awards at the Venice and Atlanta film festivals.

The movie, he later recalled, represented "an attack of crass commercialism." "When I look back at the film," he said once, "I can easily say, 'No wonder I didn't go to Kent State' or 'No wonder I didn't go to Vietnam or I wasn't protesting when all my friends were carrying signs and getting clubbed in Century City.' I was off making movies, and *Amblin'* is the slick by-product of a kid immersed up to his nose in film."

Still, *Amblin'* fulfilled its young director's purpose—it won him a contract with Universal, and Spielberg was soon directing television episodes of "Night Gallery," "Marcus Welby," and "Columbo." *Duel,* a television movie about a motorist pursued by a malevolent, phantom truck, earned him critical acclaim, and at twenty-five, Spielberg was directing his first feature film, *The Sugarland Express.*

As critics duly noted, craft and technique came easily to Spielberg: He had an instinctive ability to manipulate suspense and expectation, and a natural sense of graphic dynamics that enabled him to tell a story through striking visual images and well-timed cuts. If choreographing large-scale effects came easily, however, Spielberg says he found characterization and the examination of personal relationships more problematic. "The hard thing for me," he says of his earlier films, "was answering questions like 'Who is this person?' 'Why do we like this guy?' 'Why should we spend two hours watching these people?' So I always used to make the story or the event almost as important as the characters."

Until *E.T.*, in fact, Spielberg's films have been very much the work of a director who has felt more comfortable employing a sophisticated cinematic vocabulary than expressing personal concerns. Created by someone who has spent hundreds of hours watching movies and discussing them with friends, his pictures are not only technically innovative but also replete with allusions to other movies: *Jaws* recalls old science-fiction pictures; *Close Encounters* makes references to works by Disney and Hitchcock; and *Raiders* pays homage to, even as it reinvents, the old Saturday matinee serials.

He never believed in anything, Spielberg once said, until he discovered film, and it is only recently that exposure to friends outside the business has made him realize that all those hours spent in dark theaters as a kid left certain "emotional and intellectual gaps."

"I'm still filling them in," he says now. "But you just can't pick up twenty years of lost weekends. I guess in many ways I need less reinforcing, less patting on the head, than most people, and I was so long in my own little world, my little protected environment, that I figured everyone must be like me—they must work like crazy, go home at eight, spend an hour in conversation, and go to bed.

"Movies are my life, but I see now that for some people movies are only a twice-a-year experience and that in the rest of their lives there are great decisions to be made: when to have children, where to send them to school, are they growing up okay, and how to make enough money to provide for everyone. It's sort of made me realize that there's more to life than making movies—though it's still easier to say than to demonstrate."

While Spielberg notes that he has recently given more attention to his private life than ever before, he remains "a workaholic," incapable of taking a vacation for more than a couple of days. In addition to helping out young, aspiring filmmakers by serving as executive producer on their pictures—he helped oversee such films as *Used Cars, Continental Divide,* and *I Wanna Hold Your Hand*—he has several projects of his own lined up, including *Always,* a reworking of the 1943 film *A Guy Named Joe,* which he describes as "a love story with a slightly other-worldly twist."

For Spielberg, that project, like *E.T.*, reflects his new determination to make films more concerned with characters and their personal lives, and it also reflects a new openness, on his part, toward emotions: "I think I've opened up more in the last three or four years than I had ever before. I allowed myself to be hurt. I'd never really allowed anything to reach me before—I was always overrationalizing just in order not to deal with it—and I think that now that I'm starting to deal with basic things in relationships, I'm able to turn around and be a little more open through movies about how I feel."

"*E.T.*," he goes on, "really expresses how I feel this year about a lot of things. Five years ago, I think I would probably have been too embarrassed about what people might think of me to make *E.T.* or even respond to an idea like this. I had to essentially get over my fear of running through the world naked and say, 'Take me or leave me.' I guess my priorities have shifted over the last half a decade, and in a nice way I think it's come back around through my films. That's what I mean about running around naked for the first time—I'm saying I'm going to deal with people, with what makes them happy and what makes them cry."

May 1982

BILLY WILDER

. . .

IN *SUNSET BOULEVARD*, THE SCREENWRITER hero complains, "Audiences don't know anyone writes a picture—they think the actors make it up as they go along." Be that as it may, the author of that line, Billy Wilder, has earned international acclaim for writing and directing such pictures as *Sunset Boulevard, Double Indemnity, The Lost Weekend, Stalag 17, Some Like It Hot,* and *The Apartment.* He has won six Oscars and been nominated for twenty Academy Awards, and last night, many of his colleagues from Hollywood and New York turned out to honor him at the Film Society of Lincoln Center's annual gala.

Alternately caustic and self-deprecating, gracious and irreverent, Wilder speaks with a curious blend of Austrian formality and American slang: Though he calls last evening's celebration "that Lincoln Center shindig," he likes to refer to his colleagues in formal terms (Alfred Hitchcock, for instance, is always "Mr. Hitchcock"; his longtime collaborator I. A. L. Diamond, "Mr. Diamond"). At the age of seventy-five, he scorns all manner of pretension. He wants nothing to do with "auteur" theories and critics who call the movies "cinema": he once dismissed an artsy camera shot by saying "I can't shoot a living room from the inside of the fireplace through the flames—unless I'm shooting it from the viewpoint of Santa Claus."

"The basic point is to bring them in and keep them awake," he said in an interview before the Film Society tribute. "The picture where it starts at eight, and at midnight I look at my watch and it's eight fifteen— that's the kind of picture I hate. I don't want to bore or propound some phony philosophy, and I don't want to give them schlock. If you can do it with style, without low punches, if you can entertain them for two hours and have them talk about the picture for fifteen minutes after they leave, I'm satisfied."

In some fifty pictures, Wilder has done just that and more, and he has done it in almost every genre: farce *(One, Two, Three)*, film noir *(Double Indemnity)*, suspense *(Witness for the Prosecution)*, romantic comedy *(Sabrina)*, and satire *(A Foreign Affair)*. Yet for all their disparate forms, the movies share a distinctive Wilder touch—an acerbic wit, coupled with a desire to expose society's darker side. As the director himself puts it, "I like to mix a little vinegar in the cocktail."

More often than not, his movies involve elaborate deceptions ending in a loss of innocence, and his characters tend to be unconventional, if not thoroughly disreputable, types—insurance con men, cynical newspaper editors, tax dodgers, hookers, and gigolos. "After the whole bit in drag," said Jack Lemmon, recalling his role as a member of an all-girl orchestra in *Some Like It Hot*, "I played six more parts with Billy. These are the characters: a weakling who rents his apartment out for assignations; a guy who lives with a prostitute and pays her; a married man who follows in dear old Dad's footsteps—he arranges a yearly European tryst with another lady; a totally unethical newspaper reporter who'd stoop to any unsavory act to get a story; a cameraman in a neck brace trying to collect money for phony injuries; and a loser who wants to kill himself because his wife is holed up in a sex clinic with her therapist."

Such characters and plots, along with Wilder's savage humor, have persuaded many critics to characterize him as "cynical." But as his colleagues have pointed out, a more accurate description might be found in the lines he once wrote of a character in *The Fortune Cookie*—that is, someone "with a brain full of razor blades and a heart full of chutzpah."

"It's an old Viennese tradition that comes down from Schnitzler," says Diamond. "It is a Middle European attitude, a combination of cynicism and romanticism. The cynicism is a sort of disappointed romanticism at heart—someone once described it as whipped cream that's gotten slightly curdled."

Wilder, for his part, does not deny that he is a romantic, and he points out that a film like *The Apartment* has "as fairy-tale a third act as anything by Capra." In fact many of his heroes are opportunists who experience an awakening in the course of the movie; and while his pictures have often dwelled on the brashness and vulgarity of American life, they have also conveyed an admiration for its vitality and innocence—an admiration that has roots in Wilder's own romance with this country.

Born in Vienna in 1906, Wilder left his job as a newspaper reporter to write screenplays in Berlin and Paris. Although Hitler's rise hastened his departure in 1934, he says that, like most European filmmakers of the day, he had always dreamed of Hollywood.

"I thought that the stars are going to be running in the streets," he says, "and it would be all beautifully kept bungalows and great parties with women wearing hats with ostrich feathers. One of the things that impressed me when I was young was a silent American picture in which a bum asks a man, 'Can you tell me what time it is?' And the man takes out his watch and gives it to him. I thought of that as very American. Your concept turns out to be totally different, but I was not disillusioned one little bit. Naturally you grow up, and you see it with more realistic eyes, but I have not wavered as to which country I wanted to be a citizen of—never. I thought it was great—the energy, the generosity, even with all the foibles, the human weaknesses."

While his subject matter is usually American, Wilder's style and technique bear the imprint of those two great European filmmakers—Erich von Stroheim and Ernst Lubitsch. The legacy of Stroheim, says Wilder, was "a way of attacking a scene, a sharpness and daring"; of Lubitsch, "a bemused wit, an eroticism which is so far superior to all our efforts now that censorship has been removed."

As Wilder sees it, Lubitsch was able, in the twenties, to deal with potentially risqué subjects by handling them with elegance and sophistication. In contrast, the humor of today's films strikes him as simplistic, even crude. "Lubitsch operated on the basis that the audience is not stupid," he says. "He would not say, 'two plus two equals four.' He would just say, 'two plus two.' It's like the secret of Chinese glass blowing—he took it into the grave with him. Suddenly we are painting with acrylics—no more watercolors, no more oils. It's all posters—everything underlined, with exclamation points."

"The entire industry is in intensive care," he goes on. "Half the people in Hollywood are on their way to China to set up a coproduction deal. The other half are on their way to the Sinai for a triple-bypass operation.

So who do they call in to save the patient?—lawyers, supermarket owners, soft-drink manufacturers. These are the people who decide what gets made and what does not get made today. They operate very scientifically—computer surveys, audience profiles—and they always come up with the same answer: 'Get Richard Pryor, he's hot this week.' The truth is, though, movies are launched out of gut feeling, and the prerequisite of course is you have to have guts."

Wilder's own recent pictures have been somewhat less than successful—even such critically acclaimed films as *Fedora* did poorly at the box office—and his current difficulties underline, for him, how much Hollywood has changed. What he calls "the mezzo-educated audience" has dwindled, and "the habit"—of "It's Friday night and it's Cary Grant and Marlene Dietrich"—has also been challenged by the advent of television and other distractions. In addition, says Wilder, the breakdown of the studio system has meant that writers and directors must now spend "twice as much time trying to raise money for a picture as actually making it."

"I've been foundering," he says. "People say, 'It wasn't your year.' Well, it hasn't been my decade. I guess I lost contact with the audience—I hope, only momentarily. I don't mean I'm going to do a *Stripes* or a *Saturday Night Fever*. I do my own thing, but the big stumbling block always is if people don't like a painting, you can toss the whole damn thing into the fireplace—the canvas and paint cost four ninety-nine. But my canvas costs six million or ten million or twelve million dollars, and I have a responsibility to the investors.

"And it's not just the money, but the time. At my age, you get a bit apprehensive. You think three times, and sometimes you triple-guess yourself out of something that might be a big hit. It's hard to make that beautiful, brand-new, universally acclaimed masterpiece if you play it safe. Still, the energy, the ambition, has not diminished—you strive for a decent, preferably admirable, third act. It's the bang we're looking for, not the whimper. If you are to die, better to die with your horse winning the Kentucky Derby than to die on the subway, without even a horse running in the race.

"One day I was having lunch at the studio commissary," he goes on, "and there were three young men sitting in the other corner. I recognized their faces—they had all been mail boys at William Morris. Now they were vice presidents—you could tell from their Italian suits, their narrow ties, and their Rolex watches. I heard them whisper about me, and the essence of what they said was, 'Billy Wilder's career can be summed up in one word—over.' "

Wilder and his many fans, however, remain unconvinced. He continues to work, meeting Diamond at their office every morning at nine-thirty. The two collaborators are currently in the process, he says, of "rejecting ideas, narrowing the choices of what to do next."

"I am absolutely not retiring," he said to a standing ovation at Lincoln Center. "As far as I'm concerned, this ball game is just going into extra innings. I'm ready. I changed my stance, I shortened my grip, and I got some contact lenses. I'm sure I still have a few hits coming, maybe even a triple or a home run. So a tribute like this is like a marvelous shot of adrenaline, and for this I am very grateful."

He stopped for a moment, then went on. "Thank you," he said, echoing Norma Desmond in *Sunset Boulevard,* "you beautiful people out there in the dark."

May 1982

PLAYWRIGHTS

AND

PRODUCERS

. . .

JULES FEIFFER

. . .

H AVING DRAWN HUNDREDS OF CARTOONS ABOUT JEWISH
mothers and sons, having spent "eighty-five years in psychotherapy,"
Jules Feiffer says he was convinced that he had already come to terms with
his family problems. Then, in 1974, his mother died. The day of her
funeral, Feiffer developed bronchitis and a fever of 104, and for the next
three months he was unable to continue with a novel he had been working
on. He decided that the one way he could go back to work was "to
perform an act of exorcism," and he began an autobiographical play—a
savagely funny play, which in ripping apart the happy myth of the American family, also expiated his own feelings of love and anger and frustra-
tion.

The play, *Grown Ups*, resonates with the pain and anger of a family
that doesn't know how to express its love; it is a story of missed connections and unsatisfied needs. Helen and Jack are proud of their son Jake's
success as a *New York Times* reporter, but his success seems more important to them than his actual work. Jake, in turn, resents his parents for their
expectations, for their demands, and for the humiliations they subjected
him to as a child; and he turns his rage against his wife and child. He ends
by severing every familial and emotional tie that once defined his comfortable Upper West Side life.

Like Jake, Feiffer once lived in an Upper West Side apartment with his wife and daughter. And like Jake, he saw his marriage end in divorce. But while Feiffer acknowledges these parallels, he points out that the character of the wife is the most fictionalized in the play. "It's parts of my ex-wife, of course, but also parts of three other women I've known over the years. I was concerned about my child's reaction and what my ex-wife would think. With my parents, it was different. Since they were dead, I felt I was freer to do with them what I wanted."

"I don't think I would have had the chutzpah or the callousness to do this radical surgery on my parents while they were alive," he goes on. "And it wouldn't have been possible, really—it's only when they're ghosts that you can go back and review it all. And, you know, I found partly that I really liked them. Some people watch the play and write about the mother as some awful woman, but I find her terribly charming and attractive, and also a woman whose excesses are understandable. She's the glue that holds the family together."

In Feiffer's own case, he grew up with two sisters in the East Bronx. A genteel, educated woman born in Poland and raised in Richmond, Virginia, his mother, Rhoda, supported her husband and children by working as a fashion designer. David Feiffer was unemployed much of the time, and his son recalls that he "was a defeated man by the time I knew him." "Maybe it was that, as an immigrant, he never made an adjustment to this country," he says. "Or maybe being surrounded by wheelers and dealers, he just never had the absence of ethics to be a successful business-man. He was a sweet man, my father. He lived by avoiding living."

In *Grown Ups*, the expectations of Jake's parents continually esca-late—it isn't enough that he has interviewed Henry Kissinger; they are looking forward to the day when Henry Kissinger will interview *him*—and in one of the play's more brutal scenes, Jake finally turns to his father and cries, "You never supported me until I made it at the *Times*. I had to make it with *strangers* to be accepted by my own family."

It is a sentiment Feiffer says he knows all too well. "There was always the sense that the quality of my work was of less concern than its success," he says, recalling his parents' reaction to his cartoons. "Success is what counted—it's a lousy system of values. It's what frustrated me and what frustrates Jake. I remember my father used to say, 'I won't consider you a successful cartoonist until your cartoons appear in *The New York Times*.' Well, of course, *The New York Times* didn't run cartoons, so it was a kind of double whammy. It was saying, 'I only want the best for you, which of course you can't achieve.'"

"Both my parents were concerned about me without having the faintest understanding or interest in my interests," he goes on. "And the only advice I got from them was bad advice because it was always conservative and cautious. My mother was very ambitious for me, but being an immigrant with memories of Polish pogroms, she was never far from feeling that if you offended the gentiles, they would throw you out of the country. When my cartoons started appearing in *The Village Voice*, she was both joyous and wished I would shut up before I offended somebody."

Clearly those cartoons—which Feiffer has been drawing now for twenty-five years—share with *Grown Ups* and his earlier plays certain recurrent themes. The interest in adult responsibilities and the difficulty of "growing up," for instance, first surfaced in Feiffer's early cartoons about Munro, a four-year-old boy who finds himself drafted into the army; and it was developed further in such works as *Tantrum*, the story of a husband and father who reverts to being a two-year-old.

And while *Grown Ups* is less overtly political than a play like *The White House Murder Case*, it is animated by a similar concern with the fragmentation of society. What his work all shares, he says, is a preoccupation with "the corruption of previously sainted institutions and the fact there is nothing yet to replace them." In *Carnal Knowledge*, it's sexual disllusionment; in *Little Murders*, urban violence; in *Grown Ups*, the dissolution of the modern family.

Although Feiffer says he would next like to write a political farce about the Reagan administration—"How else can you deal with the government, except with farce?"—he has yet to find a suitable idea. In the meantime, another play called *A Think Piece* is scheduled for production later in the season at the Circle Repertory Theater. The play, he says, is a meditation of sorts on the nature of trivia—an examination of the fact that "it is not the momentous events of life, but the minutiae which govern our day-to-day existence." One of its major characters is a dog.

In the past, Feiffer's plays have met with less than an enthusiastic response on Broadway. *Little Murders* lasted all of seven peformances in 1967 before returning as an Off Broadway hit two years later. And *Knock, Knock*, which played to great acclaim Off Broadway, also fared poorly when it was moved uptown. It is a fate Feiffer has learned to be philosophical about. "For one reason or another, Broadway audiences have become programmed to be passive," he says. "They go into the theater and expect to be soothed, and for better or worse, I'm not in the soothing business. I'm in the make-them-laugh-in-order-to-make-them-cry business."

With *Grown Ups*, success may be more assured—a fact that Feiffer finds particularly comforting at this point in life. "When I was first starting out, taking my cartoons around, I knew something would pop," he says. "I don't know what gave me that fierce confidence; now, being more experienced and successful, I no longer have it—I have to keep inflating flat tires. It's probably a function of age—I'm going to be fifty-three in January and I find it less easy over the years to fantasize about rejection. So instead of becoming more thick-skinned, I become more thin-skinned. That's why the success of *Grown Ups* is so warming to me now."

In any case, he adds, one of the most trying periods with *Grown Ups* came and went during rehearsals, when he first began to worry about the consequences of writing so personal a play. "I think I felt quite scared because I didn't want my dead mother to be angry with me," he explains. "I didn't want to displease or hurt her, and when I saw the character I wrote being acted by Frances Sternhagen, I felt that's her. I felt my mother would be proud of this woman, and while the audience is recoiling, I'm enjoying her to the hilt. I love those people up there, and I think what John Madden [the director] has done is treat them with affection. One of the last notes he gave the company was, 'These people *do* love their children—they just don't know how.'

"So when I sat back and watched the play, I was no longer worried about my mother hating it. Of course, if she were alive, I'd still be worried, but the mother in my head I placated entirely. How would my parents have reacted if they saw it?" He pauses. "I think they would have been mortally offended and would have prayed desperately for its success."

December 1981

ARTHUR MILLER

. . .

IT WAS OPENING NIGHT OF *DEATH OF A SALESMAN*, and after five curtain calls, the star of the show, Dustin Hoffman, stepped forward and asked the playwright to come up and take a bow. The Broadhurst Theater began to resound with cries of "Arthur! Arthur!" and "Author! Author!" but Arthur Miller was nowhere to be seen. He had quietly slipped away.

Certainly the critical and popular acclaim received by the current revival of *Salesman* has provided Miller with a measure of gratification. But while the show almost immediately sold out its limited run and received a Tony nomination for outstanding revival, its success has been less than total. To Miller's dismay and the surprise of many members of the theater community, its stars (including Hoffman, John Malkovich, and Kate Reid) and its director, Michael Rudman, were passed over by the Tony nominating committee.

In many respects, this slight only serves to reinforce the playwright's own deep-seated doubts about working in the commercial theater and the durability of his achievement. In an interview in his East Side apartment, he spoke of times when he considered "swearing off" playwriting altogether and noted, with an ironic laugh, that the rave notices received by *Salesman* must have succeeded in irking his longtime critics.

In retrospect, Miller's career has traced a spectacularly uneven course, and he tends to regard his current apotheosis as just another swing of the pendulum of success. His recent triumphs, including the current production of *Salesman*, last year's revival of *A View From the Bridge*, and the 1980 Spoleto Festival version of *The American Clock* have been matched, almost show for show, by equal disappointments. When a refashioned *Clock* was later moved to Broadway it was dismissed by the critics as damaged goods, and a pair of one-act plays, staged in 1982 at the Long Wharf Theater in Connecticut, were shrugged off as awkward and contrived. For Miller, this experience of being "thrown back into the marketplace" with each new production has been humiliating and wearisome; and he talks wistfully of the need for a national theater that would nurture and support the artist.

"I don't feel I'm triumphant by any means," he says, speaking in the brisk, colloquial tones of a native New Yorker—tones that are echoed by Hoffman in his own portrayal of Willy Loman. "I feel I've dealt with a lot of wasting circumstances as best I could, but I've had to waste my time defending my space, so to speak. Had there been a working theater, it could have been or might have been otherwise. After all, I haven't had a continuing relationship with a director in twenty-five years, no real relationship with a critic—except with Harold Clurman in a way."

"We have no real theater," he continues. "We have shows, which isn't really the same thing. And I can say this now, in possession of a hit of phenomenal proportions, that it isn't healthy. It's wrong that for a show to be a hit, it has to be sold out. The theater is healthy when a play can run half or two-thirds full. When I came into the theater, it was a rare thing that you went into the theater and it was full. Now, if you've got four empty seats, unbought, you know your time has come.

"The number of elements that have to go into a hit would break a computer down. It has to be the right season for that play, the right historical moment, the right tonality. And think of the chances of getting the right person—it depends on who's available, on whom the director may have seen or at what dinner party he might have been at and heard of a certain person. This is why the theater is so endlessly fascinating—because it's so accidental. It's so much like life."

Miller, of course, is well acquainted, firsthand, with the vicissitudes of success and failure in American life. His father lost nearly everything during the Depression—an event that reverberates throughout his work—and that turnaround in his family's fortunes would be echoed, several decades later, by a reversal in his own career.

Having won early fame in 1949 with the original production of *Salesman*—when he was thirty-three years old, he achieved the kind of quick, smashing beginning that Willy only dreams of—Miller felt secure in the knowledge that the world was "a friendly place." It was a conviction swiftly destroyed by his sobering experience with the House Un-American Activities Committee in the late fifties. When he refused to name people he had seen ten years earlier at a meeting alledgedly held by the Communist Party, he was convicted of contempt of Congress. Although the decision was later reversed on appeal, the experience convinced him that, "whatever psychological security one has had better come from within, because the social support for it is very chancy."

To make matters worse, the political chilliness of the fifties corresponded to a growing feeling on the playwright's part that he was no longer in sync with the dominant aesthetics of the day. With the advent of such writers as Edward Albee and Samuel Beckett, and the emergence of a drama that eschewed the linearity of social realism for more innovative, modernist approaches, critics increasingly came to view Miller's work as old-fashioned, moralistic, and didactic. "There was a sudden change of social values," he says, "and for a while, I felt pretty lonely. I could make no connection with the kind of theater that we were creating, theater which had no prophetic function."

As many critics see it, Miller's better plays balance his tendency to make portentous pronouncements about society with a more personal, internalized vision: *Salesman* is as much about the love shared by fathers and sons as it is about the bankruptcy of the American dream; and *A View From the Bridge* examines the consequences of sexual obsession, even as it attempts to create a parable about betrayal in the McCarthy era.

For the playwright however, the social aspects of a play will always remain a central concern. His own unhappy experiences during the Depression and the fifties convinced him that politics "determines the exteriors of your personality." And so in his view, all serious plays must ultimately address a single question: "How may a man make of the outside world a home?"

With the exception of *Salesman, After the Fall,* and *The Price,* he says, he has never deliberately tried to focus on the interior life of his characters. If anything, he adds, he has grown more interested, over the years, in examining the mythic, rather than the personal, implications of a dramatic situation.

This concern with myth, like his conviction that the theater has a duty to address the great questions of "right and wrong," springs in part from his interest in Greek tragedy and the Bible—the two most lasting influences, he now says, on his work as a whole. "I was interested, as a student at the University of Michigan, in the way the Bible tells stories," he says. "What we take away from the Bible may seem like characters—Abraham and Isaac, Bathsheba and David—but really, they're psychic situations. That kind of storytelling was always fantastic to me. And it's the same thing with the Greeks. Look at Oedipus—we don't know much about him, apart from his situation, but his story bears in itself the deepest paradoxes in the most adept shorthand."

In writing his own plays, Miller says, he has attempted to infuse his characters with a similar mythic dimension: Willy Loman, for instance, is meant to represent both the quintessential American dreamer and the symbolic father who incorporates "power and some kind of moral law."

When he wrote the play, Miller was a young man who still thought of himself as a rebellious son; and at the time, he says, he tended to identify less with Willy than with Biff, his disaffected son. Today, at the age of sixty-eight, with children of his own, the playwright says he has "crossed the line from Biff into Willy."

"When Biff's yelling at Willy now," he says, "he's yelling at me. I understand Willy. And I understand his longing for immortality—I think that's inevitable when you get older. It's not in terms of work. It's more of a mystical sense. Willy's writing his name in a cake of ice on a hot day, but he wishes he were writing in stone. He wants to live on through something—and in his case, his masterpiece is his son. I think all of us want that, and it gets more poignant as we get more anonymous in this world. Any writer wants to write something that survives him—it's one of the reasons we go on."

May 1984

JOSEPH PAPP

. . .

P ACING BACK AND FORTH IN HIS CLUTTERED OFFICE,
Joseph Papp lights up a Havana cigar and starts reciting some of the
Duke's lines from *Measure for Measure*. Papp is directing a new production
of the play, which will kick off the Shakespeare Festival's thirtieth summer
season, and his set and costume meeting has soon turned into a one-man
exercise in acting. Playing various characters, Papp roams about the room,
punching the air for emphasis, pulling his jacket lapels up for effect. His
intermittently interrupted monologue also bounds from subject to subject
as he expounds upon his concept of the play, sandwiching his opinions
between puns, lengthy asides on the quality of sunlight in Brooklyn,
sexual imagery in *Henry IV,* and maybe a few bars from "Hallelujah, I'm
a Bum" or "Brother, Can You Spare a Dime?"

At sixty-four, Papp has the quick, controlled movements of someone
trained as a dancer or basketball player, and one might easily mistake him
for an actor, so swiftly does he slip in and out of impersonations, moods,
and poses. Listening to Papp talk is like listening to a Renaissance scholar
on Benzedrine. The voice is Brooklynese neutralized by impeccable Eli-
zabethan elocution; the delivery, brisk, verging on manic. While every
opinion is announced with authority, nothing seems to have been
analyzed or subjected to internal debate; rather, it's spilled out, contradictions and all, for the listener to absorb.

The costume designer, Lindsay Davis, a young man meticulously dressed in a suit and tie, is kneeling by the coffee table, nervously scribbling down every word Papp utters, while Robin Wagner, the set designer, who has known Papp for two decades, sits slouched on the couch, casually lobbing one-liners at the producer: "Matzohs for lunch, Joe? You're turning into a religious fanatic. I remember when I thought you were Greek." "You added a line?—so now, it's going to be by William Shakespeare and Joseph Papp?"

Papp ignores Wagner's jibes. Or perhaps he doesn't hear them. Talking about the character Angelo, he is reminded of Harry Belafonte, whom he saw the other night at a benefit. Which reminds him that he wants to try to cast more black actors in *Measure for Measure*. Which reminds him of changing demographics in the city. Which reminds him of his plan to redesign the city's educational system. Getting back to the play, he says he is most interested in the character of the Duke, the head of state who likes to go among his people, dressed in disguise. As Papp sees it, the Duke is a great leader, someone perceived by his people as "abrupt and even cruel—but who also ends up being very human." As a character, says Papp later, the Duke is totally inexplicable, a hundred times more "complex than Jesus Christ."

Davis wants to know how old Papp thinks a low comic character named Elbow is.

"One hundred," says Papp, not missing a beat. "He's a guy who falls asleep all the time, an old guy—very tall and thin."

"Those old skinny men, they don't fall asleep," says Wagner.

"This one does," says Papp. "I know he does.

"Of course," he adds, almost pausing, "everything's subject to change."

The sort of theater that Papp loves most are plays like Shakespeare's— plays that are epic in dimension, drawn with great, sweeping lines, and filled with raw emotions, plays that "have a kind of ardent compassion, where people are screaming at life." And in person, Papp himself projects a similar intensity, a kind of unaccommodated and kinetic passion. He hates being bored, hates sameness, inertia, and silence; and his own moods can vacillate between a dark melancholy and an almost electrical enthusiasm. Equally fluent in the worlds of art and business, he is decisive and direct—sometimes to the point of rudeness—impulsive, and yet somehow deeply vulnerable.

There is something about him, an imaginative sympathy that makes writers and actors want to confide in him, impress him—or simply make him laugh; and around the Public Theater (the Festival's home base on the Lower East Side in New York), they tend to pick up on his every mood, echoing his responses with their own. "I think of him as a combination of a very intense and wily Talmudic scholar and a bad vaudeville comedian," says the composer and playwright Elizabeth Swados. "I think he's very, very sentimental, which he dares to be in a time when most people are very aloof."

Although *Measure,* a dark comedy about sex and politics, is one of Shakespeare's more problematic works, Papp liked its ambiguities, and he embraced its textual difficulties as a wonderful directorial challenge. *Measure* is the forty-seventh production that Papp has staged himself, but he is not recognized, mainly, as a director. It is as a producer, a midwife to others' talents, that Papp has made his reputation, and his influence on the theater consequently remains a highly personal affair, measured less in terms of an aesthetic vision or a single body of work than in terms of projects he has assembled and people he has affected—among many others, such playwrights as David Rabe, John Guare, Wallace Shawn, Michael Weller, Thomas Babe; and such actors as George C. Scott, Colleen Dewhurst, James Earl Jones, Meryl Streep, and Kevin Kline.

If the last three decades have diminished neither Papp's energy nor his passion for the theater, they *have* witnessed remarkable changes: the Festival has evolved from a provisional acting workshop, housed in the basement of a Lower East Side church, into America's largest theatrical arts institution; and as its founder, architect, and presiding spirit, Papp has become one of the most influential men in American theater today.

While its director has been assailed for being too avant-garde on the one hand, and too commercial on the other, the Festival has developed an eclectic agenda over the years—an agenda that has included such disparate works as *A Chorus Line, Sticks and Bones, Hair, That Championship Season, Short Eyes, Marie and Bruce, Dead End Kids, The Pirates of Penzance,* and *Plenty.* Under Papp's leadership, the Festival has brought Shakespeare and revivified classics to the public for free; helped bring radical new works into the mainstream; given black, Hispanic, and Asian-American authors a valuable showcase; and provided a model for not-for-profit theaters around the country. "Joe's shown more courage to do more things than anybody else," says Bernard Jacobs, the president of the Shubert Organization. "I think he's one of the major reasons we still have a theater today."

Of course, as New Yorkers well know, Papp also exerts a presence in the city that extends well beyond the theater. A child of the ideological 1930s, Papp has always been committed to using theater as a "societal force"—he set out to open the theater to "the disenchanted and disenfranchised"—and his own taste still inclines toward plays like *Tracers* (Vietnam) and *The Normal Heart* (AIDS), plays that "have something to say about contemporary issues."

Active on nearly a dozen cultural and social committees, from the Mayor's Theater Advisory Committee to Planned Parenthood, Papp often seems omnipresent in New York, the proverbial model citizen and good samaritan. In recent years he has also emerged as one of those public figures whose name appears in *New Yorker* cartoons and elicits strong opinions from people who haven't met him—someone variously hailed and assailed as "a punk version of Diaghilev," the "Don Quixote of the Great White Way," and the "David Merrick of the seventies."

Papp does little to discourage the hyperbole; like a politician on the campaign trail, he cultivates a high visibility. "I feel it's important that the public be let in on everything," he explains. "I'm a public figure, and a public figure should be in the public eye. The theater needs it. It gives you a certain amount of power to do things you want to do."

Publicity campaigns for the Festival, in fact, have increasingly played up Papp's role as figurehead of the institution. At one point, the picture of Shakespeare that stands at the center of the Festival's insignia was replaced with one of the producer, and last year's advertising campaign for *The Human Comedy* featured a likeness of Papp on the show's program, in newspaper advertisements, and even on the Broadway marquee. Such public displays of personality, Papp explains, are just good business; and, in a sense, his role as a spokesman for the Festival did begin as a publicity and fund-raising tactic. As Merle Debuskey, a press agent associated with the Festival since its start, observes, "An institution can't be interviewed or photographed. So we consciously tried to make Joe synonymous with the institution—he had to be known so the project would grow as we hoped."

At the same time, though, Papp's identification with the Festival is much more than a public-relations gimmick; the producer himself experiences it as a visceral fact. When the future of the theater is threatened, he feels physically ill; and he has taken negative reviews of shows as personal attacks. When one critic dismissed David Rabe's *Boom Boom Room* as "an empty and poorly crafted play," Papp rang him up on the phone and shouted: "You think you're going to get me? Well, I'm going to get you!"

"The institution is Joe," observes the playwright Thomas Babe, "and Joe is the institution."

Today that institution has five stages, 110 full-time employees, and an annual budget of ten million dollars, and Papp is in a position, as the British playwright David Hare points out, to "put enormous resources into what he believes in, and withhold resources from something he doesn't believe in." Papp's faith in his own judgment is absolute, and at the Public, his judgments are the only ones that really matter. He's unhappy with how an all-male production of *Antony and Cleopatra* is proceeding and he cancels the show that afternoon. Albert Innaurato wants to write a new scene for *Coming of Age in Soho,* featuring a family of eight; Papp calls his casting department, and the next day there are twenty-three suitable actors waiting to be auditioned. He decides to move *The Human Comedy* to Broadway, and he commits four hundred thousand dollars of the Festival's money to the move.

"Here at the Public," says David Hare, "it's Ruritania, and the emperor can do as he likes."

In the beginning, when the Festival was still a small acting workshop, Papp became accustomed to doing everything himself—from directing shows to installing seats in the theater—and he still approves advertising copy for shows, tries personally to sign all production contracts, and makes a point of telling writers and actors, in person, what he thinks of their work. Sometimes his impatience with bureaucracy and the democratic process also extends to the staging of shows. In the case of *Two Gentleman of Verona,* he tore apart, and rebuilt, the production a week before the opening, and produced a Broadway hit. When he attempted the same thing with *True West,* only acrimony and nasty headlines resulted—both the author, Sam Shepard, and the play's nominal director disowned the abortive production. "If a show has problems," says Papp, "something's got to be done. And once I'm involved, it's difficult for me to get involved halfway."

All or nothing remains the principle by which Papp has run the theater and his life. If he decides to give minority performers more jobs, he doesn't cast two or three actors in a show—he announces the formation of an entire black and Hispanic company. If he wants to prevent the razing of some Broadway theaters, he doesn't just sign a few petitions—he takes a hotel room in Times Square so he can spend twenty-four hours a day on the scene. Such crusades may not always succeed, and Papp may abandon one plan for another in a second, but he says he never looks back. He is a man who tries to live as though there were no past, a man who willfully lives in the present. Were he an actor, he says, the two roles he would most like to play are Hamlet and King Lear. He would play Hamlet as someone out to usurp the throne from Claudius; Lear, as an irascible authority figure who "just wants everyone to love him."

Papp has always had a weakness, he says, for old-fashioned, Broadway-style "dash, glamour, and risk," and in a day when most arts institutions are run by committees, he has developed a personal style reminiscent of such old-time impresarios as Sol Hurok and Jed Harris. In a 1978 cabaret act, he dressed the part of an old-time showman, appearing on stage in a top hat and tails, carrying a silver-headed cane. And on television commercials for the Festival, he affects the swaggering stance of a self-made mogul by talking out of the side of his mouth and gesturing grandly with a cigar.

Even off stage, there is something insistently theatrical about him. Whether he is sweet-talking a diffident actress, threatening to lie down in front of a bulldozer during a demonstration, or presenting his views of Broadway to a reporter, his audience has the sense of watching a brilliant performance; often an entirely heartfelt performance, full of real passion and commitment, but a performance all the same. "I can't stand it when people are indifferent to me," he says. "I don't mind it if they get angry, want to kill me, but I want some kind of reaction."

Papp has peremptorily stalked out of dinner parties and Board of Estimate meetings, and written enraged letters to corporate executives who have ignored him, but most of the time such overt tactics aren't required. An astute observer of others, he uses his intuition, along with his charm and street-smarts, to get what he wants. When it comes to fund-raising, for instance, Papp will talk about "maneuvering" with the person on the other end of the phone—"tap-dancing" with their emotions, playing upon their sense of civic responsibility, their love of the arts, even their fear of letting him down.

Control matters enormously to Papp. It is the reason he gets a rush of adrenaline from persuading a new patron to give money to the Festival, the reason he works out three times a week on a Nautilus machine, and the reason, of course, that he loves to work in the theater. Art lends order to his life, provides him with a framework in which to function. "Even if a play's about a depressing subject, it's still a play," he says. "It's under your control. You know the show will be over in a certain time, and in that time, no one's going to get killed. Most things in life are totally out of control, but with a play, there's a beginning, a middle, an end. You're not just going off into the wild blue yonder."

Figuring out an approach to a play like *Measure*, negotiating the foreign rights to a new show, trying to convince Mayor Koch to help save dying Broadway theaters—all are challenges that fill Papp's compulsive need to orchestrate; and one has the sense that he welcomes crises and confrontations as additional ways to test his intellect and reflexes. In his initial fight to stage free Shakespeare in Central Park—the fight that first brought the Festival into the public eye, in 1959—Papp successfully took on the all-powerful Parks Commissioner Robert Moses. In 1973, he canceled an eleven-million-dollar contract with CBS when it postponed David Rabe's controversial Vietnam play, *Sticks and Bones*. And during his tenure at Lincoln Center (the Festival was "theater constituent" there between 1973 and 1977), he presented such grim, disturbing works as *Boom Boom Room* and *Short Eyes*—plays that seemed deliberately chosen to upset uptown audiences' complacent expectations.

There are few such battles to be fought today, and Papp acknowledges that the success of the Festival has made it increasingly difficult to take an adversarial role. "Early on," he says, "I felt, risk everything on one throw of the dice. Now I have much more to lose—I have a huge institution, I have a board of trustees. I can't just violate everything." Even though Papp still likes to think of himself as something of an outsider—he shows up at a Lincoln Center benefit wearing gray suede shoes with his tuxedo, uses a four-wheel-drive jeep as a limousine—he has nonetheless become a member of the establishment he once took on. Instead of going hat in hand to fund-raising parties thrown by rich ladies in East Hampton—like "a trained monkey," he recalls—he can now call up the president of CBS and ask directly for money. His reputation and connections are enough to move a show to Broadway; and when an attack on Mayor Koch in Larry Kramer's recent play, *The Normal Heart*, produced nasty rumors in the press, Papp settled matters by picking up the phone and talking directly with the mayor.

Not that this state of affairs makes Papp particularly happy. He talks a bit wistfully of old battles and former opponents, adding, "I feel I have to be responsible, but you also have to make sure that that word doesn't make you too cautious."

Many evenings, on the way to dinner or another show, Papp will wander through the Public Theater, through its labyrinth of theaters and lounges filled with young people dressed in sneakers and army pants and bright

T-shirts, and he will be reminded of the days when Broadway did not mean a hit show but an entire culture, the days when cafés and hangouts like the Players' Club were filled late at night with actors and directors and fans, all debating the latest performances and plays. And he will feel, too, a sense of belonging.

"It's just a matter of touching base," he says, "letting them know I'm alive, I care. When I walk through the theater, I try to make sure the public toilets are clean, the lights are on properly. It's like it's my own place, so I have a great deal of concern for how it looks."

Indeed the theater is where Papp lives. He and his fourth wife, Gail Merrifield—who is director of play development at the Festival—have an apartment three blocks from the Public but, with its pressed-wood bookshelves and a dining-room table that doubles as a desk, the place has a modest, improvised feel. His office at the Public, on the other hand, possesses all the amenities of home: a fancy stereo system, complete with a compact disk player, framed pictures of family and colleagues, souvenirs from trips abroad, as well as a wall that's covered floor to ceiling with awards (including twenty-three Tonys, ninety-one Obies, and three Pulitzer Prizes).

"I was talking to these students at City College the other day," Papp recalls, "and they asked, why did I start all this, and I said I just wanted a home. Like the first place we started at on 729 East Sixth Street, between Avenue C and D, it was called the Emmanuel Presbyterian Church, and I was so pleased to say, 'This is my place—I live here.'"

Even as a kid, Papp seemed to be in search of a surrogate home: He used to organize clubhouses on his block; and in high school, he took over a "social-athletic club" (changing its name, typically enough, from "the Mustangs" to "the Martyrs"). Papp's family moved several times a year during that period—often in the middle of the night, because his parents could not pay the rent; and he remembers longing to live in a house with real lamps, instead of bare light bulbs on the ceiling, someplace that would give him the emotional sustenance he felt he lacked with his parents.

"My father was very outgoing," he recalls, "I think he loved me a lot. My mother was very proper—she wasn't a cold woman, but she didn't know how to express her feelings. She seemed to want so much from me—I saw it in her eyes. And I'd do anything for her—I once climbed up to the fifth floor, up this pole I had to shimmy up, just to put up this laundry line for her. If she'd asked me to jump off, I would have jumped. The thing is, you give a lot and sometimes get nothing back in return.

There's this fear where you're called upon to give and give and there's no payment at all."

Because of this fear, and because he tends to experience "things very, very deeply," Papp says he learned, early on, to "sometimes avoid dealing with it by not being involved." He became a self-reliant child; and as a young man, he determined to get as far away as possible from the poverty of his family's immigrant life. Having learned English as a second language—Yiddish was spoken at home—Papp fell in love with Shakespeare's eloquent use of words, and he found in the Bard's plays a way of escaping the bleakness of the menial jobs of his adolescence: shining shoes, hawking peanuts, and plucking chickens.

Later, after a wartime tour in the navy took him to Hollywood, he returned to the world of theater as a student at the Actors' Laboratory, and he also invented a new identity for himself. "He was Joe Papirofsky out of the navy," recalls Bernard Gersten, his former associate producer, who met him in 1948. "That was it. I didn't know he was Jewish. I knew nothing about his parents." Papp would later reembrace his family's Judaism, would toy with the idea of restoring his original name (he had shortened it to Papp during the fifties when he was working as a stage manager at CBS) and he would also pay tribute to his late father in his 1978 cabaret act—singing the songs his father once had loved.

Still, the sense of detachment Papp learned as a child would be transferred from his relationship with his parents to those with the five children of his four marriages. "My personal life has been a very zigzaggy thing," he says. "It took all my children to grow up before I began to have real relationships with them. Now I have a good relationship with my two oldest daughters, Susan and Barbara. My son Tony I have a very good relationship with. Miranda, a fair relationship with. One son I haven't heard from in a long time—Michael, he's sort of just disappeared."

When she was growing up, recalls Miranda Papp, who is now twenty-seven, she felt very close to her father, though he was "rarely home." It is in recent years that she has come to feel his absence. "If I said to him, 'I'm broke, I'm desperate,' he'll obviously respond," she says, "but if I don't call him, months will go by—I don't think he even realizes it. About three years ago, we had the last deep conversation we've had. It was Christmas, and he said he realized if Gail died, he'd be alone. That was the most shocking thing he said to me—I mean he realizes he's kind of pushed my brother and me away. I told him I'd like a closer relationship with him, and he said, 'Yes, I want that, too.' We both agreed we'd make a big effort, but he was like a man who comes up out of the sea for a moment to say, 'Help me'—and since then, he hasn't come back up. This is my image of him—that he's drowning in some way."

As for her brother Anthony, who is now twenty-three, he recalls that as a child, he was jealous of the attention his father lavished on people at work: "It seemed like everyone else had him as a father for a while, and I wanted more." Papp, too, notes that it has been easier for him to develop intense relationships with artists and writers—people who are "involved in the most important thing you're doing"—than with his own children. In the theater, he says, "you're all doing the same thing, and you can talk about things directly, which you can never do at home."

Of course, the theater, by its very nature, tends to encourage paternal relationships—between actor and director, writer and producer—and as head of the Festival, Papp is in a position to be looked upon as a father figure. When a janitor in the theater got his girlfriend pregnant and needed $150 for an abortion, Papp was the one he turned to for help; and when Miguel Piñero, the author of *Short Eyes* was arrested, Papp was the one who went down to the police station and bailed him out. "There was a time," recalls one writer, "when anyone was in trouble, Joe would be the first person they'd call."

When Papp decides he likes a particular writer, he not only agrees to do his first play, but promises to do his subsequent work as well; he makes it clear that he's embracing the writer as an individual, not merely buying his work. As a result, a relationship frequently develops that is much more intense than any ordinary business or artistic alliance. "It was a kind of spiritual thing," says Albert Innaurato, recalling his experience working with Papp on *Coming of Age in Soho*. "I'd gone into it feeling my career was over—but I would only have to talk to him for five minutes to feel an incredible input of energy. He was there twenty-four hours a day—he became a colleague, rather than a boss or producer."

In a business of intermittent employment, short runs, and uncertain futures, the sense of an ongoing relationship that Papp offers can be extremely alluring—especially to writers and actors who are just starting out. "It's like a combination of high school, summer camp, and family," says Elizabeth Swados, who wrote *Runaways*. "That's why so many people fall head over heels in love with the place. The problem is that, at some point, you also have to grow up and find your own family. My personal experience was feeling confused: I wondered what was mine, before I became so involved in his incredible charisma. I think almost everybody at one time or another has said, I have to get out of here, but nearly eighty-five percent of the people come back. Joe can be very possessive, and his possessiveness has caused innumerable crack-ups in relationships."

Papp himself speaks of understanding the problems King Lear has with authority and filial affection—"He just wants Cordelia to say the right thing," he says, "and the little bitch gives him all this intellectual bull." But if he expects undivided "caring, loyalty, and friendship" from the artists he takes under his wing, he says he also has the same problems sustaining intimacy with them that he has had with his own children.

"It can be upsetting if you expect to try to hold on to something that's played itself out," says Thomas Babe. "Joe's openness can encourage people to place enormous expectations on him, and if, at that point, Joe acts as producer and makes certain decisions, it can become very confusing. I admire his deep personal involvement, but I think that means you have to protect yourself sometimes—that's why some people feel he might be cold or distant after the heat of battle."

David Rabe, who says he benefited from Papp's "real, creative insights" on his first play, *The Basic Training of Pavlo Hummel,* observes that with each successive play of his, Papp seemed to have "less and less time." "The Public had begun its huge rise to prominence," Rabe recalls, "and decisions got made quicker and quicker. Ultimately, Joe was overextended—he was doing Broadway, Lincoln Center, Shakespeare in the Park, and plays at the Public. It was too much, and if you're one of the many events and you get shortchanged, ill will develops. In the beginning, Joe offers a kind of haven; and then when you feel you're not getting it, you feel betrayed."

"I think I lost something with David," says Papp today. "I'll always love him, but I could never give him all he wanted. I was building a theater, and you cannot build a theater and have strong relationships at the same time, except with those people who are working with you. Everyone expects you to be there all the time, and it's just not possible for me to be there for one person all the time."

Some of Papp's longtime colleagues feel that in recent years, as the actress Estelle Parsons puts it, "he's become more protective of himself, more careful, more aware of his position as a leader in the theater." Certainly many of the people Papp was closest to at the Festival have fallen by the wayside. In 1978, after a disagreement over Michael Bennett's *Ballroom,* Papp fired Bernard Gersten, his associate producer and friend of thirty years. And Merle Debuskey, who has been with the Festival since its beginning, says he, too, feels increasingly distant from Papp.

"All the people he was intimate with are gone now," says Debuskey. "It's like he's one of those species of palm tree that grows very tall. All the lower leaves fall off, so only the leaves at the top are left. That tree trunk, when it grew, had to be alone—anyone that might challenge it had to be cut off. Joe can't stand there and be dragged down by anything—including people. Everything has to be discarded so you can move on."

Clearly Papp has little time, these days, to have casual dinners with friends, chat on the phone, go away on weekends. Even family matters have a way of turning into public affairs: This year, the family's annual Passover Seder was filmed by a television crew from "The MacNeil/Lehrer Report."

But while Papp enjoys being in front of an audience—he once thought of becoming a stand-up comedian—he says he could never be a professional actor because "you must be too concerned with your own psyche." He does not like to worry about himself, he says, and he has orchestrated his life in such a way that he's rarely ever alone.

Even in the midst of crowds, however, a part of him remains detached—separate and apart. It is a feeling of isolation that Papp traces back to his childhood, when he had the sense of living in a "secret world," cut off from those he loved. "I'm rather outgoing, but I don't feel that way," he says softly. "I feel very much by myself. When I was a kid, I always felt lonely, though I shouldn't have been. I had brothers and sisters and friends, but I guess it was mostly my mother who gave me that feeling.

"There are lots of times now when I feel lonely for no reason. I get plenty of attention from Gail, and people are very supportive around the office. But I don't know if that's what you're looking for, really. It's not discoverable. It's an inner place that you've already made and it doesn't matter if you're busy or surrounded by people, because you missed something when you were growing up, and there's no way to replace that. Some people try desperately to fill it up—drugs, drinking, sex. I think work is relatively healthy—at least you're productive."

The Festival, certainly, has thrived on Papp's restless need to keep moving, his single-minded devotion to its future. Life is time, he believes, and there is never enough of it. He hasn't taken a real vacation, he estimates, in two decades; hasn't visited his country house in Katonah, New York, in a year; complains he rarely gets a full night's sleep. Already, he has lined up fifteen shows for the Festival's next season, and he is working on adding another ten million dollars to the Festival's current endowment of twenty million. Income from the long Broadway run of *A Chorus Line* has dropped from six million to seven million dollars a year to about one million, and Papp points out that the Festival needs more shows "that make money." He thinks that this summer's musical, *The Mystery of Edwin Drood*, has a fifty-fifty chance of becoming a commercial hit and he believes that David Hare's *A Map of the World* has Broadway potential, too. Also planned are trips to Nicaragua and Vietnam to look for new plays, a teaching stint at the University of Florida in Tallahassee, and a blueprint for developing a new theater audience in New York that involves overhauling the entire school system. "Some of the ideas I'm working on," says Papp, "would require a whole new life to do."

In the meantime, there are more benefits, more projects, more performances at what Papp calls "culture-baron things—where you're expected to put in an appearance." On a recent Sunday, for instance, Papp's schedule calls for a speech at Lincoln Center—the event is a tribute to the children of the Holocaust—followed, immediately, by a benefit for the Williamstown Theater at Studio 54, followed by another party. Ten minutes after leaving Avery Fisher Hall, Papp is standing on the glitter-strewn floor of the disco, beneath a bank of humming red-and-purple neon lights exchanging greetings with Sam Waterston, Joanne Woodward, and Dick Cavett, making small talk about the state of Broadway and coining lots of bad puns.

The audience is quiet, preoccupied—there's "no connection," says Papp, between "them and what's going on on stage"; and he starts his speech by telling them what he thinks. "This audience seems a little quiet for Studio 54," he says, startling the sleepy patrons. "It seems like a funeral for someone dead and forgotten. It's not your fault—maybe it's the acoustics or the dinner. Anyway, I'll just get on with the songs—some golden oldies." He then begins his first number. "You've got to ac-cent-tchu-ate the positive," he sings in a loud voice, swinging the mike back and forth, working the audience. "E-lim-eye-nate the negative. Latch on to the affirmative. Don't mess with Mister In-Between."

July 1985

SAM SHEPARD

. . .

"'I DRIVE ON THE FREEWAY EVERY DAY,'' SAYS A character in Sam Shepard's *True West*. "I swallow the smog. I watch the news in color. I shop in Safeway. . . . There's no such thing as the West anymore! It's a dead issue!" For the play's two heroes—Austin, an aspiring screenwriter, intent on making it in Hollywood; and his brother, Lee, a desert rat who makes a living as a petty thief—the West represents two very different places. There is the Old West, recalled mainly through movies and cigarette advertisements as a place of new beginnings, a place that promised a way of life that was as free as the land and the sky. And there is the New West, crisscrossed by highways and pockmarked by suburbs—the West that Hollywood tycoons and tract-housing developers built on the mortgaged dreams of the pioneers.

In *True West*, which has been running Off Broadway at the Cherry Lane, Shepard uses these two contradictory visions of California to delineate the deep, contradictory craving in the American character for both freedom and the security of roots, and also to explore the gap between our nostalgic memories of the past and the bleakness of the present. Shepard himself says, "If I'm at home anywhere, it's in the West—as soon as I cross the Mississippi, I don't feel the same," but the idea of the West that he cherishes exists now only as a memory in the swiftly receding landscape;

its romantic ideals, like the old American Dream, vanished long ago with the frontier.

At forty, Shepard has won a Pulitzer Prize and emerged as one of the preeminent playwrights of his generation. In an astonishing body of work—some forty full-length and one-act plays, as well as poetry, short stories, and a volume of autobiographical sketches—he has put forth a vision of America that resonates with the power of legend. Surreal images bloom in his work—men turn into lizards; carrots and potatoes grow miraculously in a barren garden; an eagle carries off a cat, screaming, into the sky; and strange, almost hallucinatory transactions occur. And yet the work remains firmly grounded in the facts of our own history and popular culture.

He has created a fictional world populated by cowboys and gunslingers, ranchers and desperadoes, but these characters routinely find that the myths they were raised on have become irrelevant jokes. Eddie, the wrangler-hero of *Fool for Love,* discovers that he has nothing better to lasso than the bedposts in a squalid motel room. The Hollywood hustlers in *Angel City* look out their window and see, not the fertile valleys of the Promised Land, but a smoggy city of used-car lots and shopping centers; a city waiting for apocalypse. And the old-time outlaws who pay a visit to the present in *The Unseen Hand* realize that there are no more trains to rob, that there is no place for heroics anymore, that it is no longer even possible to tell the good guys from the bad.

What happens when these characters are forced to face up to the disparity between their lives and a heroic, if imaginary, past is almost inevitably violent. Indeed, violence—the emotional violence of people shattering each others' dreams with verbal volleys, if not with physical blows—is a commonplace in Shepard's insistently male world. "I think there's something about American violence that to me is very touching," he explains. "In full force it's very ugly, but there's also something very moving about it, because it has to do with humiliation. There's some hidden, deeply rooted thing in the Anglo male American that has to do with inferiority, that has to do with not being a man, and always, continually having to act out some idea of manhood that invariably is violent. This sense of failure runs very deep—maybe it has to do with the frontier being systematically taken away, with the guilt of having gotten this country by wiping out a native race of people, with the whole Protestant work ethic. I can't put my finger on it, but it's the source of a lot of intrigue for me."

As the frontier receded, so did the old values and dreams, and in that wake, says Shepard, has been left a craving for belief that makes people susceptible to the promises of fake messiahs. "People are starved for the truth," he says, "and when something comes along that even looks like the truth, people will latch on to it because everything's so false. It's very difficult to find anything with a real authentic heart. Even art has turned into applauding the superficial as being authentic. For instance, the whole punk movement—it's turning the whole aspect of trash and bad taste, falseness, into a mode of art. It's a very complex psychological trick people are playing on themselves. I'm not nailing the punk movement—but it comes down to this kind of thing where the *form* of stuff has taken on a mystique that becomes a way of life."

"People are starved for a way of life," he goes on. "They're hunting for a way to be or to act toward the world. Take anything—I don't see the punk movement as any different from, say, the evangelist movement. They're both taken on faith—on one hand, faith in costume, and on the other, faith in a symbolic Christ."

For many Shepard characters, the search for a role, for a way of acting toward the world becomes a central preoccupation. Deprived of the past and any sort of familial definition—in play after play, fathers do not even recognize their sons—they try to manufacture new identities. They make up remarkable stories about themselves, but in shedding various costumes, poses, and personalities, they often misplace the mysterious thing that makes them who they are.

"Personality is everything that is false in a human being," explains Shepard. "It's everything that's been added on to him and contrived. It seems to me that the struggle all the time is between this sense of falseness and the other haunting sense of what's true—an essential thing that we're born with and tend to lose track of. This naturally sets up a great contradiction in everybody—between what they represent and what they know to be themselves."

Victims of this contradiction, Shepard's characters live "in at least two dimensions: one has to do with fantasy, the other with reality." Some of them have the ability to conjure up their fantasy life at will—as a result, such figures as Captain Kidd, Mae West, and Jesse James frequently make appearances on stage—while others are content to simply impose their fantasies on family and friends. In some cases, the characters actually undergo bizarre transformations on stage, becoming, in a sense, who they think they are.

It is a peculiarly American notion, this belief that, like Gatsby, one can spring from the "Platonic conception of himself," that identity is not something fixed by family or class, that one can grow up to become anything—the president or a movie star. It offers, on one hand, the promise of self-made riches and fame; and on the other, the perils of dislocation and anomie. Shepard, himself, talks of experiencing "this kind of rootlessness I don't think will ever be resolved," and the facts of his own life suggest an ongoing process of self-creation and reinvention.

An army brat, whose family had migrated during his childhood from Fort Sheridan, Illinois, to Utah to Florida to Guam, the playwright spent his high-school years in Duarte, a small town east of Los Angeles, where his father had an avocado farm, but the sense of transience he felt as a boy would never disappear. He was born Samuel Shepard Rogers, a name that "came down through seven generations of men with the same name," and nicknamed Steve to distinguish him from his father. Years later, he would learn that Steve Rogers had been the original name of Captain America in the comics, but by then he'd dropped the Rogers and the Steve and reincarnated himself as Sam Shepard.

As a boy, Steve Rogers had played at being a cowboy and a musician and a movie star—for days he practiced Burt Lancaster's grin in *Vera Cruz* ("Sneering. Grinning that grin. Sliding my upper lip up over my teeth")—and the young Sam Shepard who later populated his fictional world with these same mythic figures would also try on those roles in life, moving from one to another with the same apparent ease as so many of his characters.

The kid from California, whose exposure to cowboys had been limited to "seeing Leo Carrillo, the Lone Ranger, and Hopalong Cassidy in the Rose Parade," eventually went East where, as his friend Patti Smith recalled, he became "a man playing cowboys"; he traded in his "beat" outfit of the fifties—a turtleneck, peacoat, and dark pants—for a flannel shirt, straw Resistol hat, and jeans. While he'd never achieve the success of his idols Johnny Ace, Jimmie Rodgers, and Keith Richards, he would later join a fairly well-known rock band, the Holy Modal Rounders, in the late sixties, opening for such acts as the Velvet Underground and Ike and Tina Turner.

The movie stardom has come more recently. After several "rural parts" (in *Days of Heaven, Resurrection, Raggedy Man,* and *Frances*), Shepard last year played the test pilot Chuck Yeager in *The Right Stuff,* a role that coalesced, in a single image, the archetypes of western hero and space-age pioneer. Suddenly, he was up there on the screen playing one of those "pilots with fur-collared leather jackets" he'd dreamed about as a kid, and being acclaimed Gary Cooper's heir—strong, centered, and coolly sexy.

Shepard's plays, of course, are filled with cinematic techniques and allusions to the movies, but they also evince a contempt for Hollywood as a place where people "ooze and call each other 'darling,' " a place that perpetuates "stupid illusions." People have a need for "somebody to get off on when they can't get off on themselves," he wrote in *Cowboy Mouth*, but while many of his artist-heroes aspire to fill this role, those who "go Hollywood" usually end up being corrupted or destroyed. In *Angel City*, a witch doctor named Rabbit is hired by a studio to work his magic on a film and he eventually goes mad. And in *The Tooth of Crime*, an aging rock star finds that fame has trapped him in his image, and he is soon tumbled from his pedestal by a mercenary newcomer named Crow.

Perhaps Shepard's own ambivalence toward the movie business is best captured by *True West*, in which Lee, the desert rat who despises "Hollywood blood money," exchanges identities with his brother Austin, the successful screenwriter. Like Lee, Shepard holds himself apart from the business; and yet, like Austin, he is increasingly in demand by Hollywood.

He has always written for the actor, says Shepard, and some of his work actually owes a debt to the theory of "transformations," an acting technique practiced by the Open Theater. Actors using this technique would swiftly switch personas from scene to scene, often without any apparent psychological motivation, and such early Shepard plays as *Angel City* and *Mad Dog Blues* featured characters who underwent just this sort of change. As Shepard once wrote in a note to actors, "Instead of the idea of a 'whole character' with logical motives behind his behavior which the actor submerges himself into, he should consider instead a fractured whole with bits and pieces of character flying off a central theme. In other words, more in terms of collage construction or jazz improvisation."

The analogy with jazz seems particularly apt, for Shepard's writing has clearly been influenced by his interest in music. The influence goes well beyond his use of rock-and-roll in the plays (*Cowboy Mouth*, *Operation Sidewinder*, and *The Tooth of Crime* all featured musical interludes); it extends to their actual form and language. Shepard has practiced Jack Kerouac's technique of "jazz-sketching with words," and the early plays not only demonstrate the sheer delight he takes in playing around with words, but they also have the discursive, improvisational feeling of a jam session—they are less plays in any traditional sense than an extraordinary succession of emotional riffs. Many of these early works, Shepard recalls, had their genesis in a sound, as though he could suddenly "hear" a character speaking.

"Jazz could move in surprising territories without qualifying itself," he explained once. "You could follow a traditional melody and then break away and then come back or drop in to play rhythms. You could have three, four things going on simultaneously. But more important, it was an emotional thing. You could move in all these emotional territories and you could do it with passion. You could throw yourself into a passage and then you could calm down, then you could ride this thing, then you could throw yourself in again. Music communicated emotion better than anything else I know."

In many respects, it is easier to discuss Shepard's work in terms of music or the visual arts than in terms of conventional literary sources. Certainly one can find the imprint of writers he admires in his plays. His gothic portraits of the family recall Faulkner; the menacing atmosphere, Pinter; the sense of the absurd, Beckett. But the debt to popular culture—songs by the Rolling Stones, ancient Indian legends, science-fiction novels, and old Hollywood movies—is equally pronounced.

In fact, what initially excited Shepard about the theater was its very flexibility, the fact that it was a "form where you could amalgamate all the arts." "You can show film," he says, "you can dance, you can incorporate painting and sculpture. For a renegade artist who hasn't found his niche, it's a way to engage all these things. It's very accessible and the rules are wide open."

The atmosphere in which Shepard began writing during the early sixties nurtured these eclectic impulses. When he arrived in New York, the Off Off Broadway movement was just beginning, and playwrights, actors, painters, poets, and musicians all seemed to inhabit an exciting new world. "Everything influenced me," he recalls. "There was a great makeshift quality to those days. It only existed for a few years, till Vietnam came along and everything shifted to a very grim perspective. But for a while it was like a carnival, a Mardi Gras—it made you feel you could do anything. Art wasn't a career or anything intellectual, it was a much more active, playful thing, a way to inhabit a life."

Having had little formal exposure to theater in the past—the only "audience events" he attended as a boy were rodeos, Spanish fandango dances, and basketball games—Shepard began writing plays with few preconceptions about what they could or could not be. Much of what was applauded as innovative in his early work—and also condemned as obscure—probably stemmed, he says, from simple ignorance. In those days,

Shepard wrote extremely quickly and rarely rewrote anything. *Chicago* was written in a single day. He was also taking a lot of drugs at the time, and while he never wrote while stoned, he says that "maybe certain experiences from all that fed into the work."

In 1970, after a tempestuous affair with Patti Smith, Shepard left for England with his wife O-Lan and their two-year-old son. It was during a three-year sojourn there that he first became aware that "rhythmically I was an American—the way I talk, the way I walk, everything was American," and the realization seemed to galvanize his work. While living on meager grants in London, he completed *The Tooth of Crime,* a savage fantasy about two rock stars fighting for power and fame; and the play helped to consolidate his growing reputation on both sides of the Atlantic.

There had always been critics who complained that Shepard's earlier work was unwieldy and messy, and the playwright himself observes that he is "a terrible storyteller." "The stories my characters tell," he says, "are stories that are always unfinished, always imagistic—having to do with recalling experiences through a certain kind of vision. They're always fractured and fragmented and broken. I'd love to be able to tell a classic story, but it doesn't seem to be part of my nature." With *Curse of the Starving Class,* written in 1976, and *Buried Child,* written in 1979, however, a certain change occurs—the writing has begun to grow more shapely and more naturalistic. Though the language is still idiomatic, the imagery still poetic, these elements are now grounded in narratives that evince a new discipline and a more traditional approach to character.

"I wouldn't call it a development," says Shepard, "though it's some kind of evolution. It has to do with moving inside the character. Originally, I was fascinated by form, by exteriors—starting from the outside and going in, with the idea that character is something shifting and that it can shift from one person to another. You had different attitudes drifting in and out from actors who are part of the ensemble. So in the past, it was the overall tone of the piece I was interested in rather than in characters as individuals. That sort of played itself out, and for a while I didn't know where to go from there. But then I started to delve into character and it came about pretty naturally."

As Shepard began to take a more psychological approach to character, the plays became less overtly epic and more personal. Whereas autobiographical material in the early plays is either abstracted, as in *The Rock Garden,* or mythologized, as in *Cowboy Mouth,* the later plays tend to deal more directly with details from Shepard's own life. *Starving Class* and *Buried Child,* which both depict families victimized by their fantasies and feelings of guilt, mirror the "violent, chaotic family structure" that the playwright knew as a boy, and *True West* touches upon his ambivalence toward success and his own complicated relationship with his father, who now "lives alone on the desert."

Such male relationships—between fathers and sons, colleagues and rivals—have tended to dominate Shepard's plays, and he acknowledges the special fascination that the psyche of the American male has always held for him. "You don't have to look very far to see that the American male is on a very bad trip," he says. "American women at least have the pretense of being involved in some kind of sisterhood, whereas men very, very rarely form a real strong connection with one another. With men I think it happens only very, very rarely, maybe with one or two guys in your lifetime—if you're lucky. It's like men have to have sport or drinking or something like that in order to have an exchange. Women don't seem to have that problem—they're willing to give people the benefit of the doubt. It always seemed to me that there was more mystery to relationships between men, and just now, it's coming to a territory where I'm finding the same mystery between men and women."

Indeed, with *Fool for Love*—a fierce two-act portrait of a couple who may or may not be brother and sister—Shepard set himself a specific task: to "sustain a female character and have her remain absolutely true to herself, not only as a social being, but also as an emotional being." "I tried relentlessly to stick with that in the play," he says, "and for my money it accomplishes what I wanted to accomplish. It really does sustain both sides of the issue. Neither one of them comes out heroic. They're just who they are."

One day, says Shepard, he would like to write and direct a film, and from now on, he also intends to direct all initial productions of his plays. As for the writing, "everything is wide open—I don't know where to plunge." "It's a hundred times harder than when I started," he says. "For one thing, it becomes more and more difficult to write something surprising or in a new way because people now come with expectations—they expect it will be about 'the myth of America' or something. Once you've cracked the beginning, you're on a roll, but it gets more difficult to start. You've got to get rid of all the stuff in your head that you've done before in order to start off from ground zero, and, for me, that's the only place to start."

January 1984

STEPHEN SONDHEIM

AND

JAMES LAPINE

. . .

"ART ISN'T EASY," SINGS A CHARACTER IN *SUNDAY in the Park with George*. "Having just the vision's no solution, / Everything depends on execution. / The art of making art / Is putting it together / Bit by bit . . ." Putting together a Broadway musical, of course, is itself a highly strenuous art. Bit by bit, a show is assembled, piece by piece it emerges—the product of talent, hard work, carefully calculated choices, and the fortuities of luck and timing. In the case of *Sunday,* the ground-breaking new Stephen Sondheim–James Lapine musical, the process took two years and involved an Off Broadway workshop and hectic revisions during rehearsals and previews.

The original idea for *Sunday* came from Georges Seurat's famous painting *A Sunday Afternoon on the Island of La Grande Jatte,* and the show not only depicts Seurat's creation of that canvas—in the first act, an empty white set is gradually transformed into the dazzling tableau of the painting—but also demonstrates how that painting will influence later generations, how art, like love, endures through time. As a note for *Sunday,* written by Sondheim two years ago, reads, "The show is, in part, about how creation takes on a life of its own; how artists feed off art (we off Seurat); the artist's relationship to his material."

If the show, as currently staged, fulfills its creators' initial conception, however, the process by which Sondheim and Lapine executed their vision was neither simple nor straightforward. Indeed, *Sunday*—like many Broadway shows—grew slowly over many months, undergoing a complicated series of metamorphoses in its route to the Booth Theater.

Although *Sunday* would become increasingly linear and centered around character, the collaborators' original intention was to do a highly formalized show, conceptual in form, stylized in manner. Lapine, who had never worked on Broadway before, had experimented with time and traditional dramatic structure in such plays as *Twelve Dreams*. And Sondheim, who had worked with Hal Prince on such celebrated "concept" musicals as *Follies* and *Company*, has long been fascinated by the formal possibilities of the theater; he hoped, with *Sunday*, to realize an old, unfulfilled ambition—to translate the musical form of "theme and variation" to the stage.

"Every time I listen to Rachmaninoff's variations on Paganini, I'm stunned," he says, "and I thought it would be a lot of fun to try theatrically. When we'd fastened on the idea of using Seurat's painting and showing how it was made for the first act, I was all excited because I thought the second act could be series of variations or comments on the painting—in some way, an answer to the first act." The second act, he speculated, might take a revuelike form, in which songs about different aspects of art would be delivered by actors, addressing the audience directly. Or, it might deal with a series of variations performed on Seurat's painting itself.

After discussions with Lapine, however, Sondheim says he decided that these schemes were impractical. "Jim's first response," he recalls, "was, 'We must carry some kind of storyline from the first act or there'll be no focus of interest.'

"The danger always is to impose a form on material when you're just doing it because you like the form," he goes on. "That's probably the greatest pitfall of all writing, as far as I'm concerned, but I am constantly slipping toward that quicksand or getting so excited by the formal possibilities that I always have to restrain myself and say, 'Does this idea really lend itself to that?' "

Sondheim's interest in structure and form and Lapine's emphasis on narrative was only one way in which the sensibilities of the two collaborators complemented one another. Whereas Sondheim is extremely attuned to the nuances of language and essentially writes for the ear, Lapine, who was trained as a graphic designer, tends to think in more visual terms. And whereas Sondheim prefers to write in a controlled, methodical manner,

Lapine is inclined toward a more improvisatory approach, dashing things off quickly and then going back to revise. These disparate impulses, combined with a set of shared instincts about the theater, would provide the chemistry for their successful collaboration.

Before starting to write, Sondheim and Lapine held long "spitballing" sessions, during which they discussed philosophical points they wanted to make, ideas for dialogue and particular scenes, references to Seurat's life, painting techniques, even special effects that would be fun to include.

When Lapine began writing in September of 1982, he tried to keep his language simple—to give the show the sense it had been translated from the French. He avoided Latin-root words and contractions, and made the dialogue "as sharp and pointed as possible." It was a style that also mirrored Seurat's painting technique—in which, from a distance, millions of dotlike brushstrokes in pure color mix together optically to create a glorious spectrum.

Seurat's technique similarly helped Sondheim find a musical approach for the show. Adept at writing in a variety of manners—from the highly sophisticated to the lightly humorous, from the personal to the parodic— he says he likes to write within a set of restrictions; and his earlier scores have often used a show's subject matter as a framework for composition. *Follies,* which narrated the reunion of several aging showgirls, used pastiches of old standards to recall the characters' pasts. *Sweeney Todd* employed a "gnarled," operatic score to play off the Grand Guignol nature of its material. And *Pacific Overtures* featured open, stripped-down songs that captured the feeling of traditional Japanese music.

As for *Sunday,* says Sondheim, he sought an analogue for Seurat's use of pure color in the use of diatonic—rather than chromatic—harmonies and simple triadic forms; at one point, he even toyed with the idea of composing the entire score on the white keys of the piano. "The idea was to keep the music open and pure the way the painting is," he explains, "and to give it a shimmer. I was also fiddling with chord clusters, because that seemed to me some kind of possible analogue to Seurat's close juxtaposition of different-colored dots. The closeness of the dots in the painting made me think of the closeness of the notes on the piano."

Another aural equivalent of Seurat's color scheme, Sondheim discovered, could be found by repeating musical motifs, as well as certain key words and phrases, throughout the score—much the way he did in *Sweeney Todd.* The romantic opening section of the main song ("Sunday in the Park with George"), for instance, is developed further in a subsequent number ("Color and Light"), which then becomes the basis for a later song ("We Do Not Belong Together"), which, in turn, informs the show's penultimate number ("Move On"). As a result, what may initially sound like a sequence of separate numbers actually connects, like the painter's dots, to form a highly patterned score that binds the story together and grows in resonance with the progress of the show.

Since he prefers to "interpret," rather than wholly invent, a character, Sondheim not only reads a draft of his collaborator's book before starting to write, but also asks him to overwrite, so he can then "raid" the script for his lyrics—a method that ultimately helps to integrate song and dialogue into a seamless show. In the case of *Sunday*, Lapine filled locations for songs in his script with long stream-of-consciousness monologues, which Sondheim intended to draw upon for his songs.

There were difficulties, however. Sondheim worried that his own colloquial, conversational use of language would clash with Lapine's more poetic usage; that his songs, consequently, would "tear the extremely delicate fabric of Jim's prose—have a kind of rape effect." Further, he found that Lapine's use of language was so precise, "so meticulously worked out for the ear, that by merely changing one syllable—to make it work musically—I would kill the entire phrase." In the end, the composer used very little of Lapine's prose in writing his actual lyrics; what he did appropriate, he underscored and used as little dialogue passages within the songs. By last summer, when *Sunday* began workshop performances at Playwrights Horizons, he had completed half a dozen numbers for the first act.

In deciding to develop *Sunday* at Playwrights, a nonprofit, Off Broadway theater, Lapine and Sondheim were able to circumvent the economic pressures and high visibility of usual Broadway tryouts, and present their show to a small, private audience, limited to the theater's subscribers. They would use this audience's reactions as a guide when they sat down in the fall to rework the show.

During the workshop production, the first act already encapsulated the basic storyline of the current production. It told the story of Seurat, an artist who, like many of the heroes in Sondheim shows, experiences the world as a disconnected observer. He is so obsessed with his painting that he neglects his mistress, Dot, and she eventually goes off to America with Louis, a baker of French pastries, who is more devoted to her emotional needs.

In the show's Playwrights Horizons incarnation, however, this love story was interrupted by lengthy digressions about the people whom Seurat painted in *La Grande Jatte*. As Lapine saw it, the figures—frozen by the painter's art into silent, decorous poses—were, in real life, a motley, raucous crew, all with messy little stories of their own. In this version of the show, several of these people (a boatman, a nurse, a German couple, and a soldier) had extended scenes, as well as their own full-length songs.

Though these sequences possessed a certain whimsical charm, audiences grew impatient waiting for George and Dot to reappear; and during the fall Sondheim and Lapine tried reworking the act in order to make a lengthy middle section featuring the peripheral characters seem less intrusive. Sondheim also replaced a big romantic song sung by one of these characters with a lighter number.

These changes, they realized during Broadway rehearsals, were insufficient. With the first act already running an hour and forty-four minutes, more radical surgery was called for. So, as they continued to build up the parts of George and Dot, they trimmed the peripheral characters further, eventually reducing them to sharp, bright cameos with a few lines to sing. Several songs would be dropped altogether, including two during previews.

Other ideas and theatrical conceits would fall by the wayside as well. Some ideas—for instance, showing how Seurat's other paintings might have been created—were edited out because they resulted in unnecessary digressions. Others, like an elaborate series of costume changes, depicting the difference between the characters in real life and the characters in the painting, were discarded as too expensive to realize on stage.

"Part of the problem in writing the show," says Lapine, "was the wealth of things we wanted to say. Later, when we put the show on its feet, I think my reaction was 'God, it's about too many things.' So a lot of the later decision making was about honing it down, making it specific." Specific, but at the same time, not too esoteric. Because the show is rooted in their own artistic concerns—the song "Putting It Together," for one, reflects the problems of an artist who has chosen to work in a popular, big-budget medium like show business—Sondheim and Lapine were also concerned that the show not become overly arcane. Thus, in shaping *Sunday*, they made an effort to dramatize their philosophical points through the characters' stories, and to humanize those characters' dilemmas so that the show would open out beyond specific aesthetic issues to examine the larger themes of love and art.

While work on the first act mainly entailed cutting and shaping, the second act would undergo more drastic revision. Having been performed only three times during the workshop, it still had a somewhat rudimentary form as the show went into Broadway rehearsals (only two of its songs had been fully completed) and it would remain in a state of flux throughout previews.

One of Lapine's earliest versions of the second act had traced the painting's life history. There was a scene in which the canvas left France and arrived in Chicago, and a scene set during the fifties, when the painting traveled, on loan, to New York. This historical approach proved enormously time-consuming, and Lapine quickly wrote another version that cut directly to contemporary time.

As currently performed, the modern-day scenes of the second act depict a willfully trendy art world, a world in which a word like *image* refers to the artist's public persona, rather than to what he creates on canvas, and it provides an ironic contrast to the more innocent world of Seurat depicted in Act I. But while this refracting of time past through the flawed lens of the present recalls some of Sondheim's other shows, there is an important difference. The characters in *Follies* and *Merrily We Roll Along* used the past to measure their loss of youthful idealism; the hero in Act II of *Sunday* uses the past as a means of finding redemption.

This central character is another artist named George, who may possibly be Seurat's great-grandson, and he would eventually emerge as the focus of the second act. In fact, after a working version of the act had been completed, a process similar to that involved in Act I began to occur: Ancillary scenes featuring minor characters—in this case, lengthy cocktail-party sequences featuring art-world habitués—were pared down, while scenes about George were augmented. A contrast between this George and his distinguished ancestor was established: Seurat could connect only to his artistic vision, not to the people who loved him; young George, on the other hand, is able to maintain personal relationships but has doubts about his work.

For a long time, the specific nature of that work was uncertain. At first, George was to be a performance artist with a performing-arts troupe, but as Lapine points out, that "made him too laughable a figure." Next, he became a holography expert (holograms, which use light to create three-dimensional images, are modern equivalents of sorts to Seurat's experiments with color)—an identity that was abandoned when it became clear that holograms would not work on stage. In the end, he evolved into a creator of "chromolumes"—machinelike sculptures that employ lasers and light.

Since they had spent much of the rehearsal period shaping up the first act, Lapine and Sondheim found themselves considerably behind schedule with the second half of the show. As *Sunday* began Broadway previews, the second act was still missing two songs and the collaborators had yet to settle on a satisfactory ending.

There were other difficulties as well. The move from Playwrights Horizons to Broadway required complicated technical readjustments of the show's special effects (including a laser show, pop-up figures that rise from beneath the stage, and a series of scrims), and a restructuring of speeches to accommodate new costume changes. It also became apparent as soon as *Sunday* moved into the Booth that it could not be done without amplification, as had been originally planned.

To make matters worse, the company's morale had begun to sag. Many of the actors had already seen their Act I roles diminished by various cuts, and they were now faced with constant changes in Act II. Audience reaction was dispiriting as well: There were a disturbing number of walk-outs during early previews, and word-of-mouth on the show—particularly on its second act—was poor.

After the opening was postponed, a turning point came on April 20, when two new songs were put into the show. A longtime veteran of the out-of-town tryout routine, with a reputation for procrastination, Sondheim was used to making last-minute changes—he wrote the final number of *Company* ("Being Alive") and the opening number of *A Funny Thing Happened on the Way to the Forum* ("Comedy Tonight") while the shows were on the road—and with *Sunday* he was simply late in completing the second act's score.

Rich in character and information, the composer's writing has always been distinguished for serving the dramatic context of an individual show; and in the case of *Sunday*, the missing two songs ("Children and Art" and "Lesson #8") helped to anchor the second half of the show thematically, and they also conveyed important information about young George and his spiritual dilemma.

Once "Children and Art" and "Lesson #8" went in, the emotional arc of the story suddenly seemed complete, and Lapine—working now in his capacity as director—could concentrate on polishing the actors' performances and the overall shape of the show.

He and Sondheim also continued to fiddle with the show's final scene. A tableau featuring the entire company had already been rejected as being too similar to the ending of the first act. And another scene—in which the young George returns to La Grande Jatte and draws his version of the island—was discarded as too literal and didactic. "It would have spelled everything out," says Lapine, "and we wanted an ending that would be sort of ineffable—abstract in a certain way. I think both Steve and I really like mystery. We like unexplained things."

Indeed, much of the fine-tuning that took place during the preview period had to do with the writers' attempts to balance their own love of mystery with the audience's needs and expectations. "Both Jim and I feel," says Sondheim, "that it's wonderful to be intrigued in the theater— it's just awful to feel baffled. It's finding that line where everything isn't exactly explained, and yet doesn't rouse hostility in the audience because they're confused." Additional suggestions about clarity and focus came from the collaborators' professional friends, including Michael Bennett, Hal Prince, Tom Stoppard, and John Guare, who saw the show late in previews.

At some point, says Lapine, "the one thing you don't want to do is go off and keep rewriting. If something's not quite right, it's often about modulating what's already there." During the final two weeks of pre- views, this was largely done by perfecting technical aspects—something highly important in a show as atmospheric as *Sunday*. Numbers were "buttoned"—that is, their beginnings and endings were defined by light- ing, musical, and blocking changes—and scene-to-scene transitions were refined.

Bit by bit, as the last pieces of the show clicked into place and the process of putting together *Sunday* came to a close, Lapine says that he and Sondheim were able to step back a little and see the show as something separate—as something created and whole. "It's like making a painting," he says. "You go through the process of doing what you do, and then finally, you just have to put it out there and hope others respond. The irony is, you want it to look effortless, and to get that, it's such hard work."

June 1984

TENNESSEE WILLIAMS

.   .   .

SUCH WAS THE VITALITY OF THE LATE TENNESSEE Williams's work that his plays not only shaped the aspirations of an entire generation of playwrights, directors, and actors, but they also redefined the scope and poetic possibilities of the American theater. His vision was an unaccommodated one—a vision of the world as a kind of jungle, in which shafts of sunlight illuminated oases of extraordinary beauty, but also disclosed the ugly consequences of memory and passion. Williams once announced his intention to air all those "closets, attics, and basements of human behavior" that had previously been bolted and dark, and what he usually found inside was guilt and desperation—the pain of individuals longing for intimacy, but trapped inside their own frailties and lies. And yet, there was no real despair, for Williams's voice—alternately lyrical and ribald, urgent and romantic—also promised compassion and earthy vigor, and a hint of transcendence, too.

"In order to negotiate life," says the actress Elizabeth Ashley, "most people sort of chart an emotional course to avoid the rocks and shoals, so your ship doesn't crack up. But Tennessee wrote about all of those shoals and the monsters in the sea that come up and eat the boat. He went into the taboos of the heart and let us know that we don't have to carve out of our souls the innocence and the madness—the things society wants to amputate. He saw life whole—not just the skin on the hand, but the bones and the blood in the veins beneath."

Given their exploration of the existential confusions of living and other matters polite society would rather ignore—nymphomania and rape in *A Streetcar Named Desire,* for instance—Williams's plays initially provoked indignation, but they ended up changing the way the theater portrays sexuality and violent emotion. The nightmare images—the gothic blossoms of the playwright's rebellion against the puritanism of his youth—were nonetheless mediated by a sense of affirmation. In *Camino Real,* Don Quixote announces that "the violets in the mountains have broken through the rocks," and his other heroes, sinners though they may be, never stop looking for salvation, for a chance to embrace those "superior things! Things of the mind and the spirit!" Indeed Williams could have been talking about his own work when he wrote in *Streetcar* that a lyricism "gracefully attenuates the atmosphere of decay."

Whether it is elegiac as in *The Glass Menagerie* or sensual as in *Cat on a Hot Tin Roof,* atmosphere always defines Williams's plays. "The straight realistic play with its genuine Frigidaire and authentic ice cubes" never interested him at all, and his own work consistently employed a poetic symbolism—a rose, a bird, a street car, take on metaphysical resonance—that lent his characters a mythic dimension.

These expressionistic tendencies became more heightened in later years, for Williams, like many artists, gradually moved away from the pseudorealism that distinguished his early, more popular works. Following *The Night of the Iguana,* his work became increasingly abstract, the action more internalized. *Small Craft Warnings,* which portrayed the loves and losses of a group of barflies, had hardly any narrative line at all. *Vieux Carré* traced a young artist's coming of age by chronicling, through a series of vignettes, his encounters with ghosts from his own past. And *Clothes for a Summer Hotel* was essentially a "tone poem" about madness and death, wandering back and forth through time to recount the story of Scott and Zelda Fitzgerald. "There's a coeval quality to events as one grows older," Williams once said. "The past and the present begin to merge. Also, there comes a time when you want to give yourself more license. Though you often take more than the critics will allow, I felt I had acquired a craftsmanship that enabled me to do it."

The later plays also appeared to grow more concerned with the playwright's inner history. *Something Cloudy Something Clear* drew heavily on the playwright's own experiences as a young man in Provincetown, and

Clothes used the story of the Fitzgeralds to examine his own fears about failure and the loss of creativity. In a sense, though, these plays only accentuated an autobiographical impulse that had existed from the beginning. The family portrayed in *The Glass Menagerie*, after all, bore a remarkable resemblance to Williams's own. "You can't manufacture unreal people," he said. "You have to transmute their reality through your concept of them. They became sifted through myself so that something of my own life went into their creation."

A sickly child who grew up alienated from the stuffy, moralistic world around him, Williams watched his sister Rose slip into madness—later cruelly cauterized by a lobotomy—and he developed a special sympathy for the lonely and dispossessed. Trapped by circumstance and torn between the irreconcilable demands of the spirit and the flesh, his characters are all marginal people—the damned, the misplaced, the incomplete, and the frail.

For them, God's presence is uncertain, and they flee the fact of their mortality, seeking solace in sex and rouged illusions. Blanche, the southern gentlewoman turned nymphomaniac; Maggie, the "Cat," spurned by her handsome husband; Big Daddy, the terminally ill master of "twenty-eight thousand acres of the richest land this side of the valley Nile"; and the Princess, the aging actress who takes a younger lover—all belong to that gallery of lost souls.

"I have always been more interested in creating a character that contains something crippled," Williams said once. "I think nearly all of us have some kind of defect, anyway, and I suppose I have found it easier to identify with the characters who verge upon hysteria, who were frightened of life, who were desperate to reach out to another person."

Those characters, of course, have provided actors with rich canvases to work from, and in some cases have also given them new or revitalized careers. Jessica Tandy says the role of Blanche "changed my professional life." Maureen Stapleton regards the role of Serafina in *The Rose Tattoo* as her "first big break," and Geraldine Page thinks of Alma in *Summer and Smoke* in much the same way.

When she played that role, Page recalls the playwright complimented her on it, saying she had given the finest performance since Laurette Taylor in *The Glass Menagerie*. "I told that to my acting teacher Uta Hagen," says Page, "and she said, 'He tells that to all his leading ladies,' but I was happy about it anyway."

Although Williams was devoted to the rehearsal process—he usually stayed on hand to provide rewrites if required—he also suffered from what he called "tongue-locking, face-flushing timidity," and he dealt uneasily with actors. "He'd often say the wrong thing," recalls Charles Bowden, a producer of *Iguana*. "You had to keep him away from the actors, though he could tell them on paper exactly what they should do. I remember he felt Bette Davis's approach was wrong, and he wrote a note that nailed Maxine to the wall."

The note read, "Everything about her should have the openness and freedom of the sea. . . . She's the living definition of nature—lusty, rapacious, guileless, unsentimental. Her hair ought to look like she went swimming without a cap and rubbed it dry with a coarse towel and not bothered to brush or comb it. . . . She moves with the ease of clouds and the tides."

"He could never have said that," adds Bowden. "He would have said 'Your hair's all wrong,' when that wasn't what he meant at all."

Self-conscious and "morbidly shy," Williams responded to stress with laughter—what he called "my substitute for lamentation"—and self-deprecating wit. "His humor was unfailing," says the director José Quintero, recalling a snowy day in Chicago. "Tennessee loved to swim, and I remember I found him on the steps of the Art Institute, sitting there as if there were no snow, and he said, 'It's a place for art—they will have compassion for the artist. They will have a pool.' That was the Tennessee I loved."

Indeed what many of Williams's colleagues remember best was his marvelous laugh—a nervous, funny laugh, halfway between a guffaw and a cackle, that erupted at the most improbable times. "The more intense the work became, the more Tennessee would laugh," recalls Robert Whitehead, the producer of *Orpheus Descending*. "There was a minor-key quality to it—a kind of humorous sense of human frailty. In the beginning, it never seemed maniacal, but in later years, it had a kind of edge."

The last few decades of Williams's life would become increasingly dark. The plays after *Iguana*, for the most part, received poor reviews, and the fact that the playwright was always having to compete with a younger, more vital self caused him bitterness and fears about the resilience of his talent.

The death of his lover, Frank Merlo, in 1963 also diminished Williams's world, and he began to rely more and more on alcohol and drugs. That period, he later said, contributed to the increasingly impressionistic nature of his plays: "I was on speed and my mind started going too fast for the typewriter—the work was different after that."

Still, Williams was not unacquainted with the fickleness of success.

His life before his triumph with *The Glass Menagerie* had been one "of clawing and scratching along a sheer surface and holding on tight with raw fingers," and while he complained about the critics, he faced the new disappointments with a similar resolve to persevere.

"When I saw him," says Elia Kazan, "we'd start talking and feeling happy again. But I think it upset him that his plays were less successful. It left a hole in him, and the melancholy grew over him in those last years when he worked and worked and no one liked his plays very much. Still, Tennessee kept up pretty well—he wrote every day."

Like those of his characters whose outward fragility belies a great strength, Williams struggled on, getting up at five every morning to write. After the disastrous Broadway run of *Clothes* in 1980, the theaters grew smaller and the productions less elaborate, but he continued to work.

"Whatever his personal pains were, he went on writing," says the playwright John Guare. "You know the bird in *The Fugitive Kind,* who doesn't have feet and has to stay all its life in the sky? Well, Tennessee was not that fugitive kind because he always had a place to land—he had the theater. I think he is a model to us all."

Certainly Guare and his colleagues drew inspiration from the productivity of Williams's life and his artistic achievement. The playwright's luxuriant delight in language, his ability to strip his characters of illusions, his idiosyncratic alloy of lyricism and violence—these formed his legacy to another generation.

"I grew up during the so-called golden age of television when naturalism was the thing," says Guare. "And Tennessee showed us that naturalistic speech did not have to be a collection of hems and haws. He could find an extraordinary fire in ordinary speech. And I think a play like *Glass Menagerie* showed you that it was possible to make drama out of the life around you—wherever you were growing up. Life suddenly became something to be transformed."

That same play, it turns out, also gave the playwright Lanford Wilson his start. "My first play was very much like *Glass Menagerie,*" he says. "Tennessee was how someone seriously interested in the theater wrote. Later I started writing from myself, but Tennessee was the one who taught us what to do. It's hard to define exactly what I learned—I don't know if I got it directly from him or from the climate he created—but he made you understand that you must empathize with all your characters and that all your characters are really you."

Williams shared many of his characters' vulnerabilities, and also their heightened awareness of what Chance in *Sweet Bird of Youth* called "the enemy, time." The playwright once described himself as "an avid collector of memories," and as he grew older, his sense of mortality—as a boy he was afraid to go to sleep for fear he would die—grew more pronounced.

"Over the thirty years I knew him, he was always saying he was dying," says Page. "I'd say, 'You look wonderful, Tennessee,' and he'd say, 'No, no, I'm not well—I'm dying.' But he was a poet—he saw things entire—and poets see things more from the point of view of eternity. With someone who doesn't have that kind of view, it's plain hypochondria. But with someone like Tennessee, it's something else again."

As for Williams, he remained haunted by the realization that "the past keeps getting bigger and bigger at the expense of the future," but he did keep the viewpoint of eternity in mind. "I'm very conscious of my decline in popularity," he said in an interview shortly before his death. "But I don't permit it to stop me because I have the example of so many playwrights before me. I know the dreadful notices Ibsen got. And O'Neill had to die to make *Moon for the Misbegotten* successful. To me, it was providential to be an artist, a great act of providence that I was able to turn my borderline psychosis into creativity—my sister Rose did not manage this. So I keep writing. I am sometimes pleased with what I do—for me, that's enough."

March 1983, on his death

LANFORD WILSON

. . .

TWENTY YEARS AGO, THE OFF OFF BROADWAY movement was just beginning to come into its own, and such young writers as Lanford Wilson, Sam Shepard, John Guare, Megan Terry, Maria Irene Fornes, and Jean-Claude van Itallie all shared an exciting new world—a world in which improvisation was as much a way of life as it was a theatrical technique. Although some of these writers would later emerge as America's preeminent playwrights, they worked, in those days, as hotel clerks and waiters and short-order cooks to support their aspirations.

"I can't believe the energy we had then," recalls Lanford Wilson. "I remember running around shouting, 'Theater should be a circus.' It was all very intense and exciting. There was a kind of independent collective Off Off Broadway: if one of us discovered something, it belonged to everyone. We were all ripping each other off, but it didn't matter in the least because we were all so strongly what we were. I felt like we were what the Impressionists must have been." Out of that hectic, fertile atmosphere came Wilson's first full-length play, *Balm in Gilead*—and the show remains, as he notes, "a homage to what we were all doing back then."

Set in one of the all-night cafés where Wilson and his colleagues used to congregate, *Balm* is a young man's play, a play full of the exuberance

Wilson then felt about the technical possibilities of the medium, and the exhilaration a boy from the Middle West felt on discovering that the streets of New York were themselves a wonderful "museum."

The play's thirty-odd characters—drug addicts, hustlers, pimps, prostitutes, "the bums, the petty thieves, the scum, the lost, the desperate, the dispossessed, the cool"—were inspired by people Wilson used to spend time with on the Upper West Side. And while the play is a work of art that bears all the thematic seeds of his later work, it is also a kind of journalistic document, a carefully orchestrated montage of conversations overheard.

"A lot of the play is dictation," Wilson says. "I was just trying to take things I'd heard and adapt them to a flow. Fick's monologue at the end of Act I was said to me verbatim. I remember it was like four in the morning and raining, and I got off the subway, and this guy was walking along next to me, like Ratso Rizzo [in *Midnight Cowboy*]. He didn't want money—he wanted a buddy or something. I went home and took a hot bath and sat down at the typewriter and wrote down everything he said. It was an exercise in getting down exactly what he said, exactly the way he said it."

This ear for conversation, Wilson discovered at the age of twenty, was a kind of natural gift. "I didn't realize it until I started writing plays," he recalls. "I said, 'Not only do I hear the way people talk—and the specific rhythms of their speech—but I have a talent for reproducing that in an organized and exciting way.' *That* is a talent—everything else is work."

In some forty full-length and one-act plays, Wilson has used this talent to create a remarkable gallery of ordinary people—people who together make up a portrait of America as the playwright sees it today. Sally, the reclusive spinster in *Talley's Folly*, Kenny, the crippled Vietnam veteran in *Fifth of July*, the shabby residents of *The Hot L Baltimore*, the aging female impersonator in *The Madness of Lady Bright*, the disaffected archaeologist in *The Mound Builders*, and the sophisticated suburban couples in *Serenading Louie*—what these disparate characters all share is a peculiarly American sense of dislocation, a sense of having lost connection with their pasts. Haunted by memories of how things used to be, these characters spend their days searching after their misplaced dreams, and they talk nostalgically of the time when "everything was an event," when "we were very young, we were very merry."

In using memory to romanticize the past, however, Wilson's characters perpetuate their illusions—the same way they so skillfully use verbal pyrotechnics to conceal their vulnerabilities and to shut out the very individuals who might make them feel less alone. Matt Friedman in *Talley's Folly* has developed a nimble way with jokes and shaggy-dog tales to avoid confronting painful truths; Jackie in *The Hot L* talks a tough game to present a self to the world that hides her real naïveté; and the two estranged couples in *Louie* use language not to communicate with one another, but to ensure their mutual isolation.

For Wilson, speech patterns form the basis of a character; and characters form the basis of a play. It is an approach that tends to result in discursive works, often more musical in structure than conventionally plotted. In some cases, a play springs from a single line of overheard dialogue; in others, from one or more individuals whom the playwright knew in real life. D. K. Eriksen, the lapsed novelist recovering from alcoholism in *The Mound Builders*, Wilson observes, was "one-third Tennessee Williams, one-third Jane Bowles, and one-third me." And the incestuous brother and sister in *Home Free* were composites of two pairs of friends, "I sort of schmoozed together."

Having laid the groundwork for a character, Wilson then shapes the role further with a particular actor in mind—drawing upon the actor's idiosyncratic gifts, as well as his own perceptions. "What it is," he says, "is observation of the outside, filtered through things you've experienced yourself. It's the same thing as acting—you make these substitutions. You know intuitively what it's like having something stolen or stealing something or being a member of a minority race, because there are specific instances in your life where you *were* that person in a certain situation. Actors remember that moment, while they're playing a particular scene, and that's how they get this incredible truth. It's the same thing for me."

In Wilson's case, this process has yielded characters of extraordinary humanity and depth. He has a difficult time, he says almost wistfully, creating out-and-out villains; and he attributes his gift for empathy to a tendency to automatically pick up moods and emotions from people around him. "I'm a sponge," he says. "Someone comes into the room and has a headache, and within a moment I have a headache, too. Just listening to people, I become them. I go away from parties so depressed, because someone's told me a depressing story. It's like I had to write it or something—I've had to go through all the corresponding feelings. Fortunately, if I'm around someone really happy, I can pick that up, too."

When he first began to write, Wilson was still spellbound by the incredible diversity of people he was meeting and their varied use of language. He recalls that as a young man of nineteen, even "sarcasm was a major revelation—to someone from Ozark [Missouri], it was astonishing that people could say, *'Right'* and mean 'no way.' "

This Dickensian delight in personality was reflected in his early plays, which featured large, sprawling casts of characters, sketched-in quickly with a couple of lines or speeches. *Balm* conjured up an entire lowlife world in Manhattan; *The Rimers of Eldritch* suggested a tiny Midwest town, population seventy; and *Hot L* evoked the teeming life of a residential hotel. In addition to honing Wilson's ability to draw thumbnail sketches, such collage-form plays also gave him a chance to experiment with overlapping dialogue techniques, the musical repetition of scenes, and movement back and forth through time.

By the late sixties, however, Wilson had started to worry that he'd been "using theatrical gimmicks to avoid examining character at sufficient depth." He tried to limit the number of characters in his plays and to write those characters in greater detail—and as he did so, he slowly moved toward a more linear narrative structure. Although later works like *Talley's Folly* and *A Tale Told* would retain certain expressionistic touches, the well-made play became a model of what he wanted to achieve.

At the same time, a new optimism had crept into his work. Given his strongly religious upbringing, Wilson has always been inclined to regard his plays as "Baptist sermons" that raise the question "Why are we behaving this way?" and his early plays purveyed a tragic view of life, featuring abrupt, violent endings that emphasized the dark consequences of human actions. In *Balm*, a young man is stabbed to death in a scene that is repeated three times; in *Rimers*, the hypocritical citizens of a small town murder the local eccentric; and in *Serenading Louie* a man murders his wife, then commits suicide.

As Wilson recalls, the 1970 opening of *Louie* in Washington, D.C., was "devastating. There was a line of people with tranquilizers in their hand at the water fountain, and I said, 'That wasn't my intention, to ruin someone's evening.' At that moment, I decided I wanted to find something you could examine and be absolutely truthful about, and still find something positive to say. It was a very conscious decision."

Quite possibly, he adds, there was a more personal reason for this philosophic shift as well. It wasn't so much that he had suddenly achieved a newly affirmative view of life; it was more, he suspects, that "a huge event" in his life had left him vulnerable and in need of "self-protection." In 1967, while Wilson was working on *Louie,* his friend and mentor Joe

Cino—the founder of the Caffè Cino—committed suicide; and his death, says the playwright, "showed me things that I didn't want to know, that I didn't want to think about." "One is kind of in danger of becoming unglued all the time," he explains, "and so I'm hoping that it's really not just self-preservation that is responsible for the plays trying to be a little lighter. Still, there's a possibility that I said, 'What positive things can I dwell on?' because the negative things were doing me in."

Whatever the underlying reasons, Wilson took a decidedly more up-beat approach in his next play, *The Hot L Baltimore*. Though the play is an aching lament for the loss of the past—as represented by a once grand hotel, turned seedy and now awaiting the wrecker's ball—it is also a tribute to the romanticism and plucky courage of the hotel's inhabitants, these "losers who refuse to lose." The play ends with an image of the hotel's residents drinking champagne and turning slow circles on the dance floor.

Fifth of July, the first of the Talley plays to be written, possesses a similar Chekhovian air of regret, combined with humor and an insistent sense of redemption. Its characters—a group of disaffected exiles from the sixties, whose idealism has since turned sour—must come to terms with the not-so-pretty facts of their radical past and accept some unpleasant truths about themselves; and yet in doing so, they achieve at least a glimpse of a brighter future. Kenneth Talley, who lost both legs in Vietnam, resolves to continue his teaching career, and decides not to sell the family homestead as he had originally planned; his lover makes plans to work on its gardens; and his Aunt Sally spreads her husband's ashes on the land, thereby validating the continuity of time past and time present. If the play implies that the day of independence must be followed by a spiritual hangover, that the price of the freedom conferred by America is rootlessness and anomie, then it also acknowledges the possibility of celebrating what remains good and true in the country and its people.

As far as Wilson is concerned, recording contemporary history—"where we are today"—has always been an animating impulse, and he says he wants his work to "be responsible to the times." "If I can get it down accurately," he says, "it's going to reflect something larger than the microcosm we're dealing with. Someone like Tennessee [Williams]—he wrote himself *that day*, the way he was perceived by the world. To me, that's so egotistical. I write the world as I see it around me."

Wary of being didactic, Wilson usually grounds his examination of social issues in intensely personal situations: a checkers game, for instance, sums up the generational conflict in *Hot L*, just as a series of dissonant conversations between former lovers conveys the aftermath of the sixties in *Fifth of July*. At the same time, his plays delineate a mythic vision of America as a country, in Wilson's words, that "is trying to reverse the myth of Jupiter; instead of the old man eating his children, the children are eating their grandparents." A condemned hotel *(The Hot L Baltimore)*, a family home for sale *(Fifth of July)*, or a parcel of historic land *(The Mound Builders)*—these remnants of a more gracious past stand threatened by change and flux in Wilson's plays; and his characters mourn the loss of the old certainties on which they were raised—their beliefs about the family, about America, about the way things would turn out.

That sense of loss and rootlessness stems from events in Wilson's own life. Born in Lebanon, Missouri, Wilson was five when his parents got divorced, and he recalls that the thing he "wanted most as a kid, was a father." He and his mother moved from Lebanon to Springfield, Missouri, to Ozark, Missouri, all before he was twelve; and in 1955, he went west to California in search of his father, whom he had not seen in thirteen years. Their reunion was a disappointment, and after a year Wilson headed back east—to Chicago and then New York.

The sucession of rented houses that Wilson lived in as a child would give him a lasting sense of impermanence; and he has returned again and again in his plays to the theme of "why it isn't all right to live in a trailer and move from one place to another—why we need that feeling of land." To this day, the one place he thinks of as home is his grandmother's house—until it burned down in the mid-fifties, it was the oldest house in Lebanon, Missouri—and Lebanon, he says, still remains the compass point of his imagination.

He has commemorated the town, of course, in the Talley plays, but when he later returned for a visit, he found that Lebanon was not nearly as beautiful, as idyllic, as he had remembered it. Classmates had succumbed to alcoholism and divorce; and the open, hilly land was now spotted with neat little houses and landscaped yards. Like so many of his characters, Wilson realized that "it wasn't at all like what I thought it was"—memory and reality no longer coincided.

In addition to contemplating two more Talley plays—one set during the Civil War, another during World War I—he says he would also like to concentrate on writing a play with "immediate, obvious overt action" and at least one character who may "not be a villain necessarily, but someone who's powerful, who really does not care what happens to other people as long as he gets his way." "I think I've been avoiding that," he explains, "and I want to try these things I haven't done before."

Like Zappy, the tennis player in *Angels Fall*, who realized the instant he hit a ball that "this is what I do," Wilson knew that he had found his vocation the moment he started writing. He was twenty or so at the time, and one day, during his lunch hour—he was working in an advertising agency in Chicago—he began writing down what he thought was a short story. "By page two," he recalls, "everything just fell into place, and I realized I was writing a play. If someone had asked me what I did, twenty minutes after that experience, I would have said, 'I write plays.' I didn't know what a playwright was then, or what a play was, but I realized that it would always challenge me, that it was something you could spend your entire life doing and never totally learn."

"It's more difficult than when we were starting out," he goes on, "because we're now a little more critical of ourselves. You don't have the energy you had back then, and you probably discard things you'd have leaped at twenty years ago. You're never really happy with any of it, but you think, If I keep at it, I'm eventually bound to write something decent."

June 1984

PERFORMERS

. . .

MERCER ELLINGTON

. . .

As he lay dying in a New York hospital, Duke Ellington turned to his son, Mercer, and asked him to finish editing the tapes of the Third Sacred Concert. Although Mercer had long been a composer in his own right, it was the first time that his father had ever really acknowledged his musical judgment, and his words of recognition were to be among his very last. Duke Ellington died several days later, and after more than fifty years in the shadow of his famous father, it seemed that Mercer was finally on his own.

"Over the years, we'd had so many arguments," said Mercer, recalling his father's domineering pride. "But the only time you feel at a loss is when you don't have anything to fight, and one of the things that made me feel so lost was that when Pop passed away, I was left without an argument. My thought of what to do never really went past him. He was supposed to last forever."

It has now been seven years since Duke died, and in death, as in life, he continues to haunt his only child. Eight times a week, when the curtain goes up at the Lunt-Fontanne, Mercer Ellington is there on stage, conducting the band as it performs some forty Duke Ellington pieces. *Sophisticated Ladies*, a revue of Ellington's music, has been acclaimed as Broadway's newest hit, and Mercer Ellington is suddenly in the spotlight, a spotlight really focused, as it always was, on his father. "My son Mercer Ellington is dedicated to maintaining the luster of his father's image," wrote Duke in his autobiography, and Mercer has indeed become, as he says himself, "the keeper of the keys," a loyal custodian of his father's memory and his music.

Like most sons, Mercer Ellington loved and admired his father, and sought his love and admiration in return. Yet at times, he says, he also hated his father—a feeling he explains by quoting a family friend who once said, "Hate is such a luxurious emotion, it can only be spent on one we love deeply." His ambivalence toward his father is reflected by the fact that he sometimes refers to him as "Pop," sometimes as simply "Ellington." In Mercer's case, all the usual filial emotions were heightened further by his father's remarkable achievement—an achievement that Mercer, having chosen the same profession, would encounter again and again in the form of invidious comparison. Just as there were special privileges attached to being the son of Duke Ellington, Mercer found, there were also special expectations and doubts.

Duke Ellington, after all, was blessed with rare genius. As a composer, he wrote some three thousand original works, ranging from such popular hits as "Mood Indigo" and "Satin Doll" to the religious pieces of the Sacred Concerts. As a conductor, he nurtured one of the finest bands ever, a band that included such outstanding talents as Johnny Hodges, Harry Carney, Ray Nance, Cootie Williams, and Jimmy Hamilton. In the view of his colleagues, he had won all the awards and enjoyed every honor. He was, as the noted jazz critic Ralph Gleason once observed, "a musician's musician and a composer's composer. And one incredible man."

Even as a young child, Mercer was aware of his father's singular reputation. He heard the band on records played on his grandmother's old Victrola, and when he finally saw his father on stage, Duke seemed to personify all the glamour and wonder of show business itself. He was handsome and charming and he made the audience applaud by doing what he loved, and young Mercer knew then that more than anything in the world he wanted to be a part of the band. "The shock came when I came around people who didn't know how great Pop was," he says. "It was like you were born into royalty or something. Your father was a king."

The king, however, was not a very attentive father. He was fond of saying, "music is my mistress," and he let nothing interfere with that love. According to his son, he never particularly wanted children—Mercer was conceived out of wedlock—and he particularly did not want a son. Duke was always "girl-conscious," says Mercer, and would have preferred a daughter. As a result, Mercer's hair was kept in long braids so his father "would tolerate [his] presence."

In any case, Mercer saw little of his parents during the first seven years of his life: He was left with his grandparents in Washington, while his parents—Edna Ellington was one of Duke's "showgirls"—played the clubs in New York. Around 1928, when his parents separated, Mercer began spending half a year with his mother, half with his father. Even then, he says, his father had little time for him. Mercer signed his own report cards and turned to his father's sidemen for companionship and solace. They were the ones, says Mercer, who actually introduced him to his father "as a person"—they explained Duke's music, and they told Mercer about his likes and dislikes.

As for his parents' separation, it would become another source of tension between Mercer and his father. Although Duke supported Edna until her death, he tended to avoid her, going so far as to ignore her in his autobiography. Mercer, on the other hand, remained a devoted son, sending her money every week so she could refurnish her apartment. "Mercer always remained loyal to his mother," says Stanley Dance, Duke Ellington's biographer. "And this may have been the source of some irritation. Duke loved the ladies and that made for a kind of divisive thing between them."

Still, Mercer was always eager to win his father's affection, and he quickly discovered that music was the way to his father's heart: If Duke were expected home at four, Mercer would sit down at the piano at ten minutes to four and begin playing, in hopes that his father would stop and listen. Curiously enough, he never felt the impulse to rebel, never really thought of abandoning music altogether. Although there would be brief stints as a liquor salesman and a semiprofessional football player, Mercer would always return to music.

Music was such a part of his childhood that it must have seemed there was no other real choice: His grandfather played the piano, his mother played the piano, and his childhood friends spent their afternoons in the park, figuring out chords on their ukuleles. By the time Mercer was seven, he was already serving as an assistant band boy with his father's orchestra. "It seemed to me that everybody was just supposed to love music," he recalls. "You know, get up in the morning, practice on his horn, go to the job, and then come on back home. I just didn't know anything other than that."

Duke, too, encouraged Mercer's interest in music, sending him to Columbia and Juilliard for formal training—training which, given Duke's antipathy toward rules, eventually led to further differences. From 1940 to 1941, however, while the band was playing on the West Coast, Duke himself began giving Mercer lessons in composition and arrangement. He would write out various harmonies and instruct his son to compose an appropriate melody. "I learned enough from him at that point to teach myself from his work," says Mercer. "It was never a question of competition—he was much more a genius than I. The things I was working at were to gain his approval."

Under his father's supervision, Mercer wrote such well-known pieces as "Moon Mist" and "Things Ain't What They Used to Be," and began to enjoy a close relationship with the band. By the forties, however, Duke had adopted Billy Strayhorn, the talented young composer of "Take the 'A' Train," as a kind of second son, and Mercer says he found it increasingly difficult to get the band to play *his* compositions.

In order to hear his own music performed, Mercer began writing for other groups without pay—he discovered they would accept his tunes on the basis that he was "Ellington's son and must have some ability"—and finally decided to organize a band of his own. At first this endeavor appeared to have Duke's blessings: he "loaned" Mercer the singer Al Hibbler, and suggested that the new band print the "Mercer" very small and the "Ellington" very large and accept some of his own lucrative dates. Mercer, however, struck out on his own, and began touring small towns in the South, which his father had refused to play.

As Mercer's band began to establish a reputation of its own, Duke's displeasure grew. For one thing, says Mercer, he "snatched Hibbler back." "I had signed contracts to produce Hibbler," Mercer recalled in a memoir of his father. "But now I couldn't make the dates and was sued for two months. We got into all sorts of predicaments. My father would never do anything overt or bad enough to really hurt, but if my foot slipped he would let me go all the way down."

Certainly that was the case with Mercer's attempt to record on his own. Although he had an offer from Savoy Records, his father persuaded him to go with his own label, Musicraft. Mercer agreed, only to find that production of his records was sabotaged. "In each case the worst track was used," says Mercer. "And if I know Ellington, this was one way of making sure we would never get anything worthwhile. Pop had this terrible superstition that any time you had more than one band with the same name, it was just bad luck. We finally came to an agreement: We would just play closed affairs with no advertising, while he would do the big commercial dates."

Why did Duke Ellington treat his only son in such an unfatherly manner? The music critic and biographer Derek Jewell offered one theory in his book, *A Portrait of Duke Ellington*. "It's likely that Duke's behavior toward Mercer ultimately sprang from the fact that his son wasn't as brilliant a musician (or, perhaps, was *almost* as brilliant a musician) as he was," writes Jewell. "He'd pushed Mercer toward music, and now his son hadn't reached the standards Duke demanded. Ellington was forever impatient of anything but the absolute best."

Then again, Mercer's band represented competition, and competition was regarded by Duke Ellington as a threat to his role as family patriarch. "Selfishness," he said once, "can be a virtue. Selfishness is essential to survival, and without survival we cannot protect those whom we love more than ourselves." Given the vagaries of the music business, Duke argued, his ability to support his family could be maintained best by remaining in a position of unquestioned power.

Over the years, in fact, Duke *had* provided very well for Mercer, making sure that he had a fine home, elegant clothes, lots of pocket money, a car, and a good education. This was no mean feat at a time when people were still suffering the effects of the Depression and blacks in particular were subject to all sorts of discrimination, and to this day Mercer says he feels a deep emotional debt for his father's largess.

Duke's paternalism, however, had its oppressive aspects as well. It meant that Mercer could never be independent, that attempts to develop a life of his own were regarded as acts of ingratitude. "In the final analysis I don't think he wanted me to do anything," Mercer explains. "I think he thought that as long as I was devoted to him, that was enough—he was capable of supporting me. He said once, 'You have the children, I'll take care of them.'"

"It made me angry," Mercer goes on, "but more than anything, it made me more furtive. I started reading psychology books, and my being versed in this subject put me in a peculiar relation to Ellington. I knew all the various ways you could trade on other men's weaknesses. But if anything, it probably made matters worse between us. Before, he used to pull these little tricks and I'd be the victim and the relationship would be good. But to rise up against him really made the old man mad. It became a cold war."

Nonetheless, in 1964, Duke Ellington asked his son to become his road manager. "I've had so many managers turn left on me," he said at the time. "And I thought if anyone is going to steal money off me, I'd keep it in the family." Although he was then a successful disk jockey at WLIB, Mercer decided "to put an end to going upstream." His own band had been playing his father's music anyway, and he was tired of the comparisons, tired of all the struggles. Besides, he argued, he had proven that he *could* earn a living on his own, and having accomplished that, he felt ready to serve his father.

"Pop had never asked me to do anything for him before," Mercer recalls. "I would rather have stayed where I was, but all my life he'd taken care of me, and I always felt I didn't even know what to give him on Christmases because he could just go out and get whatever he wanted himself. I was glad to just do something. In a sense, Ellington was very possessive and saw to it that I never got so far from his sphere. I'd wander, but not too far. I guess you don't want to go away really, you just don't want to be taken for granted."

Not that the job of road manager made for better relations with his father. Discipline in the band was virtually nonexistent—an old superstition that the first man on stage was the man most likely to lose his job, for instance, made for chronic lateness—and Duke, used to being surrounded by yes-men, did not welcome criticism. Mercer found himself chastising the same band members who had taken care of him as a child, and he also found himself playing a kind of father to Duke. "In a sense I became more mature than Pop," he says. "He remained the baby because I had to take care of things, had to take the complexities out of life so he could remain totally creative."

Mercer had to do this, of course, without appearing to, for little passed Duke's scrutiny without an argument. He and Mercer argued about money; they argued about booking engagements and travel plans and sometimes they even argued about nothing. "Ellington wouldn't ever say I'm lonesome or let's talk," says Mercer. "That would demonstrate a point of weakness. So sometimes, in the middle of the night, he'd call me up from his hotel room, start an argument, and in the middle of it say, 'Well, bring your ledger down here—let me take a look at it.'

"So I'd go over to his room and in the middle of looking at the numbers, he'd say, 'Do you want some coffee or something?' Having gotten me over there, he would transpose the argument into a social conversation." These visits frequently entailed a walk of several blocks:

Duke usually stayed at one hotel; Mercer, along with the band, at another down the street.

Duke worked up to the very end, and the band played a scheduled IBM convention date in Bermuda the day after he was buried. Although Mercer fully intended to break up the band after his father's death, request after request for memorial concerts arrived, and the band continued to play. "I was too busy to feel the full impact of his death until two or three years later," Mercer says. "It was missing his telephone calls at four A.M. or finding yourself in a concert hall you'd played with the old regime. Everything comes back to you, and there you are standing all alone."

For all his quarrels with Duke, Mercer Ellington had always wanted a band like his father's, and now he had one. He had resented his Dad and fought with him, but he had always known he would have to come to terms with his overwhelming presence. And now that his father was gone, he embraced everything he had once tried to escape. After Duke's funeral, Mercer's daughter asked him, "Do you need to be exorcized?" and, in fact, says Mercer, he has found himself becoming more and more like his dad: the mannerisms—an ironic mode of expression, a guttural hesitation in the voice—are increasingly the same, as are the careers, so shaped and focused on the music.

"All along I think I tried to be as much like him in every aspect as possible," says Mercer. "Like the only way to dress was to dress the way Ellington dressed. I never felt I could get away from it. Even in music: I would discover something new and when I'd take it to Pop, he'd say, 'Look at what I did in 1935,' and there it'd be. I'd think I'd found a new direction and he'd say, 'That's nothing—I did it in 1947.'

"You are gradually absorbed and as the years go by, I become him. I'm not saying I'm as great as he was, but as I get older I become Ellington and there is no difference of individual ego. What's different is that his task was how to compete with his achievement in the earlier days when he could come up with those startling hits, one after another. My job is not self-comparison so much as comparison to Duke Ellington. Whereas he had to prove he could do something better than he'd done before, we have to prove we're capable of doing what he's done already."

March 1981

JOHN GIELGUD

. . .

FOR THE FIRST TIME IN HIS SIXTY-YEAR ACTING
career, Sir John Gielgud was out of work. It was not the lack of parts that
had left him in a Manhattan hotel room feeling like "a beached whale,"
and it certainly wasn't age—at seventy-six, nattily turned out in tweeds
and a jaunty silk ascot, he says he feels as sprightly as ever. It was something considerably more mundane, namely the two-month-old actors'
strike, which had temporarily halted production of the film *Arthur*, his
latest acting project.

Even so, there was a whisper of good cheer in his voice. He was
cheerful because, strikes aside, he did have plenty of work these days,
because he felt fortunate at his age to be fruitfully employed, and because
he had recently finished his autobiography, *An Actor and His Times*.

He had taken pleasure, he says, in reminiscing about the people and
plays of his past, but he was also saddened by how much the theater had
changed. It made him feel old.

What today seemed like so much "romantic hoo-ha" were the very
things that had attracted him to the theater in the first place, and now they
were gone—the gilt boxes and big curtains of the old theaters in London,
the sentimental melodramas with their noble heroes and evil villains, the
old-time stars with their fur coats and grand gestures. He had been part

of it all, and he remembered all the details because, being a good actor, he says, he had always tried to be observant, planning to use on stage what he had seen around him.

Because Gielgud has no immediate family, the theater has not only been his work, but also a way of life. For the last four years, he has lived quietly in an eighteenth-century carriage house just outside Oxford, and it is only recently, he says, that he has begun to realize just how rarified his existence has been.

These days there are few trips into London, for the actor says he finds the noisy, crowded city—so different from the London of his youth—vaguely unsettling, and in any case feels "there is not much I want to see in the theater there anymore." When he is not working, he stays home, where he does a bit of work around the garden and watches a lot of television—a convenient device, he says, for keeping up with all the new actors and actresses "without the embarrassment of having to go round and say what I thought of the play."

"The only thing I'm ashamed of is that really the whole drama of the world has passed me by," he says. "It wasn't so much till I began living in the country and began having a television set that I think I allowed myself to be aware of the troubles and the horrors of the world. Because I've always been so concentrated in the theater—it's a wonderfully escapist job, you know—and it takes up your whole time, and it makes you very selfish."

"From my own point of view," he adds, "I also have much more authority when I'm in the theater. Actually, I'm very helpless as a person. I've never understood politics. I was never any good at games or sports. I can't drive a car. Except for reading and doing puzzles and going to picture galleries, I've never even had any hobbies. I love to have everything done for me. Until I get to the theater—and then I want to do everything myself."

Gielgud, in fact, knew almost from the start that the theatrical life was the only one for him. Having what he once called "the foresight to be born into the right family"—his great-aunt was the famous nineteenth-century actress Ellen Terry—he inherited the mellifluous Terry voice and the Terry "gift for tears." Although his first ambition was to be a set designer, to create "ideal physical settings for an ideal theater," he soon realized that he lacked sufficient mathematical abilities, and so turned to acting instead.

"I wasn't skillful in the beginning," he recalls. "I wasn't very good-looking. And I was rather self-consciously spoken—a show-offy kind of person, really. But I did come out at a very fortunate time, because the twenties, when I began to play the West End, was the time of what you would call the bright young people, when everyone drank cocktails and danced all night, and I was one of them, so it wasn't difficult for me to play those rather dense, neurotic young men."

From such roles as the Poet Butterfly in the Capek brothers' *The Insect Play* and Nicky Lancaster in Noël Coward's *The Vortex*, however, Gielgud moved fluently to the classics and the great Shakespearean roles, and in time, of course, became one of that remarkable trio of actors who have dominated the English stage—the others being Laurence Olivier and Ralph Richardson. His 1936 *Hamlet*—cerebral, musical, and graceful—would dazzle Broadway audiences and earn the actor lasting acclaim as one of the definitive portrayals.

But if the young Gielgud was once a kind of mirror for his age, it seems that during the fifties theatrical fashion temporarily passed him by. With the advent of John Osborne's *Look Back in Anger* in 1956 and an upheaval in English aesthetics, there came a rebellion against virtually everything the classical actor once stood for. "When the angry young men came along," he says, "I thought I'd probably end playing fathers and diplomats. I thought my number was up."

Though he says he did not always understand the strange new plays, though he was afraid of appearing "old-fashioned and hammy," Gielgud learned, nonetheless, to adapt. He developed a more naturalistic style of acting. He worked with such innovative directors as Peter Hall, Peter Brook, and Lindsay Anderson. And he appeared in plays by David Storey, Edward Bond, and Edward Albee. In his last Broadway appearance, in 1976, he starred with his old friend Sir Ralph Richardson in a highly acclaimed production of Harold Pinter's *No Man's Land.* At the age of seventy-two, he had a new career.

"I have a theory about why I started getting offered some awfully good parts again," he says. "My theory is that the playwrights, who were writing about their contemporaries and who'd had rather an extraordinary contempt for the older generation, were suddenly getting concerned about age themselves."

In the last year or so, Gielgud has found that his stamina has diminished, and while he hopes to do another play, he adds that "one must husband one's energies more carefully these days." He feels that he is too old to direct Shakespeare on stage—"I don't have a sufficiently new kind of vision that's required nowadays; I'd fall back on the old-fashioned scenic spectacle"—and last year he reluctantly turned down an offer to perform King Lear at the British National Theater, saying he was "frightened of not being up to it."

Since appearing as Cassius in Joseph Mankiewicz's film of *Julius Caesar* in 1953, Gielgud has turned increasingly to the movies—a medium he finds congenial and somewhat less taxing than the theater. Someday, he says, he would like to play Prospero in a film version of *The Tempest*, but in the meantime he is occupied with television commentaries for the BBC and supporting roles in such movies as *The Elephant Man* and *Arthur*.

"Now I don't plan anymore," Gielgud says, almost apologetically. "I just wait and see what crops up. It's not the same as the eight times a week in the theater, of course, but it's great fun, and I rather enjoy the smaller roles because they haven't got the responsibility of a longer part. In the old days, actors kept on playing the star parts even after they were too old. We don't do that anymore. On the other hand, we play cameos for which we're really more suited, and if one plays them with taste and sensitivity, one can be quite useful." He hesitates for a moment, then adds, "I think that's how I should like to be remembered. As an actor—a somehow useful actor."

September 1980

AUDREY HEPBURN

. . .

THIN, GRACIOUS, AND VERY EUROPEAN, SHE USUALLY wore Givenchy gowns or maybe just slim black slacks with a shirt tucked inside, but she always looked elegant, with just the right touch of mischievous wit. Men almost always named her as their idea of the ideal woman and women always said they would love to look like her. Eating lunch at a Swiss ski resort with Cary Grant or driving along the French Riviera in a Mercedes 300 with Albert Finney or just taking breakfast at Tiffany's—she seemed to lead the pretty, sheltered life of a modern princess.

Last week, Audrey Hepburn was back in New York, completing another movie, a comedy written and directed by Peter Bogdanovich, and she was sitting in the Café Pierre, eating mint chocolates and macaroons. It was an appropriate setting—the dusky pink walls reflected the glow of candles, and musicians played a sarabande. Self-conscious by nature, she is overcome, she says, by size and strangers, and the intimacy of the hotel makes her feel safe.

"I love making movies," she says in that famous, distinctive voice. "When I'm not working, I miss it like I'd miss chocolate or a concert. But I could survive without working and I couldn't survive without my family. That, I suppose, is why my private life has always taken precedence, why I've done so few films in recent years."

Since she married Andrea Dotti, an Italian psychiatrist, in 1969, Hepburn has been living a quiet, private life, the life of a wife and mother of two boys. Dividing her time between a flat in Rome and a country house in Geneva, she attends medical conventions with her husband, works in her garden, and occasionally paints. "Movies have no bearing in my private life," she says. "The fact I've made movies doesn't mean breakfast gets made or that my child does better in his homework. I still have to function as a woman in a household."

Since *Wait Until Dark* in 1967, the actress has made only three pictures: *Robin and Marian* in 1976, *Bloodline* last year, and this latest film, *They All Laughed.* She has not appeared on the stage since she played the title role in *Ondine* on Broadway in 1954. Theater, she explains, is far too time-consuming even to consider, and in the case of recent movies, she has only accepted parts that do not commit her to lengthy stays away from home. Audrey Dotti, as she calls herself, is reluctant to give interviews or speak about her personal life.

But while she is shy about talking to people, the doctor's wife actually seems to relish all the attention she receives in New York. Of the crowds of admirers who wait in the hotel lobby to give her gardenias and other tokens of affection, she says, "I'm fascinated by them—it's not embarrassing at all. It creates atmosphere. I'm thrilled to see that people aren't jaded."

In *They All Laughed* Hepburn portrays a European tycoon's lonely wife, who comes to New York for a short interlude of romance and escape. It is a role not unlike her very first in an American film—that of a frustrated princess who takes off on a brief escapade with a journalist in *Roman Holiday*—and Bogdanovich says he created it specifically for her. "All the things I could say about Audrey could also be said of this character," the director says. "She's witty and fragile and strong. What I think is interesting is bringing an actor and character together so you don't know where one leaves off and the other begins."

Pointing out that she is an actress who relies on instinct rather than technique, Hepburn agrees that she is most comfortable with roles that match her own personality. "You have to refer to your own experience—what else have you got?" she says, recalling her title role in *Sabrina*, Billy Wilder's Cinderella story of a chauffeur's daughter who marries the rich employer's son. "Sabrina was a dreamer who lived a fairy tale and she was a romantic—an incorrigible romantic, which I am. I could never be cynical. I wouldn't dare. I'd roll over and die before that. After all, I've been so fortunate in my own life—I feel I've been born under a lucky star."

Certainly it has been a charmed, if not altogether happy, life. Born in Brussels in 1929 to a British businessman and a Dutch noblewoman, Hepburn attended schools in England as a child. When she was ten, her parents were divorced and she was sent to Arnhem, the Netherlands, where her mother's family had an estate. During the Nazi occupation, she says, her family faced "death and privation and danger," and the experience left her with a craving for security and an acute appreciation of "safety and how quickly it can change." One of her brothers was taken away to a labor camp; her uncle and a cousin were executed. Hepburn earned money for the Dutch Resistance by giving ballet recitals.

After the war, Hepburn returned to England and continued her dance studies, but found that the years of hunger and illness had stripped her of the stamina necessary for a career in ballet. She became a chorus girl on the London stage. In time, there were bit parts in British movies, and during the filming of one she happened to meet the French author Colette, who asked her to play her heroine Gigi on the Broadway stage. Hepburn agreed; she came to the United States; and at the age of twenty-two she found she had become a star.

Having never studied acting formally, Hepburn says she depends to a great degree upon simple discipline—discipline acquired from her years as a dancer. Meticulous in her work, she always arrives early for her calls, never does a scene until she is sure she understands it, and oversees every detail of her own performance—including the selection of her wardrobe. She credits her directors—among them Billy Wilder, William Wyler, and George Cukor—with her early and continued success.

"I'm not trying to be coy," she says, pouring herself a cup of mint tea. "But I really am a product of those men. I'm no Laurence Olivier, no virtuoso talent. I'm basically rather inhibited and I find it difficult to do things in front of people. What my directors have had in common is that they've made me feel secure, made me feel loved. I depend terribly on them. I was a dancer and they managed to do something with me as an actress that was pleasing to the public."

She paused to recall some of her film roles—Eliza Doolittle in *My Fair Lady,* the book clerk turned high-fashion model in *Funny Face,* Rima the bird girl in *Green Mansions*—and then, returning to her own story, continued, "My own life has been much more than a fairy tale. I've had my share of difficult moments, but it's like there was always a light at the end of the tunnel. Whatever difficulties I've gone through, I've always gotten a prize at the end." She sat quietly for a moment, then pulled a tiny silver compact from her purse and carefully retouched her lipstick. She had one more chocolate, and then she was gone.

June 1980

LENA HORNE

. . .

AT SIXTY-THREE, LENA HORNE HAS BEEN IN SHOW
business for nearly five decades, and for black entertainers in particular,
it has been a half century of remarkable change. In the beginning, Horne
was called a "chocolate chanteuse" and a "café au lait Hedy Lamarr," and
for many years, she was denied a room in the very hotels that billed her
as their star attraction. She was invited to Hollywood parties with the
understanding that she "sing for her supper," and she performed in
U.S.O. shows where German prisoners of war were given better seats
than black enlisted men. White club owners suggested that she invent a
Spanish name for herself and try to "pass," while the black press criticized
her for marrying the composer Lennie Hayton, who happened to be white
and Jewish.

All that is now behind her, but in preparing for her new Broadway
show, Horne recently found herself taking inventory of the past. *Lena
Horne: The Lady and Her Music* is a musical retrospective of her own
career, and Horne will be singing a selection of songs from the Cotton
Club era and old MGM numbers, as well as such recent hits as "If You
Believe" and "Watch What Happens."

The prospect of reinventing a former self on stage is one Horne finds
amusing in an ironic sort of way. She says she feels no connection at all

with the sleekly coiffed, elegantly dressed MGM star who used to lean against a pillar and sing songs like "Stormy Weather."

"It's like looking at someone else," she says. "She's young and dumb, but working because it's the only place she could work and feed her family. She looked like a little brown copy of the other leading ladies. MGM didn't want any blackness in those days, except in the role of being some native in the jungle or a loving, confidential maid. So I was made into a kind of neuter. In the old days, I thought, really, that by being a good girl and minding my mother, it would open doors for others, that it would maybe do some good. I used to sing about things like the moon in June and airy-fairy sort of stuff, but I don't do that anymore because life isn't that way. My expectations are less fairy tale-ish now."

Although the times have changed, emotional scars remain. Afraid of being hurt, afraid of letting her anger show, Horne says she once cultivated an image that distanced her from her employers, her colleagues, and from her audiences as well. If audience members were going to regard her as no more than an exotic performer—"Baby, you sure can sing, but don't move next door"—well, then, that's all they'd get. By focusing intently on the notes and lyrics of a song, she was able to shut out the people who were staring at her, and over the years, she refined a pose of sophisticated aloofness, a pose that said, "You're getting the singer, but not the woman."

"I used to think, I'm black and I'm going to isolate myself because you don't understand me," she says. "All the things people said—sure, they hurt, and it made me retreat even further. The only thing between me and them was that jive protection. The audience would say, 'She looks great, but she's cold as an iceberg.' It was like they were looking at a plant or something."

The result was distance, but distance at cost. By the late fifties, she says, "I was literally freezing to death. I could feel nothing except my lack of love toward anybody or anything. I went so far as to see my husband Lennie as this foreign white creature. And my work was affected, too. I thought, How can I sing about a penthouse in the sky, when with the housing restrictions the way they are, I wouldn't be allowed to rent the place?"

There followed a period of years during which Horne questioned her ability to sing honestly anymore, and for several years she stopped performing altogether. It was the civil-rights movement of the sixties that finally provided her with a means of turning her anger into something useful, and the camaraderie of the cause slowly renewed her trust in others. Her antipathy toward whites, she says, gradually diminished, and she went through what she calls "a gentling, a leavening of the spirit." She began singing again, and her singing, this time, was different. She finally allowed herself to feel and in doing so, she found she could actually enjoy her work. It was no longer a necessary job, but a means of communication.

"When I exposed myself to the person in the audience, I felt something different," she says. "It was an acknowledgment—We're not really alike, but maybe you can understand. Whereas the song used to be a selfish piece of property, it became a way of reaching out. It's taken a long time and I still have my defenses very high about certain things, but I want to be as open as I can."

Some of those defenses, says Horne, developed very early. Born into the hermetic world of the black middle class, she belonged to one of the "first families" of Brooklyn. Her black friends—she was not allowed to play with white children—belonged to organizations like the Peter Pan Club and later, Junior Debs, and they all attended dancing school. Her father's mother, who was an activist in the NAACP and an early feminist, gave her one piece of lasting advice. "You will look people in the eye," she said, "and speak distinctly, and you will never let anyone see you cry."

When Lena was still a child, however, her parents separated, and the security of Brooklyn was soon left far behind. Her mother, an aspiring actress, headed south in search of jobs, and she took Lena along, boarding her with a succession of local families. It was a peripatetic life and it was also a lonely one, instilling in the young girl the sense that she would always be an outsider.

Certainly her protected life in Brooklyn had in no way prepared her for the harsh facts of the jim crow South. She learned that blacks were not allowed to try on shoes or clothes before buying them. She learned that lynchings were a part of daily life. And she learned that if one followed certain patterns of behavior, if one "fitted the white people's idea of what a good black kid was, you would be all right."

By 1933, Lena's mother had remarried, and the family returned to New York, settling in Harlem, where her white stepfather was regarded as a social pariah. In order to help support the family—they were then living on groceries from relief organizations—Lena went to work as a dancer at the Cotton Club.

The Cotton Club in those days was a Harlem nightclub that advertised "the cream of sepia talent, the greatest array of Creole stars ever assembled, supported by a chorus of bronze beauties." It was run by whites, exclusively for whites, and it derived its cachet from offering them a safe glimpse of the exotic "other."

Friends and relatives of the black performers were not allowed to sit in the audience, and bouncers vigorously enforced this policy. Although the working conditions were poor and the pay was low—Horne did three shows a night, seven nights a week, for twenty-five dollars—the club was able to attract such gifted artists as Duke Ellington and Cab Calloway. Its appeal was obvious: In those days, there just weren't many other places for black entertainers to work.

"I was choice because I was sixteen years old and the Cotton Club was about flesh," Horne recalls. "It was a very glamorous show for the customers to watch: the girls all fitted the image white people decided they wanted—glamorous, sort of half-white-looking girls. We all dressed upstairs above the show section, and the conditions were really terrible. We couldn't even use the toilet, which was for the customers.

"It was like you were this great, glamorous jewel: glamorous so long as it was out in front in its showcase. Behind that, the jewel lived in a pigsty. But I was young and less aware, and it seemed normal. None of those things really shocked us. It was just inconvenient. We were used to the put-down. Besides, I didn't feel too lonely, because I was with my own people. The only contact you had with whites were the hoods who owned the place and the people in the audience who stared at you."

As the months passed, however, it became clear that the club's owners had no intention of allowing Horne to break into the shows as a singer. One day, she recalls, her stepfather tried to press the issue, and the owners "beat him up and they pushed his head down a toilet and told him to shut his mouth." "I knew then," she adds, "that I had to get out."

Fortunately, a way out was soon provided by the black bandleader Noble Sissle, who hired Horne to sing with his Society Orchestra. Touring with him, she found, was no great improvement over her previous travels through the South. It was 1935 and blacks were not permitted to stay at most hotels. She and the band members usually ended up at rooming houses in the black sections of town; in Indianapolis, they were forced to spend the night at the local circus grounds. Such indignities were then routine and were borne in silence. To protest in those days would have simply resulted in the loss of a much-needed job.

"We did it for survival," says Horne. "We were to be exemplary and demure so the white society types Sissle worked for wouldn't say, 'There go those black people messing up again.' For me, it was the beginning of the middle-class image. The thing is, I was with black men I admired as really fine musicians, and when I saw the contempt white people had for these black men, it just broke my heart. I had taken sides then. That's when I really saw how bad it was—this was *work,* after all, and I saw those wonderful musicians I respected having to play that game."

Although such discrimination gradually faded, Horne found that as late as 1942 she was denied a room at the Savoy Plaza, where she was then performing, and was forced to commute from her quarters at the Theresa Hotel in Harlem. Other hotels, she says, would permit her—as their featured attraction—to take a room, but barred her black musicians. Still others would give them all rooms on the condition they not use the front entrance, not eat in the main dining room, not use the public elevators, and not drink at the bar.

If the inequity of these arrangements was all too apparent, the question of negative stereotyping in the material black entertainers were asked to perform was less readily acknowledged. As Horne points out, Noble Sissle, who collaborated with Eubie Blake on *Shuffle Along*—a musical that featured numbers about "pickaninnies" and "dear old bandana days"— would have been shocked to think he was perpetuating a racial stereotype. In her own case, she adds, it was Barney Josephson, the white owner of Café Society, who first encouraged her sense of "professional self-respect." Having selected "Sleepy Time Down South" as an audition song, she was chastised by Josephson for singing something with such reactionary lyrics.

To see this in context, one must recall just how pervasive prejudice in the entertainment world once was. When Horne arrived in Hollywood during the early 1940s, the only roles black actors were allowed to play were those of low comics, servants, or natives in Tarzan movies. None had long-term contracts with the studios, but were hired in anonymous groups as extras for individual movies.

It was the hope of Walter White, then head of the NAACP, that Horne's glamorous good looks would prove an "interesting weapon" in his campaign to bend the color line in movies, and the singer reluctantly went along with him. Yet, as she recalls, many of the black actors who were part of the old system greeted her with suspicion. As far as they were concerned, she was an "eastern upstart," a troublemaker who was likely to antagonize the studios, and they were quick to dissociate themselves from her.

White Hollywood, it seems, didn't know what to make of Horne either. For her first screen test, makeup artists smeared dark coloring on her face in order to match her complexion to that of her black costar's, and they told her that her features were too small to photograph properly. With the exception of such black pictures as *Stormy Weather* and *Cabin in the Sky*, her roles were limited to musical cameos in scenes that southern distributors, who objected to seeing a black woman on the screen, could neatly excise from the films.

Her social life was little better. She attended her first Hollywood party at Cole Porter's house, knowing that in return for the invitation she would be asked to sing. "I don't mind singing at a party with close friends," she says, "but it's different when you walk into a room where you don't know anyone and you're presented as sort of the dessert. But I knew I'd be asked—I was the hit of the season. The whole thing was sort of awkward. Miriam Hopkins was there and she started telling me how I was different from other black people she knew in the South. She was maybe being sweet, but it was very condescending. Tallulah Bankhead [later] made the same comment. She'd been raised in the South where the educated slaves were separate from those who worked in the field, and it was like she'd already made me into a house black. Later, we got it straight and became good friends."

To make matters worse, Horne's movie image, which possessed as she puts it "glamour but no threat," had brought her unwanted acclaim as "the first Negro sex symbol." In the past, sex had been carefully segregated in the context of the all-black show, but with Horne's film and cabaret appearances, audience members were suddenly invited, in her words, "to entertain the possibility of involving themselves imaginatively in miscegenation." The allure of the "exotic," so crudely exploited at the Cotton Club, had been given another dimension.

By 1950, Horne's own marriage to Lennie Hayton—they were actually married in 1947, but waited three years to announce it—had become the center of considerable controversy. There were threats of violence, as well as obscene mail, and Hayton built a wall around their California house and bought a shotgun.

No doubt Horne's attitude toward the marriage complicated matters further. "At first, I became involved because I thought Lennie would be useful to my career," she says. "He could get me into places no black manager could. It was wrong of me, but as a black woman, I knew what I had against me. He was a nice man who wasn't thinking all these things, and because he was a nice man and because he was in my corner, I began to love him."

Over the years, though, that love would be subject to many stresses. At times, says Horne, she grew impatient with black critics, who in questioning her marriage seemed to be putting racial solidarity before individual passion. At other times, she says, she would use her husband as a kind of "whipping boy," making him "pay for everything whites had done to us."

As a black woman, recalls Horne, she had begun to feel alienated from the white world of her husband, and as a wealthy celebrity, alienated from the black community around her. The cruises to Europe, the furs, the jewels, the fact that she was one of the few black millionaires—these new realities had separated her from her past, and once again, she felt like an outsider. She turned her bitterness against her husband.

"Lennie had washed me," she says. "He didn't see me as black, and I realized that was part of my feeling of this whole sterility. I suddenly wanted him to see how different I was. I wanted him to *feel* I was black. That he could say to me the day that Malcolm X was killed—'Those radicals, they're always killing each other off'—as though I were another white person, was like a blow. He didn't see that to me Malcolm was a kind of hero. I knew it was wrong to feel that anger against him, but I was sick of being taken for granted. I was sick of conforming."

For years, she had tried to hide this racial anger. She had tried to be polite and grateful, and to maintain the role expected of "a good little symbol." She had tried to "make all the right moves in hopes it would help others," but suddenly, she says, she realized it hadn't done any good. By the late fifties, she was convinced that she and the other "firsts" had been no more than tokens. In 1960, when a man at the Luau Restaurant in Beverly Hills referred to her as "just another nigger," her anger, so long suppressed, finally exploded. She jumped up and threw a table lamp, several glasses, and an ashtray at the man.

She began traveling. She spoke at rallies and sang at demonstrations, and she started to work with such organizations as the National Council of Negro Women, the Delta Sigma Theta sorority, and the Urban League. Becoming part of the movement, she says, helped her to realize she "was not alone anymore." "It suddenly didn't matter anymore that I was Lena," she says. "The image no longer mattered, because the image hadn't done anything for anybody. I was able to join the movement as a private black person, not as some tired old symbol."

As for her marriage to Lennie Hayton, she says, "we became close again, but in a different sort of way." "He had to go beyond this whole thing of being liberal and thinking we're all nice people. He had to see that under the civility, this nice black woman he was married to was mad as a bitch. I think he began to understand my anger better: Before, he'd just think, Oh, she's tired and sort of crazy. He finally had to come to terms with the depths of my own prejudice."

In 1972, Lennie Hayton died. It was the same year that Horne's twenty-nine-year-old son died of kidney disease, the same year that her father died. "I let myself feel all that hurt and the hurt seemed to release me," she says. "Maybe it weakened me. It let me feel sorry for a whole lot of people and things I couldn't do anything about. When I finally woke up and realized there was only me and I was still awake morning after morning, I did what I had to do—I went back to work."

Having recently decided to give up club appearances, Horne decided to return to Broadway and the city where she grew up. "There was only one place to finish and the place was Broadway," she says. "I never thought I'd be working at my age, but you get caught up in the gratification of feeling you're a worker. Maybe it's from having been a black woman in the fifties and sixties—you learn not to depend on anything. I've been a working woman since I was sixteen, and after what I've been through—well, you get into a habit of surviving."

May 1981

LIZA MINNELLI

.   .   .

DAUGHTERS GROW UP FASTER THAN MOST MOTHERS like to admit. All at once, they are no longer children, no longer protégées, but equals—maybe even competition. Few, however, saw the change as dramatically as Liza Minnelli did on November 8, 1964. Judy Garland had asked her eighteen-year-old daughter to guest-star with her at the London Palladium, and suddenly, in a single instant, as the two women stood there on stage, everything between them changed.

"We went through what women go through for years in literally two hours," recalls Minnelli. "It was like Mama suddenly realized I was good, that she didn't have to apologize for me. It was the strangest feeling. One minute I was on stage with my mother, the next moment I was on stage with Judy Garland. One minute she smiled at me, and the next minute she was like the lioness that owned the stage and suddenly found somebody invading her territory.

"We were singing, and I looked at her and the killer instinct of a performer had come out in her. For some reason, it made me laugh because I knew the imitation of her I was going to do for her afterward, and we both howled. She said, it's true. She said, 'Liza, I thought you'd be so cute out there and so darling—my little baby girl. And then you put one foot forward and one hip went back just on the right beat, and the hand went out, and I thought, Oh, my God, I've got to be good now—this kid ain't fooling around.' I think that what Mama was saying was, 'You're everything I wanted you to be. You're a force to be dealt with and I created it, and now I've come up against it.' "

Though she was terrified at the time, Minnelli would look back on her mother's momentary display of jealousy as "a great compliment." Just a year earlier, she'd made an appearance on her mother's television show and she had come across as a gawky, somewhat hesitant teenager, gifted but immature; and it was as though, with the Palladium show, she had finally won recognition from her mother as a performer in her own right. It would take more time—plus a Tony for *Flora, the Red Menace* and an Academy Award for *Cabaret*—for audiences to accord her that same respect. They would ask her to sing "Over the Rainbow," as though she were her mother; and even today, she complains about hearing people mispronounce her name as "Lisa," instead of "Liza." In reaction to the public's hunger to see her as "Judy Garland's daughter," Minnelli seemed, for many years, to make a conscious effort to dissociate herself from her mother. As a teenager, she practiced varying the vocal patterns she'd learned from her mother; she took on movie roles—the sexily decadent Sally Bowles in *Cabaret* and the kooky, melancholy Pookie in *The Sterile Cuckoo*—that contrasted sharply with the ingenue parts made famous by Judy Garland; and in concerts, she avoided performing her mother's best-known numbers.

As Minnelli has come into her own as an entertainer, however, all that has begun to change. In her latest Broadway appearance (she is starring with Chita Rivera in *The Rink*) she plays the role of a headstrong daughter, attempting to come to terms with her feisty, spirited mother—a role that requires her to draw upon her own memories of growing up. In addition, she now sings such famous Garland songs as "The Boy Next Door" and "The Trolley Song" in her own cabaret appearances.

"If Liza respected you, she'd follow you over a cliff," says Fred Ebb, who's worked on many of Minnelli's concert shows. "But in the past, when I'd urge her to do one of Judy's pieces, she'd always say she wasn't ready—either psychologically or as a performer. Then one day about two years ago, she just felt she was, and at the end of this number called 'Show-stoppers,' she made this speech. She said, 'There's one show-stopper I left out, and frankly I left it out because I never felt ready to do it before. But I am ready now, and I'd like to sing this show-stopping song by a show-stopping lady, who was the best friend I ever had.' And then she sang 'The Man That Got Away.' "

Although she was well aware of the emotional toll that show business had taken on her mother, Minnelli says she never considered another line of work, never really thought of rebelling. Earning her mother's approval had always meant a lot to her, and what better way to do that than to excel in Mama's own profession? Besides, she had grown up in Hollywood— her father is Vincente Minnelli, the film director—and nearly everyone she knew was connected with the business. She made her own movie debut at the age of two-and-a-half in *In the Good Old Summertime;* and began singing as a toddler, repeating her own name—Liza May Minnelli—over and over in place of the lyrics. Her dreams of becoming an ice skater gradually gave way to a determination to become a dancer and singer and actress.

As for Garland, she had been pushed on stage at the age of five by a domineering mother, whom she hated, and she once wrote: "I look at my three fine children and wonder whether I would want them to be entertainers, too. Applause alone doesn't sustain you at 3 A.M., when you can't sleep." Aware that Liza wanted to leave the Sorbonne, where she was then studying, to go into show business, Garland began rehearsing "what I would say—all sorts of motherly things about going back to school." And yet, when they actually sat down to talk, she said she found herself giving Liza her consent. She added one piece of advice: "Watch me, learn from me, and learn from my mistakes."

Having decided to try to make it on Broadway instead of in Hollywood, Minnelli left for New York at the age of sixteen. Her parents offered no financial support, and her mother "was smart enough to stay out of it—she never made calls. She said, 'I never want to be guilty of getting you a job,' and she's not." If the simple fact that people were curious about Judy Garland's daughter nonetheless opened many doors, it caused Minnelli little if any guilt.

"Producers are tough," she says. "They don't care who your parents are. They're out there to make a buck, and if you're not good, you're not going to get a job. If someone allows you an audition, that's one thing, but you have to come through and perform." With her first Broadway show, *Flora, the Red Menace,* Minnelli did indeed come through: she became the youngest performer to win a Tony award.

Precocity, of course, had long since become a habit for Minnelli. Like the fictional heroine Eloise—whom her godmother Kay Thompson actually based on her—Liza was a "very hip kid." At six, she knew how to dial room service and quote Oscar Wilde; at eleven, she was hiring and firing servants.

"I was always treated like a grownup," she recalls. "There was no baby talk—ever. My mother said, 'Why start out on the wrong foot? Enough people are going to say goo-goo, ga-ga, when you're older.' In other words, they'll double-talk you when you're older. So, I'll talk to you straight when you're young."

Garland not only leveled with her daughter but after her divorce from Vincente Minnelli came to rely, increasingly, on her for comfort and advice. It was Liza who was the strong and sensible one—the one who dealt with unpaid bills and missed appointments, the one who was always ready with reassurance when everything seemed to be coming apart. As a baby of three, Liza had played the role of psychiatrist—silently listening to stories about studio atrocities and mean-spirited producers—and she later grew adept at coping with her mother's pill-taking and suicide attempts.

By the time she was a teenager, she had become her mother's best friend and confidante. The two would spend hours sitting around the house or talking long-distance by phone—exchanging jokes and gossip, and comparing crossword-puzzle clues.

Life with mother, Minnelli has recalled, was a constant melodrama of highs and lows, of painful falls from grace and even more dazzling comebacks: "There were no middles, no times when I was just tranquil. I was used only to screaming attacks or excessive love bouts, rivers of money or no money at all, seeing my mother constantly or not seeing her for weeks at a time." As a consequence, Minnelli later discovered, it would be difficult to "adjust to normality."

Whatever anxieties she felt as a child were rarely articulated; fearful of adding to her mother's worries, Liza tended to keep her own problems to herself. "I didn't want to hurt anybody's feelings," she explains. "I was shy and very introverted, and Mama would have to pull it out of me. I wouldn't talk about things that bothered me, but she could see everything in my eyes."

Though her mood swings made her behavior erratic and sometimes frightening, Garland tried hard to be an exemplary mother: She nursed Liza through various illnesses, sitting up with her all night, and took an active interest in everything from her schoolwork to her dates. Though her self-absorption, her sense of being threatened by a younger version of herself sometimes made for hurtful, angry scenes, she also gave her daughter encouragement—"She was so supportive, she'd congratulate me if I walked across the room"—and advice about singing and acting. In addition, says her daughter, she passed on her sense of humor, her resiliency, and her ambition.

"I got my drive from my mother," says Minnelli, "and my dreams from my father. Mama was really Mama. It wasn't Mother or Mom. It was Mama. You know, for Christmas, you got gloves and talcum powder. My father, on the other hand, would give me a scaled-down version of what someone wore in *The King and I*. Mama would give me Mother Goose to read, and Daddy would give me Colette."

It is such happy memories that Minnelli prefers to dwell on; she possesses, she says, "a good filter for keeping out the bad stuff and remembering the good." Alluding to recent news stories about the pope's visit with his would-be assassin, she explains, "All that stuff about forgiving and letting go and going forward is what I've always believed—and may be the reason I've survived."

"There's nothing I can say to convince people that I had a happy childhood," she says, her whispery voice, suddenly reminiscent of her mother's. "They don't want to believe that, and part of the reason for that is because Mama said, 'I don't want them to believe that I'm happy or else they won't cry when I sing "Over the Rainbow." ' But she ensured my happiness as a kid. I know what happened to me, and I know that I'm fine—you know, working and going forward. And I'm sorry—I'm terribly sorry if I'm not unhappy. It's not my fault I'm happy and I have been for most of my life."

"It's your life, and there aren't any comparatives," she goes on. "I mean, how do you ask a princess what it's like to be a princess—she doesn't know, it's the only thing she's ever been. You do have a choice, though, and I made the choice to be proud of my heritage, instead of rebellious. To tell you the truth, I'm bored with all these people saying, 'Oh, I've had such a sad childhood.' I was around half of them, and that's a lot of baloney. We had a swell time—we all had the same drunken clown at our parties. I just had too much respect and I was raised with too much love to be rebellious. And also there was nothing to rebel against."

Audiences and critics, of course, have always been quick to point out just how closely Minnelli has followed in her mother's footsteps. Although her voice possesses a slightly harder, 1980s edge, it carries echoes of the throbbing emotion that Judy Garland imparted to all her songs; her stage presence, too—histrionic, nervous, at once vulnerable and brassy—can also conjure up images of her mother.

Minnelli, on her part, vacillates between anger at being regarded as a kind of reincarnation of her mother ("Someone once asked me, 'When did you feel you were your own person?' and I felt like saying, 'Hey, there's five-foot-five of human being here. You're not talking to a ghost' ") and pride at embodying a family tradition. "When I walk outside the theater," she says, "and see a lady, someone of another generation, who's been standing there, waiting out in the cold—if I've given her just one touch of anything, because through my mother, through me, she chooses to think, 'Life goes on,' well, that's wonderful. It really is. Things do go on—and on. I guess what I'm trying to say is that I'm trying to be a good daughter."

A decade and a half have passed now since Judy Garland's death, and yet Minnelli still thinks of her at least a dozen times a day. In an odd way, she believes, her mother's death actually brought them closer together. "What it did was it took away space, it took away miles," she says. "Back then, I'd have to go through long-distance operators and all that to get through to where she was on a boat or someplace—just to call to tell her something funny that I'd read. We were always doing that. We were always doing *The Times* crossword puzzle together, and we'd call each other all over the world to say, 'Have you figured out what twenty-nine down was?' Mama's death took that away, because now I just look up and ask. I just ask in my own head. It took space away, and also now no one can harm her."

If she ever has a daughter of her own, adds Minnelli, she would name her after her mother. She would name her Judy.

March 1984

PAUL NEWMAN

. . .

ONE DAY, THIS JANUARY, PAUL NEWMAN WAS SIT-
ing in a hotel room in Florida, taking a break from his latest film and
thinking desultorily about leaving the movie business. These were hardly
new thoughts for Newman; they had occurred frequently over the last
few years. Still, it seemed ironic that the fifty-six-year-old actor should be
entertaining such thoughts at the very moment critics were hailing his
portrayal of a police officer in the movie *Fort Apache, The Bronx* as one
of his finest performances in years.

At first the notion of Paul Newman playing a cop seems somewhat
incongruous. In his best-known pictures, the actor has always portrayed
rebels living on the margins of society—the delinquent-turned-boxer in
Somebody Up There Likes Me, a pool shark in *The Hustler,* a chain-gang
member in *Cool Hand Luke,* and the wise-cracking outlaw in *Butch Cassidy
and the Sundance Kid.* Yet as portrayed by Newman, Patrolman Murphy
in *Fort Apache* is also a kind of loner, a man set apart by his convictions,
his humor, and his own thoughtful nature.

Clearly, there's something of the loner in Paul Newman, too. While
he likes to call himself an "ordinary guy" who can drink two six-packs
of beer a day, while he has a penchant for locker-room banter and practical
jokes (he once sawed George Roy Hill's desk in half because the director

failed to pay back a liquor bill), those who work with him say they find him intensely private. He rarely attends parties, always chooses tables in the back of restaurants, and confides in very few. This is partly a reaction to the demands of celebrity—"It makes you feel like a piece of meat when people ask you to take off your glasses to see your baby bloodshots"—and partly a by-product of his own detachment.

If he identifies with anyone, says Newman, it is not with any character in the movies but with Tonio Kröger, the introspective hero of a story by Thomas Mann. Like Tonio, Newman says, he has deeply ambivalent emotions about his life and his art.

"Sometimes I feel it's all here," he says, "the next day, that it's garbage. One minute you take all this stuff you've been through—all the experience, some of the pain, some of the laughter—and you put it all out on the floor for everyone to look at; the next minute, you say it's just a game. Even in a really emotional scene there is fifteen to twenty percent of you standing back like a camera. One side of you is always looking at the other and going 'tsk, tsk, tsk.' It's a funny existence—you can't feel very stable about yourself."

For several years now, that attitude has been reflected in Newman's growing ambivalence toward acting. Beginning in 1972, he started lavishing increasing amounts of time and enthusiasm on his new hobby, car racing. He began choosing films that would not conflict with his racing schedule, and many of the films he chose, such as *Quintet* and *When Time Ran Out*, were neither critical nor popular successes. While his acting career seemed to languish, his racing career began to flourish: his record now includes two Sports Car Club of America national amateur championships and second place in the Twenty-four Hours of Le Mans.

Newman learned to race, he says, the same way he learned to act—by methodical study and lots of slow, hard work. "I became an actor for one of two reasons," he says, recalling the day he left the family business in Cleveland to enroll as a graduate student in the Yale School of Drama. "Either I was running away from the sporting-goods business, or I was going back to do the only thing I ever approached doing very well in college."

Still, Newman adds, he was never an instinctive actor like Joanne Woodward, his wife of twenty-three years. He found he had to "think" his way into a part. "I've always considered myself an emotional Republican," he says. "I'm not very good at revealing myself. I cover up for it by telling terrible dirty jokes. That first time, when I read a stage direc-tion—'Weeping is heard off stage'—I didn't know what to do. But there I was in drama school. I'd left a good-paying job and I said, 'Well, kiddo, better do it or go back home.' So I took the script down to the basement and worked on the scene, and that performance was probably as full and rich as anything I've done."

In the thirty-odd years since, Newman has achieved acclaim on the stage in *The Desperate Hours* and on the screen in *Sweet Bird of Youth*. Psychiatry, he says, helped put him in touch with his emotions, and time and practice have turned a difficult skill into a kind of habit. He finds he no longer needs to lock himself away in a hotel room for three or four days at a time, studying a script from eight in the morning until ten at night. Nor does he need to spend one night getting drunk in order to overcome blind spots about a role.

Yet as his facility for acting grew, the pleasure of the challenge dimin-ished. It was getting easier and easier, he found, to fall back on the same mannerisms and the same gestures, and he suspected he was beginning to repeat himself. "At some point," he said, "I'd begun to feel restless. I couldn't crawl out of my skin anymore."

In the last decade or so, since his auspicious directing debut with *Rachel, Rachel* in 1968, Newman has been spending more and more time behind the camera: His most recent project was the highly praised televi-sion version of *The Shadow Box*, which starred his wife. What he says he really wants to do, however, is "find some sort of profession completely outside of the theater, acting, cinema"—not an "avocation," like racing, but an entirely new career.

One profession he says he's considered is aquafarming. Raising oys-ters, he points out, not only fulfills certain humanitarian impulses—"Just think, fifty tons of protein per acre per year!"—but would also enable him to give up the peripatetic life of an actor and spend more time at home. "You ask yourself, 'How long do you think you could do something like that, kiddo? The idea of sitting around reading all day is such a luxury now, but would it be a luxury after a year? To what extent do you actually feed off all this movie business—being a public figure?' I don't really know the answer."

So, for the time being, Newman is in Miami, starring in Sydney Pollack's new film, *Absence of Malice*. "There's an old joke about a trav-eling salesman," he says. "He comes home to find his wife in a state of dishabille and the bed slightly rumpled. He throws open a closet door and sees this guy standing there, his knees shaking. 'What are you doing here?' he demands. And the guy says, 'A fella's gotta be someplace.' So why am I still acting? Well, like he said, a fella's got to be someplace."

February 1981

LAURENCE OLIVIER

AND

JOAN PLOWRIGHT

. . .

It was a gray, damp, very London-like day, and Laurence Olivier and his wife, Joan Plowright, were taking afternoon tea—coffee, actually—in their temporary home at a hotel on West 58th Street. She is starring in the Broadway comedy *Filumena*, which he has directed, and they were both talking now, as they have throughout their nineteen-year marriage, about their shared work, their mutual passion—acting. More specifically, they were talking about green umbrellas. Not the practical ones for rainy days like this one, but the theatrical kind.

The green umbrella, Plowright was saying deliberately, could be anything that somehow helped an actor focus on his role. It had to do with "a bit of folklore," she said, concerning a thoroughly miserable actor who one day was late for rehearsal and dashed on stage, an umbrella still hanging from his arm. "For some reason that morning, he acted *miraculously*," she went on, "and Max Reinhardt, the director, looked at him and said, 'Keep the green umbrella—something to do with it made you transformed.' So in approaching a part—Filumena or any part—we talk of *finding* the green umbrella."

Olivier, who at seventy-two looks frail but quite unvanquished, after several serious illnesses, was having none of this folklore talk. "It's one of those picturesque, rather sentimental sidelights on things," he said, set-

tling down on a chintz-covered couch and fixing his wife with a look that
Peter O'Toole once described as "that gray-eyed myopic stare that can
turn you to stone." "I'm not *denying* the existence of inspiration, darling,
but I think illuminating feelings can come out of practice more likely than
waiting for them to strike you like a flash of lightning. Craft. Yes, that's
it, and there's nothing wrong with craft, is there?"

Indeed, in both his directorial and acting careers, Olivier has remained
a dedicated purveyor of craft, technical craft. Unlike those trained in the
Method, he would rather rehearse a scene ten times than spend an hour
discussing it; rather focus on the verbal pacing of a speech than probe its
psychological subtext. As his wife said to him, "I think I tend to start from
inside and put on an outside, but you've said you start from outside, then
find an inside."

Practicable and necessary—these are Olivier's favorite adjectives, and
his chores as director of *Filumena,* an Italian tale of domesticity, stand as
a kind of testament to those virtues. Having taken over the play following
previews in Boston, where it was dismissed by critics, and its original
director, Franco Zeffirelli, departed for other assignments, Olivier set
about "making myself useful." "It wasn't terribly inventive on my part,
since the production was already set," he added, "but I realized the actors
needed somebody there who was an understanding sort of person."

As a director, Olivier tried to impart to the cast an appreciation of the
sort of external artifice he uses in his own performances. He speeded up
the dialogue, suggested that the actors use Italian accents, and he wedded
appropriate gestures to the actors' speech. A gifted comedian who once
said he wished his epitaph would read, "He's funny," he also restored, says
his wife, the comic nuances that Zeffirelli had elected to play down.

The fact that his wife was playing the title role, Olivier maintains, was
not an incentive for him to direct the play. If anything, it was the opposite.
"It was just as if she were being directed by someone else entirely," he
explained. "The thing we've *never* done is to make a partnership of our
two careers. It becomes a rather boring situation for her in which, if I'm
always directing her, then I'm obviously the genius and she's the dumb
little clerk who has to be told everything."

He paused to consider other theatrical couples such as the Lunts and
perhaps even his own marriage to Vivien Leigh, and then went on. "With
people who nurse ambitions to use their relationship as a professional
partnership, it's usually founded on very romantic terms—they start by
playing Romeo and Juliet or something, and marry each other's style. But

I think that wouldn't be right in our case because Joanie's got entirely her own style, which is much more interesting than being a companion star with mine, and I'm too old now, being twenty-five years older than she is, to change *my* style. Therefore it's much better to exercise our separate things."

Yet if the Oliviers have made a point of keeping their professional careers separate and distinct, they have also found, in acting, a matrix for their lives together. "We have a mutual understanding of that compulsive need to act," Plowright said. "And our life is a shared love of the job. I gave up working for two years each time I had a child, and it was Larry who encouraged me to return to work. Perhaps it's that he missed me not being involved.

"One sometimes falls into a kind of theatrical stance even at home. He says he's not quite sure when he's acting and when he's not, and I can't always tell. It's a bit eerie, really. As for the children, we've tried to keep them away from acting as much as possible. Neither of us came from theatrical families; it was a desperate need for it that made us choose it, and we didn't want the children to think it was the only profession there was." While the Oliviers' daughters, Tamsin and Judy-Kate, sixteen and thirteen years old, have yet to feel such a need, it seems that their eighteen-year-old son, Richard, has. He is planning to study film at the University of California at Los Angeles.

By now the gray light outside had begun to fade. Plowright got up to fetch her husband another cup of coffee and they began to talk about what they planned to do after *Filumena*: her intention to take voice lessons to prepare for the possible role of Miss Adelaide in a London revival of *Guys and Dolls*; his determination to spend most of the coming year writing his autobiography. "I'm rather bored by the subject—meaning me," he said, almost to himself. "It's just more work, and thank you very much, I live for it, but it *is* work."

His remark suddenly reminded Plowright of a certain Russian author. "That's why we both adore Chekhov, isn't it, darling," she said gently. "How did he put it—'Work, my dear, is the only thing we really have, apart from one another.'"

Olivier murmured something and got up to go out into the damp—no umbrella necessary, thank you—for a meeting on his latest acting project, a new movie version of *The Jazz Singer*. "It's sort of a yoke, but at times, you know, a yoke is a kind of comfort," he noted. "And it's always there. It's a bit like climbing the Himalayas, if you get my drift. On the way, you think, 'This is agonizing—I can't get my breath.' And when you scale the top, I suppose you're relieved. 'Yes,' you say, 'it *was* rather nice.' But then you have to start thinking how to make your way down. *That* is the only satisfaction for an artist—the fact that you are making a continuous effort. And I suppose as you get on, it gets harder—there's more to lose. It's cruel, in a way, but then, there it is."

February 1980

MICHIKO KAKUTANI
GRADUATED FROM YALE UNIVERSITY IN 1976.
SHE IS CURRENTLY A BOOK CRITIC
FOR *The New York Times*.